Marketing Management and Communications in the Public Sector

The fields of marketing and communication have become increasingly important for modern public administrations in recent years but the focus on these subjects has been geared mainly towards the generation of outputs, leaving somewhat behind the analysis and deeper reflections on the impact they make and their limitations.

This book provides a thorough overview of the major concepts in marketing and communication, which is done by utilizing an exclusive and decisive public-sector approach, with an unambiguous international outlook. The possibilities and limits of the application of marketing and communication, from strategic aspects to the more concrete questions of instruments and implementation, are discussed, and if the realities of the public sector are the key to any understanding of marketing and communication, the international scene is the only possible ground in which to do this.

Aided by a multitude of pedagogical features, *Marketing Management and Communications in the Public Sector* is a key read for all students, practitioners and scholars working or studying in this field.

Martial Pasquier is Professor of Public Management and leads the Public Marketing Chair at the Swiss Graduate School of Public Administration (IDHEAP), Switzerland. He also teaches in other academic institutions and directs the Swiss Public Administration Network (SPAN). Professor Pasquier is vice-president of the Swiss Competition Commission and sits on numerous Boards and Foundation Councils.

Jean-Patrick Villeneuve is Professor of Public Management at the Swiss Graduate School of Public Administration (IDHEAP), Switzerland and leads the International Public Governance unit. He additionally teaches at other academic institutions in Europe, North America and Asia.

ROUTLEDGE MASTERS IN PUBLIC MANAGEMENT

Edited by Stephen P. Osborne, Owen Hughes and Walter Kickert

Routledge Masters in Public Management series is an integrated set of texts. It is intended to form the backbone for the holistic study of the theory and practice of public management – as part of:

- a taught Masters, MBA or MPA course at an university or college
- a work-based, in-service, programme of education and training or
- a programme of self-guided study.

Each volume stands alone in its treatment of its topic, whether it be strategic management, marketing or procurement, and is co-authored by leading specialists in their field. However, all volumes in the series share both a common pedagogy and a common approach to the structure of the text. Key features of all volumes in the series include:

- a critical approach to combining theory with practice, which educates its reader rather than solely teaching him/her a set of skills
- clear learning objectives for each chapter
- the use of figures, tables and boxes to highlight key ideas, concepts and skills
- an annotated bibliography, guiding students in their further reading and
- a dedicated case study in the topic of each volume, to serve as a focus for discussion and learning.

Managing Change and Innovation in Public Service Organizations
Stephen P. Osborne and Kerry Brown

Risk and Crisis Management in the Public Sector
Lynn T. Drennan and Allan McConnell

Contracting for Public Services
Carsten Greve

Performance Management in the Public Sector
Wouter van Dooren, Geert Bouckaert and John Halligan

Financial Management and Accounting in the Public Sector
Gary Bandy

Strategic Leadership in the Public Sector
Paul Joyce

Managing Local Governments
Designing management control systems that deliver value
Emanuele Padovani and David W. Young

Marketing Management and Communications in the Public Sector
Martial Pasquier and Jean-Patrick Villeneuve

MARKETING MANAGEMENT AND COMMUNICATIONS IN THE PUBLIC SECTOR

Martial Pasquier and Jean-Patrick Villeneuve

Routledge
Taylor & Francis Group

LONDON AND NEW YORK

First published 2012
by Routledge
2 Park Square, Milton Park, Abingdon, Oxon OX14 4RN

Simultaneously published in the USA and Canada
by Routledge
711 Third Avenue, New York, NY 10017

Routledge is an imprint of the Taylor & Francis Group, an informa business

© 2012 Martial Pasquier and Jean-Patrick Villeneuve

British Library Cataloguing in Publication Data
A catalogue record for this book is available from the British Library

Library of Congress Cataloging in Publication Data
Pasquier, Martial.
   Marketing Management and Communications in the Public Sector/
   Martial Pasquier and Jean-Patrick Villeneuve.
   p. cm. – (Routledge Masters in Public Management)
   Includes bibliographical references and index.
   1. Government publicity.   2. Communication in public administration.
   I. Villeneuve, Jean-Patrick.   II. Title.
   JF1525.P8P37 2012
   352.7'48 – dc23   2011026032

ISBN: 978-0-415-44897-0 (hbk)
ISBN: 978-0-415-44898-7 (pbk)
ISBN: 978-0-203-14492-3 (ebk)

Typeset in Perpetua and Bell Gothic
by Florence Production Ltd, Stoodleigh, Devon

MIX
Paper from
responsible sources
FSC® C004839
www.fsc.org

Printed and bound in Great Britain by
TJ International Ltd, Padstow, Cornwall

Contents

CONTENTS

Plates, figures, tables and boxes

PLATES

FIGURES

TABLES

BOXES

Part I

Chapter 1

Public management and marketing

LEARNING OBJECTIVES

By the end of this chapter you should:

- Be able to identify the distinctive features of the public sector.
- Understand the various management models used in the public sector.
- Have considered the organizational and marketing implications of a public-sector setting.

KEY POINTS OF THIS CHAPTER

- Marketing in the public sector is directly affected by the characteristics of the overall managerial framework present in a public-sector setting.
- Elements specific to public-sector organizations include: legal status, objectives, tasks and environment.
- Three general management models can be identified in the public sector. The Weberian system (bureaucratic and traditional), New Public Management (private sector inspired, emerged in the 1990s) and Democratic Governance (participatory approach, emerged in the 2000s).

KEY TERMS

Public service organization – a public body that implements public policies, generally through the production of goods and services, by coordinating resources available to it. The classic type of public-sector organization is the central public service organization. It is directly dependent on political authority and generally has very little autonomy regarding the way its work is organized and carried out.

continued . . .

KEY TERMS ... *continued*

Weberian (or Classical) model – model structured by sociologist Max Weber. The defining characteristics of this model include a stable, neutral civil service – hierarchically organized and specialized by function – and a clear separation between a function and the individual holding the position.

New Public Management – model inspired by private-sector practices and premised on the notion that competition in the public sector is the best guarantor of greater efficiency.

Democratic Governance – model that developed in the 1990s and 2000s, mainly in reaction to criticisms levelled at New Public Management. Based on notions of accountability, transparency and citizen participation.

THE DEVELOPMENT AND CHARACTERISTICS OF PUBLIC ORGANIZATIONS

Discussion of marketing in public organizations requires an understanding, on the one hand, of the role of public organizations in democratic political systems and, on the other hand, of how management is conceived of and defined in these organizations.

Very broadly speaking, central public service organizations, defined independently of political institutions, came into being with the development of the liberal state. This is a conception of the state in which the principles of liberty and individual responsibility take precedence over the power of the sovereign. The members of a state (citizens) therefore enjoy fundamental rights that no power may violate. Indeed, by the end of the 19th century and the start of the 20th century in many countries it had become necessary to define the boundaries of state power for the government and for central administrations and thus to impose the principle of their subordination not to the monarch or dictator but to the letter of the law. As a result, relationships between the state and its citizens are generally governed by administrative law. The management of public organizations is thus greatly influenced by the application of corresponding rules of procedure. In the United States, it is particularly under the influence of future President Wilson that the structure of the public administration developed in a more professional and pragmatic manner (Chevallier, 2002, p.16).

One further aspect to consider is the growth of the public sector. With the development of the state's economic activities (electricity, telecommunications, postal service, etc.), and with the advent of the welfare state after World War II, the state's functions grew considerably, a fact that had a number of consequences. First, administrative structures diversified and delivery of public services was entrusted to organizations with specific statuses (publicly funded bodies, public corporations, etc.)

■ **4**

or a degree of managerial independence. Subsequently, the relationships between public organizations and the beneficiaries of public action broadened and could no longer be based solely on administrative law. The emergence of more informal relationships no longer linked entirely to a political process but more directly to services offered made it possible to take into consideration such marketing elements as analysis of users' needs, differentiation of certain services, performance of communications activities, etc.

These developments intensified in the wake of frequent criticism of the classic functioning of administrations (bureaucracy, inefficiency, etc.). Solutions that have been proposed since the 1980s have focused on the growing autonomy of public organizations, putting them into competition with one another, and the adoption of a 'consumer-driven' model for the provision of services. These changes, generically grouped under the term 'New Public Management', have led to the introduction of new management concepts and more widespread use of marketing and tools (satisfaction analysis, fee systems, promotional activities, development of brands, etc.).

Despite the many changes that public organizations have undergone in recent decades with the introduction of management methods and techniques akin to those of private enterprises, they still have distinctive features that affect the possibilities for adopting marketing concepts and using marketing tools:

- the status of public organizations
- their objectives
- their tasks
- their environment.

Status of public organizations: Their public nature means that the behaviour of public organizations is primarily the result of the political process subject to control or close monitoring by parliament. It also entails that public law applies in case of conflict between the organization and the beneficiaries of its actions (primacy of principles over processes). In this framework, the public organization and its employees may be called upon to use measures of constraint against individuals, organizations and institutions (arrest, fines, specific prohibitions). As a result, these organizations' managerial autonomy may be severely limited by the fact that compliance with rules and procedures takes precedence over managerial choices.

Objectives: Unlike private companies, which can rank objectives in the service of maximum profitability, public organizations must generally manage a complex system of sometimes contradictory objectives (offer high-quality services, provide identical services to all citizens, manage a budget with numerous constraints, etc.).

Tasks: A public organization's tasks must have a legal basis (lawfulness of action), failing which it cannot act. In addition, unlike private organizations, it is not restricted to producing goods and services and making them available (output-oriented logic). It must also design and implement public policies to satisfy collective needs (outcome-oriented logic). Consequently, measurement of its performance cannot be reduced to the relationship between a service and its beneficiaries. It must also include the capacity to increase collective welfare.

Environment: Generally speaking, private companies are active in a competitive situation and choose their partners (suppliers and customers). In contrast, public organizations do not normally operate in a market situation, cannot make services available selectively, and face a large number of stakeholders. Moreover, public organizations are increasingly being made accountable not only to political authority (vertical accountability) but also to all their partners, the media and the general public (horizontal accountability).

Consequently, although marketing concepts and tools may be used by public organizations, the framework in which they are used is not homogeneous and highly restrictive conditions may be placed upon their use: organizations may be forbidden from developing services, from differentiating services on the basis of their beneficiaries, from selecting beneficiaries, etc. To quote Allison (1979): '[P]ublic and private management: are they fundamentally alike in all unimportant respects?'

MANAGEMENT MODELS IN PUBLIC ORGANIZATION

Three distinct management models can be identified in public organizations: the Weberian model, the New Public Management model and the Democratic Governance model (see Figure 1.1). The reference standard for the management of public organizations was inspired by the work of the sociologist Max Weber (1921). From his studies of the structures of major military, religious and administrative institutions, Weber arrived at a model which offered the most appropriate means of administering laws effectively and coordinating complex activities.

The Weberian model, also known as the Classical model of public administration, is characterized by a centralized, hierarchical specialization of functions, professionalism, a hiring and promotion system based on competence, the impersonal nature of rules, and a clear separation between the function and its incumbent. Because this principle

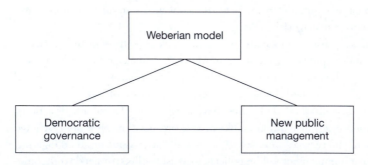

Figure 1.1 *Management models in the public sector*

prohibits any personalized or differentiated professional relationship between the organization and the beneficiaries of its action, thereby, as we shall see later, it considerably limits the application of marketing concepts.

Three types of criticisms have been levelled at the Weberian model: criticisms of the model itself, of its inability to account for the way organizations operate and of its failure to take into account changes in the relationships between the public organizations and society. Criticism focuses primarily on an assumed absence of harmony inside the organization and the existence of parallel powers that act outside the hierarchical rules. Organizations cannot simply be summed up as a set of formal rules. Moreover, they are becoming less and less impervious to economic and social organizations and powers. In addition, the application of bureaucratic principles can lead to expedients that are deleterious to the functioning of the politico-administrative system (strict application of bureaucratic rules leading to abuse of power, use of administrative jargon creating an unnecessary barrier between the administration and the individual, etc.). Box 1.1 shows a classic example of that strand of criticism.

■ BOX 1.1 EXAMPLE OF CRITICISM DIRECTED TOWARDS THE WEBERIAN MODEL OF ADMINISTRATION

In a US state it was discovered that a certain employment office had succeeded in finding permanent jobs for many people out of work over a period of 18 months. It was noted not only that this office succeeded in placing more jobless people than other offices, but also that the new employees kept their jobs longer in comparison with those who had been placed by other offices in the same state. During a biennial visit to examine the office's records, a state auditor found everything in order. But he also discovered that the director was using an unusual motivation system that seemed to hold the key to her success: she rewarded employees with an extra day's leave as soon as they had found jobs for a set number of jobless workers who kept their job for longer than the average period recorded for all the offices in the state. Despite the director's success, the auditor was obliged to inform her that she was breaking the law and that she could not use such a reward system. One year later, this office's performance was slightly below the state average, in respect of both the number of placements and the average duration of jobs. Everybody firmly believed that the special reward system was the cause of the office's success and that its abolition had immediately led the office into mediocrity. All they could do was nod, shrug their shoulders and say, 'It was a great idea but it was illegal.'

Source: Gortner *et al.* (2002).

Other criticisms are directed at the manner in which public organizations operate. Such organizations frequently have no clear objectives and it is difficult to establish links between resources made available and results. Moreover, they are seen as lacking innovation and transparency with regard to the quality and cost of services delivered.

Lastly, this management model has been criticized for its failure to adapt to the evolution of public organizations. Among the questions relevant to the subject of this book, we can cite costs generated by regulatory activities, a misalignment between the Weberian model and the service society, and above all the fact that numerous economic functions assumed by the State during the twentieth century can now be performed at lesser cost and with higher quality levels for beneficiaries (telecommunications, electricity, etc.) outside the state.

Although the Weberian model has been strongly criticized from the 1980s onwards, it served as a reference for most Western countries throughout the twentieth century and many of its principles continue to form the basis of the functioning of public organizations.

In the face of all these criticisms, to which can be added objections of a more theoretical nature arising out of neo-liberal thought (Buchanan, 1962), proposals for sweeping reform of the management of public organizations have been made since the mid-1980s and have been initially implemented in a number of English-speaking countries (New Zealand notably). The book of Osborne and Gaebler (1993) codified these new management principles for public organizations and made them both accessible and popular. The New Public Management model places efficiency of public action at the centre of the organization's concerns and is based in large part on the management principles of private enterprise. It purports that to be efficient and able to adapt to change, public organizations must be made autonomous and have much freer choice of management tools to perform tasks (e.g. autonomous human resources management, the ability to introduce merit pay). The process leading to greater autonomy is framed within a contractual relationship between political authority and the public organization – a service provision contract – which should explicitly set out the performance indicators to be used in measuring the organization's performance and its capacity for fulfilling the terms of the contract. To ensure that the organization works more efficiently, competitive principles should be introduced inside the public service between public organizations or between public and private organizations. With the same aim, the activities of public organizations should be much more strongly oriented towards users' needs.

This model, radically different from the classical model, greatly facilitates the introduction of marketing concepts and tools: beneficiary satisfaction is included in performance measurement (importance of more personalized relations) and organizations have the autonomy to adapt or even differentiate services provided on the basis of their beneficiaries.

Numerous experiments with New Public Management have been carried out, the extent varying from country to country. However, assessments of the model have differed greatly (Wollmann, 2003; Boyne *et al.*, 2003) and many criticisms have sought to put the potential benefits of the model into perspective. The chief criticisms are aimed at a legitimacy deficit in public action and at a loss of democratic control. For example, in the name of efficiency some public organizations may prefer to concentrate on certain tasks to the detriment of others that benefit either few people or marginal groups. Other criticisms are aimed at the difficulty experienced by organizations that must adapt, often in an artificial manner, to a falsely competitive environment; opportunistic behaviour to fulfil contract terms; an expansion of the service offering to the detriment of the requirement to produce and coordinate public policy; and the emergence of a new form of bureaucracy, known as managerial bureaucracy. The fact that organizations must be governed by means of service provision contracts and performance indicators requires them to develop complex information management and reporting systems that are sometimes relatively abstract in relation to their basic missions.

Faced with these criticisms and in order to respond to developments observed during the past two decades, new proposals have been made that are intended to serve as a complement to, rather than a replacement for, the Weberian and New Public Management models.

Although they lack the homogeneity of the other models, these proposals, which can be grouped under the umbrella term 'Democratic Governance', centre on the following principles:

- accountability
- transparency
- networked governance
- co-production of public policies (from definition to delivery)
- implementation and superposition of various managerial approaches.

The accountability principle refers to an organization's capacity to account for its decisions, use of resources, and actions, not only to political authority (vertical accountability) but also to all its partners (horizontal accountability).

The transparency principle requires that an organization's processes and internal decisions be open to third parties, whether or not they are involved in the organization (Florini, 1998; Pasquier and Villeneuve, 2007). This transparency can be documentary, financial, legal or deliberative. Documentary transparency, for example, enables people to request documents or information held by the administration without having to justify their reasons for asking and without the administration's being able to refuse access to these documents unless overriding public or private interests are at issue.

Networked governance consists in concluding arrangements between actors at the same level or at different institutional levels for the performance of public tasks (e.g. collaboration between municipalities on waste management, or between police forces on security at very large demonstrations). These arrangements, which may evolve over time, are necessitated by the complexity of, and changes in, our society.

Whereas the Weberian model sees beneficiaries as subjects and New Public Management sees them as consumers, Democratic Governance considers that

9

beneficiaries must be involved right from the start of the process of defining a public policy and in its implementation, so that needs expressed can be met while taking into account political, social and financial constraints. In this way beneficiaries are not merely individuals or organizations able to use a public service: their involvement makes them true participants in public action.

The diversity of a state's tasks, the complexity of environments in which public organizations deploy their activities, and the speed of change in its environment mean that several different methods of managing public organizations must be developed, and that several management models must be allowed to coexist in the same politico-administrative system – a principle that obviously renders political control of administrative bodies more difficult, or at least more delicate. Some public organizations operate in a highly competitive environment (e.g. universities) while others carry out their mandates outside any competitive context (e.g. state archives). It is difficult to find a single management model for such widely differing organizations. The situation is sometimes even more complex: some organizations, such as meteorological departments, have to fulfil both missions in a monopoly situation (weather reports, development of forecasting models, warning systems, etc.) and missions in an open-market context (forecasts for specific target groups such as farmers, hoteliers, media businesses, etc.).

In complex situations where public organizations enjoy a degree of autonomy, marketing functions come into their own. For an organization, uncertainty generally increases with autonomy, and marketing – by studying the needs of beneficiaries, offering differentiated services, facilitating access to services and so on – makes it possible to reduce the risks by generating the necessary information and insights.

Table 1.1 gives an overview of the three main management models for public organizations: the Weberian model, New Public Management and Democratic Governance. The models are compared with respect to administrative bodies' basic structure (size, degree of centralization and autonomy, etc.) and on the basis of the relationships that these bodies develop with supervisory authority (political institutions) and beneficiaries of services.

The last criterion, relationships with beneficiaries, is of greatest importance for this book because it will directly influence marketing activities (see Chapters 2 and 3 in particular).

In the Weberian model, an organization develops standardized services for all citizens and marketing considerations are virtually absent. Standing in stark contrast is the New Public Management model, where the development and production of services is aimed at satisfying the organization's clients and where a degree of individualization of the relationship can be envisaged. In this case marketing assumes great importance for the organization precisely because it is evaluated on its capacity to satisfy clients. Bridging the two approaches and giving greater consideration to institutional aspects, Democratic Governance allows room for a special relationship between the administration and beneficiaries, while keeping this relationship within a stable institutional framework.

Table 1.1 *Comparison of public organization management models*

	Classical model	New Public Management	Democratic governance
Politico-administrative structures	■ Public service as an institution ■ Large, complex departments/ ministries ■ Centralization and hierarchy	■ Universal service ■ Small-sized units ■ Decentralization and autonomy ■ Privatization of some services	■ Democratic service ■ Differentiation in structures ■ Some units given autonomous powers of coordination
Government–administration relationship	■ Logic of separation ■ Hierarchical authority (politico-administrative unity)	■ Logic of separation ■ Contractual authority (politico-administrative dichotomy)	■ Logic of interaction ■ Institutional and professional authorities
Administration–citizen relationship	■ Collective relationship with all citizens	■ Individual relationships with specific sub-groups	■ Holistic relationships with all citizens

CONCLUSIONS

Management in the public sector has numerous specificities, making it distinct, in all important things, from management in the private sector. These specificities (status, objectives, tasks and environment) have a preponderant impact on the strategies and tools that can effectively be used by policy makers and public managers.

Three specific models of public sector management, Weberian, New Public Management and Democratic Governance, all entail specific approaches and objectives and all define the beneficiary of public services in a slightly different way. These models and their overlapping nature in today's public administrations frame the way in which marketing in the public sector can be envisaged. It is on these specificities, and with these limitations in mind, that this book explores the realities and possibilities of marketing in the public sector.

EXERCISE 1.1

On the basis of the description of the three models of management (Weberian, New Public Management and Democratic Governance) identify specific practices in your organization that would fit into each of these models, focusing on elements related to:

- the organizational structure
- human resources strategies
- communication initiatives
- service delivery.

DISCUSSION QUESTIONS

1   What are the implications, from both management and marketing points of view, of operating in an organization inspired by a Weberian, New Public Management or Democratic Governance approach?
2   Do organizations define themselves according to one particular management approach, or do they mostly combine features from more than one? If so, how are these features being combined in your organization?

REFERENCES

Allison, G. T., Jr. (1979) Public and Private Management: Are They Fundamentally Alike in All Unimportant Respects? *Public Management Research Conference,* Washington, DC, Office of Personnel Management.

Boyne, G. A., Farrel, C., Law, J., Powell, M. and Walker, R. (2003) *Evaluating Public Management Reforms,* Buckingham, Open University Press.

Buchanan, T. G. (1962) *The Calculus of Consent: Logical Foundations of Constitutional Democracy,* Ann Arbor, University of Michigan Press.

Chevallier, J. (2002) *Science Administrative,* Paris, Presses Universitaires de France.

Florini, A. (1998) The End of Secrecy, *Foreign Policy,* 111, 50–63.

Gortner, H. F., Mahler, J. and Nicholson, J. B. (2002) *La Gestion des Organisations Publiques,* Sainte-Foy, Presses de l'Université du Québec.

Osborne, D. and Gaebler, T. (1993) *Reinventing Government: How the Entrepreneurial Spirit Is Transforming the Public Sector,* New York, Penguin Group.

Pasquier, M. and Villeneuve, J.-P. (2007) Organizational Barriers to Transparency: A Typology and Analysis of Organizational Behaviour Tending to Prevent or Restrict Access to Information, *International Review of Administrative Sciences,* 73, 147–62.

Weber, M. (1921) *Wirtschaft und Gesellschaft: Grundriss der Sozialökonomik,* Tübingen, Mohr.

Wollmann, H. (ed.) (2003) *Evaluation in Public-sector Reform: Concepts and Practice in International Perspective,* Cheltenham, E. Elgar.

Chapter 2

Marketing and public marketing

LEARNING OBJECTIVES

By the end of this chapter you should be able to:

- Understand the evolution and transformations of the concept of marketing.
- Identify the elements that have led to the development of public marketing.
- Identify situations in which public-sector marketing is possible.
- Analyse the characteristics of a public marketing setting and identify the limits they impose.

KEY POINTS OF THIS CHAPTER

- Marketing deals with three fundamental questions surrounding the notion of exchange: its nature; the partners involved; and the processes to put in place for a satisfactory exchange.
- It is in large part the enlargement of the concept of exchange in marketing, the increasing importance of the beneficiary of public services and the reactivity to its needs that public-sector marketing has emerged.
- The logic of marketing is not applicable to all public-sector settings: the type of exchange and nature of relationships define when marketing is possible, notably in situations of free exchange and free relationships.
- The characteristics of public marketing must be well defined in terms of market, organization, exchange and relationship.

KEY TERMS

Marketing – the activity, set of institutions and processes for creating, communicating, delivering and exchanging offerings that have value for customers, clients, partners and society at large.

continued . . .

KEY TERMS ... *continued*

Exchange – trade that must respect the following criteria: two or more parties; each have something that is of value to the other; each derive benefits from the exchange; the exchange is voluntary. The contents of the exchange are elements being traded in a relationship. They can have tangible aspects and value, but also represent symbols, ideas and values.

Parties to the exchange – individuals and/or an organization involved in the trade. The exchange can be 'restricted' (two parties), 'generalized' (at least three parties) or 'complex' (numerous partners and an ensemble of interconnections).

INTRODUCTION

Marketing is a widespread concept, and its role is becoming increasingly important to the commercial success of private-sector firms. Its use in the public sector is far from simple, given that marketing is associated with advertising, sales, persuasion and even manipulation.

This chapter introduces the general concept of marketing and how it has evolved, before discussing ways of using marketing in the public sector, reasons for its development and its corresponding limitations.

THE CONCEPT OF MARKETING

There is no single recognized definition of marketing. Depending on the object of study or the chosen theoretical orientations, marketing may take different forms; hundreds of definitions have been proposed and analysed (Ringold and Weitz, 2007; Grundlach, 2007). The American Marketing Association (AMA, 2007) defines it as follows: 'Marketing is the activity, set of institutions and processes for creating, communicating, delivering, and exchanging offerings that have value for customers, clients, partners, and society at large.'

We need to understand the main developments of marketing as a concept since it first appeared, and identify the central issues. Given the goals of this book, the next two sections concentrate on the main reasons that explain marketing's interest for public-sector organizations.

Development of the concept

The first writings about marketing were produced in the United States in the early 20th century by Sparling (1906), Hoyt (1912), Weld (1916), Copeland (1920) and White (1921) – followed by the *Principles of Marketing*, a work of synthesis by Beckman,

■ **14**

Maynard and Davidson (1927). Research focused on the question of distribution (primarily of agricultural products), market observation and sales force management.

Without wishing to write a history of marketing one may highlight three different developments, as illustrated in Figure 2.1.

Marketing developed considerably in the 20th century with the emergence of concepts and models that are still used today (see Box 2.1). All these developments have continued to the present day by integrating deeper analyses of distribution systems and competition strategies; the internationalization and globalization of companies' commercial activities; marketing within companies' functions as a whole; new modes of communication; and a systemic approach to ecological, judicial and societal aspects of the corporate environment.

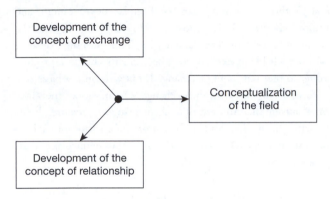

Figure 2.1 *Main orientations in marketing development*

■ BOX 2.1 MOST IMPORTANT DEVELOPMENTS IN MARKETING

- Products' life-cycle (Dean, 1950)
- Market segmentation (Smith, 1956)
- McKitterick's marketing concept (1957) putting client orientation within an integrated approach
- The marketing mix, involving the homogenous regrouping of the entire range of marketing instruments (McCarthy, 1960; Borden, 1965)
- Study of lifestyles as a basis of segmentation (Lazer, 1963)
- Analysis of buyers' behaviour (Howard and Sheth, 1969)
- Positioning of the product (Ries and Trout, 1976)
- Initial reflections on the marketing of services (Shostack, 1977) as increasingly separate from the traditional marketing of consumer goods.

Without questioning the conceptual developments cited above, various post-war authors looked at the content of the exchange between an organization and its clients. Gardner and Levy (1955) and Levy (1958) first drew attention to the fact that the object of the exchange exceeded the utilitarian function of a product by integrating reflection about the brand and the symbolic element of the goods exchanged. Kotler and Levy (1969) broadened the field of marketing study by redefining the concept of exchange content. To these authors, organizations do not merely exchange products with their clients, but also symbols, ideas and values. This broader concept of marketing has, among other things, made it possible to transpose it in other sectors (non-profit, social, political and public sectors).

The third development concerns the relationship between the organization and its clients. With products and services of different brands becoming increasingly interchangeable, along with the increasing costs of brands' development and management, several authors (Berry, 1983; Jackson, 1985) have highlighted the importance of the relationship established within (and above all outside) the exchange rather than that of the object itself being exchanged. Many clients choose a product or service not just according to the item being exchanged, but also on the basis of a relationship established before, during and after the exchange. Organizations therefore develop marketing activities outside the moment of exchange, so as to acquire clients and retain their loyalty, with the quality and intensity of the relationship taking precedence over the value of the object exchanged. Marketing is thus defined as a social process composed of exchanges *and* social relationships.

Content of the concept (or basic paradigm)

Although marketing concepts vary, it is nonetheless possible to highlight the leading questions marketing is dealing with today:

- What is the nature of the content of the exchange?
- What are the relationships between the various exchange partners?
- Which processes need to be introduced for the partners to be satisfied by the exchange?

Given that marketing aims, through an exchange, to transfer something of value from an organization to a client or beneficiary, it is particularly important to look at what this 'something' involves. Although basic works on marketing concentrated on material products or tangible goods, later studies have shown this approach no longer suffices to deal with the increasingly complex reality of organizations' marketing. In 'Marketing as Exchange' (1975), Bagozzi – carrying on where Kotler and Levy (1969) and Kotler (1972) left off – highlighted various exchange characteristics, suggesting that exchanges include a growing share of intangible and symbolic elements while often, at the same time, involving more than two parties. This is clear, for instance, when buying a gift, when the ultimate beneficiary also participates in the exchange.

On this basis Bagozzi defined three types of exchange: 'restricted exchange' involving just two parties; 'generalized exchange' involving at least three parties, each making a contribution to the exchange while receiving something in return (e.g. a gift); and a 'complex exchange' involving numerous partners organized through an ensemble of interconnections and relationships (as with ordering a book by internet, when various actors take part in the exchange: the operator with an internet catalogue who receives the order; the publisher or distributor who has the work in stock; the shipper[s] in charge of transporting the order; the financial service used for the payment, etc.). Redefining the object exchanged, and the framework of the exchange, have helped broaden the notion of marketing and, as Kotler (1967) notes, apply it to 'any social unit keen to exchange values with other social units'. Thanks to this approach, marketing can be applied not just to goods and services but also to events, persons, places, information and ideas.

Marketing is also concerned with the relationship that develops between exchange partners, independent of the content of the exchange. How much one party knows about the other; their social relationship outside the exchange process; how often they meet, and what form these meetings take (physical or not); and the formal context of the relationship are all key factors that can influence the degree of client loyalty, the moral constraint of the exchange (linked to the relationship with the vendor) and the perceived value of the elements exchanged. Relational marketing thus looks to create, and above all conduct, a relationship established with a client, whether actual or potential, so that the relationship provokes and maintains the exchange process.

This relational aspect has assumed considerable importance in marketing, especially in services marketing, but the concepts used and the tools developed may be applied to any area where the relationship between the parties is just as, if not more, important as the elements of the exchange.

The third question which marketing deals with – the one most widely taught and treated in print – concerns the tools and processes behind a satisfactory exchange for the parties, and how the relationship between the parties is conducted. It involves themes linked to market structure (segmentation and positioning); processes for analysing market actors and their behaviour (clients, competition, intermediaries, suppliers); acquiring and managing market information; the conception of the offer exchanged and establishing of marketing strategies; instruments that may enhance this offer such as price, communication or distribution; and systems for controlling and piloting marketing activities. This more instrumental approach to marketing is, of course, fundamental for organizations, and a number of instruments are used in both the commercial and non-commercial sectors (obtaining data about clients or users, analysis of satisfaction, planning an advertising campaign, etc.).

Although marketing has naturally developed its own tools (see Chapter 4), it has also extensively borrowed concepts and tools from many other fields, which have found in marketing a rich field of application. Take, for example, the growing use of statistical and mathematical tools in modelling and understanding marketing phenomena; ethnological, anthropological and semiotic contributions to understanding and

17 ■

structuring the behaviour of the parties involved in an exchange; or aspects taken from management science, even for marketing activities (controlling, organization, etc.).

FROM MARKETING TO PUBLIC MARKETING

The application of marketing tools and concepts to the public sector has followed three paths or trends. First, according to Kotler *et al.* (2002), Butler and Collins (1995) and Burton (1999), marketing should be very broadly defined, and consequently include all the exchanges between social units. The public sector may therefore be contextualized within a marketing approach, allowing all public services – whether of a social, cultural, sporting or educational nature – to be included in marketing. Others have been more critical of such an acceptance of marketing, and consider that exchange criteria (product, price, etc.) and relationship criteria need to be fulfilled before the corresponding tools can be applied. Finally, Cousins (1990) and Greffe (1999) concentrate solely on how appropriate marketing tools can apply to public body dynamics; if they are relevant to the context and goal, the more fundamental question of pertinence does not arise.

Applying marketing to the public sector is the result of developments in both marketing and public management (see Figure 2.2).

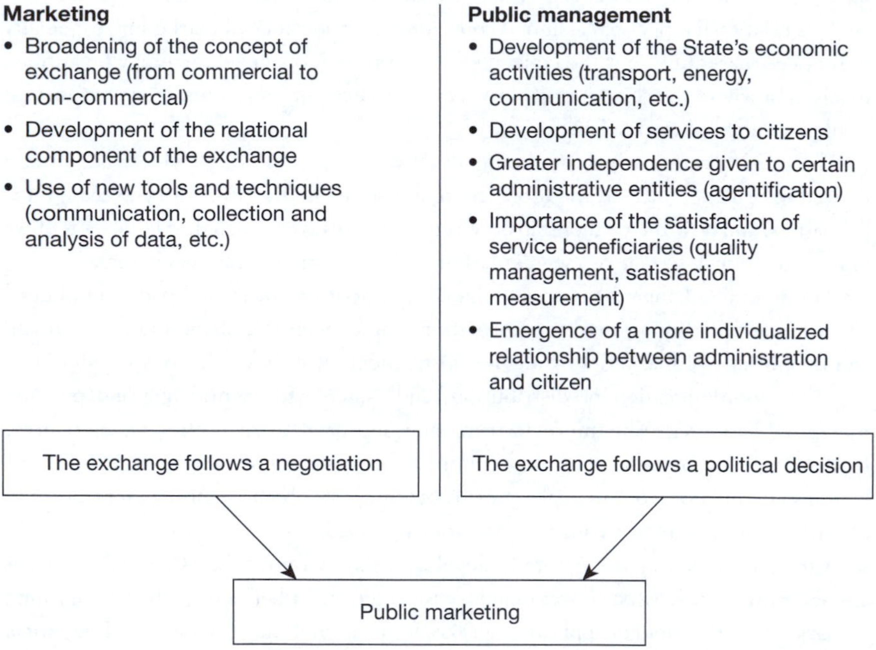

Marketing
- Broadening of the concept of exchange (from commercial to non-commercial)
- Development of the relational component of the exchange
- Use of new tools and techniques (communication, collection and analysis of data, etc.)

Public management
- Development of the State's economic activities (transport, energy, communication, etc.)
- Development of services to citizens
- Greater independence given to certain administrative entities (agentification)
- Importance of the satisfaction of service beneficiaries (quality management, satisfaction measurement)
- Emergence of a more individualized relationship between administration and citizen

| The exchange follows a negotiation | The exchange follows a political decision |

| Public marketing |

Figure 2.2 *Bases of the development of public marketing*

The broadening of the concept of marketing, along with the reinforcement of the relational aspect of the exchange and the powerful development of marketing tools and techniques (systems for obtaining and handling information, cost-analysis systems, communication and distribution tools, etc.) enables non-commercial aspects of exchanges to be taken into account. These tools and concepts may then be applied to the public sector.

At the same time, the notion of public administration and its management models have changed considerably over the last 20 years. The State has developed its economic activities and services for citizens – requiring the use of tools (notably marketing tools) from the private sector. At the same time many administrative units have been rendered partly autonomous (creation of agencies), giving them the chance to take a different approach from that of the traditional public administration model. Some of these agencies have developed hybrid management models which reflect the public nature of their organization while developing exchanges of a more commercial nature, above all by customizing the relationship with service beneficiaries. Furthermore, given the ideas of New Public Management – and the fact that service quality is no longer measured by the authority but by the beneficiary – administrative units have been encouraged to take account of the relational aspects of the exchange, and apply the corresponding tools for measuring service quality and the satisfaction of beneficiaries.

Along with these aspects, linked to the developments of the marketing concept and public administration models, two other points should be considered in order to understand the growing use of marketing in the public sector: the growing uncertainty affecting public bodies; and the need to strengthen social ties.

Given politically defined requirements for public bodies to improve the quality of services and pay attention to citizens' needs, and also because governments have introduced competition to the provision of public services, these bodies face increasing uncertainty – exacerbated by their financing often partly depending on results. By better appreciating the needs and expectations of the beneficiaries of public action, by detailing the content of the exchange (offer) and improving communication about the offer, etc. – in short, by using traditional marketing tools – public bodies are able to reduce this uncertainty to some extent (see Box 2.2).

Along with the specific roles of public management, it is still worth considering the new roles it has assumed, notably those involving social ties. Given the destructuring of social ties, and their 'virtualization' through social networks like Facebook or Twitter, society needs to maintain – if not (re-)create – social links between its members. Public management can play a key role here by promoting discussion, encouraging citizens' participation, seeking to remain close and accessible to persons who are socially and physically isolated, etc. In such situations, and outside all form of exchange, relational elements are very important, and are useful lessons for relational marketing.

It is not possible to determine whether marketing can really be applied to the public sector or not – for two main reasons. First, the public sector is not a homogenous entity, as it includes both services of a commercial nature (hospitals, tourism, etc.)

19 ◾

■ BOX 2.2 INTRODUCING COMPETITION TO SWISS UNEMPLOYMENT FUNDS

Like most countries Switzerland offers unemployment benefit, providing benefit payments to the unemployed and counselling to help them find new jobs.

The Swiss benefit-payment system involves competition between public and private funds. Each Canton is legally required to have a public fund for its residents; the social partners (employers' and workers' unions) may also create an unemployment fund. The unemployed therefore have a free choice of fund (some Cantons have only a public fund, while others have a public fund and more than ten private ones). Although benefit assessment may not differ from fund to fund, competition exists with regard to the service provided (how quickly benefit is accorded and paid out, proximity to one's home, etc.).

At federal level, the State regulates the system by paying each fund compensation for the service provided, based on the fund's average costs over the previous year. A fund whose costs were above average must therefore finance the shortfall itself; while funds whose costs were below average may keep the profit (some public funds even pay out part of this profit to their employees).

---

and activities involving constraints (prison, taxation, etc.). So some elements of the public sector are very close to the private sector, with the application of marketing tools posing no real problem – for example the postal services, which remain a public entity in many countries.

Secondly, the same public body may also, in some cases, offer both freely available fixed-price services, and at the same time oblige citizens to respect norms or provisions. This is true, say, of the police, who may use force to inspect vehicles or stop drivers, arresting the latter if they break the law; yet who may also charge an event-organizer for their services in ensuring an event's safety. So generalizing marketing throughout the public sector, without deeper analysis of the notions of exchange and relationship, is not easy.

Several pre-conditions, needed to create an exchange in the broader marketing sense, have been defined (Kotler, 1967; Kearsey and Varey, 1998; Gilly and Dean, 1984):

- ■ At least two parties are involved.
- ■ Each party owns something that may be of value to the other.
- ■ Each party derives benefit (monetary value, satisfaction) from the exchange.
- ■ The exchange must be voluntary, with the parties free to accept or decline the other's offer.

Similarly, two conditions are required for us to speak of a relationship in an exchange:

■ personal interaction
■ freedom within the relationship (which must not involve constraint).

Although these criteria are fulfilled in a number of cases, enabling Buurma (2001) to structure the objects exchanged and steps of the exchange in the public sector, authors like Scrivens (1991) or Kearsey and Varey (1998) are highly critical, insisting that many services provided by public bodies do not fulfil these conditions – either because there is no satisfaction for one of the parties to the exchange (paying taxes); the exchange is not voluntary (a vehicle's MOT test);[1] or the relationship involves constraint (police stopping a vehicle on the road).

Chapman and Cowdell (1998) aimed to delimit the fields where marketing can be used by constructing a model based on possible relationships between the user and the organization providing the service (see Table 2.1).

Although this proposition helps establish a typology of public-sector relationships, it only allows for limited integration of the exchange issue. To be able to define situations where marketing *can* be applied, from situations where the basic conditions are not fulfilled, we need to confront the types of exchange and the nature of the potential relationships between the parties. Table 2.2 presents the results of this confrontation.

The first case, corresponding to a forced relationship where there is no exchange, occurs frequently in the public sector. A police arrest and a summons from a judge are concrete, important events where marketing is absent from public-sector considerations as there is no satisfaction for one party, or freedom within the relationship. Also, so as to protect people from arbitrary use of force, situations are clearly codified in democratic systems, with strict rules about the use of force (procedural codes, administrative directives, etc.). This obviously does not mean that

Table 2.1 Public-sector provider–user relationship

		PROVIDER		
		Active	*Inactive*	*Reluctant/restricted*
USER	*Active*	**Private sector** Opt out of public sector	**Political demand** Lobby groups generate social demands	**Rights** As provider's duty; as user's privilege
	Inactive	**Societal marketing** 'It's good for you'	**No transaction**	**Resignation** User must accept, provider cuts costs
	Reluctant/ restricted	**'We know best'** Legislation makes it work	**Distress purchase** Dire necessity	**Hostility** Mutual distrust

Source: Chapman and Cowdell (1998, p.42).

21 ■

Table 2.2 *Potential areas for applying marketing to the public sector*

	Absence of exchange	*Forced exchange*	*Free exchange*
Forced relationship	No marketing	Selective use of marketing tools	
Semi-free relationship tools	Elements of relational marketing	Possible application of the conceptual approach to marketing and corresponding tools	
Free relationship			

public administration and public agents do not have to follow principles which are elementary in modern society – such as respect for others (listening, showing a minimum of empathy, bearing in mind other people's characteristics should they have a handicap or not understand the language, etc.), or an ability to communicate (clearly explain a situation and expectations, justify decisions taken in a comprehensible fashion, point out individual rights etc.). But, even if some of these elements are used in relational marketing principles, they are not enough for such public service activities to be approached from a marketing standpoint.

In a situation where exchange is absent, but where there is no constraint, it is possible to have an approach that treats aspects of relational marketing more systematically: as we shall see later on, some of the activities of public bodies do not involve providing services for inhabitants, but the developing, setting up and monitoring of public policies. All these activities, which do not lead to an exchange, may involve persons or groups of people, as they require data to be collected and analysed, discussions held with representatives of these persons, etc. When an expanding municipality needs to review its public transport network, or has to organize a bid for the corresponding concession, it can send inhabitants a questionnaire to learn about their transport habits, stage an information session, or encourage dialogue (internet forum, suggestion box, etc.). Depending on the activity and the institutional context, relational marketing principles may be used to help establish a long-term relationship of confidence.

Another situation, involving a similar lack of exchange within a relationship, can be found in social links maintained by the administration. Through its physical presence (opening times, listening to isolated persons, internet access-points or post offices) the administration helps maintain a social link without providing a tangible service. Again, some aspects of relational marketing may be useful in providing clarity and follow-up within these relationships.

It is a different matter if the relationship involves constraint, although a degree of exchange nonetheless exists. This is the case, for instance, with the periodic technical inspection that is obligatory for vehicles in many countries, and which involves an actual service (permission to drive the vehicle, guarantee that the vehicle respects safety norms). Given the frequent lack of freedom in the relationship between the administration and the service beneficiary, it is not possible to apply all marketing principles – like segmentation of needs, expectations or behaviour patterns, or the positioning of the offer (no or little competition, no possible differentiation as to the price of the service, etc.). Yet bodies may apply a number of marketing tools, e.g. by trying to adapt parts of the offer according to the beneficiaries (garage owners versus individuals); intensifying the use of communication tools to improve and simplify processes between the body and beneficiary (possibility to make an appointment by internet, pre-payment possible via modern means, etc.); or by introducing measures that systematically improve the service and relationship with beneficiaries (surveys of satisfaction or quality of service). The same situation occurs with children's schooling, taxation, etc.

If the relationship is partly free and an exchange takes place, a more constructed marketing approach can be adopted. The simplest case occurs, of course, when both the exchange and relationship are totally free, and the public body can act largely like a private enterprise (albeit within the existing legal context). Short-term professional training courses in universities fulfil such criteria, as they have tremendous latitude to accept participants or not, and are free to decide the offer's content and form. Yet, in the public sector, freedom within the relationship is often limited to accepting the corresponding service or not: whether to be connected to the electricity grid or telephone network or not. On the other hand, the choice of operator is not always open, and the offer and terms of the exchange are imposed. The capacity of public bodies to use marketing tools, and their interest in doing so, lie in introducing differentiation criteria to the offer, and the potential involvement of beneficiaries in the exchange. Table 2.3 outlines some relevant situations.

Public bodies have more and more opportunities to introduce elements of differentiation to their offer, providing they respect the basic or minimal offer as legally stipulated; for instance, by offering complementary or free services, or by differentiating prices or access to the service:

■ *Differentiation in the offer of services:* universities must adapt their course offers, develop a specific profile, provide training that respects laws of the market, etc.

■ **Table 2.3** Differentiating offer and personal involvement of beneficiaries

		Degree of involvement in the relationship	
		Low	High
Degree of differentiation in the offer	Nil/low	Restricted marketing	Primacy of relational marketing
	High	Primacy of the offer and of the content of the exchange	Full marketing

■ *Differentiation of price:* public transport bodies have complex pricing systems based on socio-demographic criteria (young people, families, unemployed, pensioners etc.), intensity of use and even time of use (evening, weekend, etc.).

■ *Differentiation in access to the service:* in recent years fiscal authorities have developed a range of ways of completing tax forms (the traditional written form, software, declaration online, etc.).

The beneficiary's personal involvement is often used in marketing, especially in communication (Kapferer and Laurent, 1985). It corresponds to a person's (or organization's) level of engagement in a process of buying and/or consuming. If purchase or consumption present major risks (financial, social or personal) for the beneficiary, the person is likely to be closely involved in the decision or consumer process (active research for and analysis of information, bargaining, etc.). If someone needs a building permit, they seek out the relevant information or pay a third party (architect, solicitor) to ensure the procedure is respected. Conversely, if the risks are limited or non-existent, people tend to reduce their involvement as much as possible (routine behaviour). This is the case with household waste disposal: inhabitants want to know when and how it is collected, and adopt a behaviour pattern accordingly. A distinction is usually made, therefore, between *high* or *low involvement* situations (Rossiter *et al.*, 1991).

The first case to consider occurs when a public body has no way of differentiating between the offer of services, and the beneficiary's involvement is minimal. Marketing activities in such a case are limited merely to clear, transparent information, and to developing the simplest possible procedures. Take renewing a passport or ID card. The administration cannot differentiate this service (identical document and fee for all), and citizens' interest is limited to wanting clear information about the process, the waiting time, cost and, above all, to have access to the service as simply and quickly as possible.

The second case again concerns a weak level of beneficiary involvement, but a greater possibility for the public body to differentiate the service. In the case of collecting household waste, some local communities have developed their services (systematic collection on a particular day of the week, by a simple phone call, information about collecting by SMS, etc.) so inhabitants can dispose of their waste as quickly and easily as possible.

A third situation occurs when beneficiaries are strongly involved, but the organization cannot differentiate the offer. A typical example is mandatory children's schooling. Basic public school services are generally homogenous and may be only slightly differentiated. On the other hand, the involvement of parents – and pupils, when possible – means that relational aspects become very important, and may be considered from a marketing standpoint.

A fourth and final case should be considered: when the public body can differentiate its offer according to beneficiary, and when the latter is closely involved in providing the service. This involves the usual examples mentioned in articles about public marketing, and concerns promoting 'places' (country, region, town) from an economic or touristic point of view (Kotler *et al.*, 1993; Ashworth and Kavaratzis, 2009). Companies looking to set up in a new area seek a range of information, look to benefit from fiscal competition between regions, etc. The regions, meanwhile, adopt sophisticated marketing strategies to convince companies to select them.

CHARACTERISTICS OF PUBLIC MARKETING

Public marketing and marketing of public services

Given the strongly heterogeneous nature of the public sector as a whole, and the individual characteristics of each field within the sector, one may distinguish between public marketing in the narrow sense, and public service marketing in the broad sense of the term (see Figure 2.3).

Public marketing involves marketing services provided by public bodies, and the marketing of specific public-sector domains like social marketing, place marketing or museum marketing. As the characteristics of these domains are important in the development of marketing, and the corresponding organizations often enjoy a certain autonomy in performing their assigned tasks, they tend to be treated in academic studies in a specific way, even if the proposed tools differ only slightly from one domain to the next. Box 2.3 takes the example of place marketing, which includes marketing activities aiming to promote a geographical entity such as a country, city or political region.

However, the marketing of public services is not limited to the services provided by public bodies, as a number of public services are delegated to non-profit organizations (NPOs), which enjoy greater autonomy in conceiving, delivering and promoting these services. Finally, a certain number of public services, like the postal service, telecommunications or energy, are provided by public or private bodies, but based essentially on traditionally marketing.

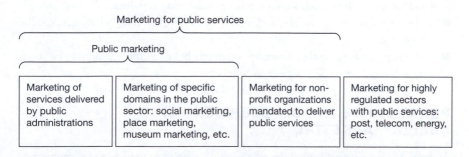

Figure 2.3 *Public marketing and marketing for public services*

■ BOX 2.3 PLACE MARKETING

Place marketing is probably the sector of public marketing that has received the widest attention. The marketing of a place can be decided for a number of reasons: to attract foreign investors, to attract a certain type of tourism or to give and/or enhance a city's reputation along a certain number of lines. Many initiatives have been launched. The most famous is that of New York with its 'I love NY' logo.

At the end of the 1970s the State of New York was in a dire financial situation and dealing with problems of criminality and general insecurity that caused businesses and tourists to stay away. According to a survey made for the State, the situation in the tourism industry represented a net loss of some $16 billion. Following that, a large marketing campaign was launched to find a logo and slogan. The campaign was launched in 1977 with the slogan rapidly appearing on all sorts of merchandise from bumper stickers to coffee mugs. It is to this day the most recognized emblem of the Big Apple.

Source: Godfrey, 1984.

Main characteristics

As described in the previous chapter, the public sector differs from the private sector on several counts. Similarly, characteristics of the marketing of public services must be differentiated from those of private products and services. Table 2.4 offers a synthetic overview of the characteristics of marketing of public services by identifying four types of characteristic:

- *Characteristics linked to the 'market':* elements concerning service offer and demand.
- *Characteristics linked to the organization:* elements that correspond to the possibilities and limits for the organization to develop marketing activities.
- *Characteristics linked to the exchange:* aspects concerning elements of the exchange.
- *Characteristics linked to the relationship:* elements linked to the relationship between organizations and public service beneficiaries.

REASONS FOR THE DEVELOPMENT OF PUBLIC MARKETING

Along with elements explaining the overall development of marketing in commercial organizations (development/content of exchanges, social relationships, intermediation

Table 2.4 *Characteristics of public service marketing*

'Market' characteristics	Relationships between offer and demand are particular, sometimes non-existent (offer and demand for a paying service, like an ID card, are practically linear)
	Demand does not just depend on individual needs, but on the devolution of some individual rights by the state
	Access to the 'market' is limited, both at offer level (monopoly, licences) and demand level (the law defines access rights)
Organization's characteristics	The law defines the framework/limits of the action of the organization providing the service
	Limited autonomy and flexibility in conception of services, setting prices and possibilities of access to service
	The organization must tackle multiple goals, mostly of a non-commercial nature
	Marketing activities and measures hard to evaluate
	Sizable political control of the organization
Exchange characteristics	Public services are collective entities (non-rival, non-exclusive, indivisible)
	Offer is usually unique and non-competitive (no or little differentiation in the offer, and no or few competing offers)
	No exclusion from use of services
	Balanced exchange is hard to estimate and attain
Relationship characteristics	Target-groups are numerous and cannot always be differentiated
	Relationship not generally commercial
	Personal involvement often strong
	Negotiations are collective, not individual

systems, etc.), various elements explain the development of marketing in the public sector more specifically.

The first reason can be found in increased competition in the public service offer. This approach, derived from New Public Management (NPM), looks to offer service beneficiaries a choice between various public and/or private services (e.g. giving parents vouchers for young children to be looked after, for use in public or private kindergartens). This trend is accentuated by the fact that choosing the body to perform a public task, and the relationship between the public body and the individual, are subject to increasing analysis and discussion steeped in economic terms (costs of the transaction, agency costs). Consequently, the operator chosen to perform a public task is no longer automatically the central public administration, but can take varied forms (public or private operators, hybrid system, etc.). Furthermore, rather than assign these tasks to private operators, the State encourages competition by introducing internal markets and quasi-markets, obliging public operators to take management and marketing elements into account.

Independently of the influence of NPM, several public-sector domains have embraced direct competition. This is the case, say, with countries, cities and regions competing to attract or keep residents and companies, host sports or cultural events, congresses, etc.

Even if public services are not the same as private ones, the attitude of beneficiaries as consumers is increasingly similar. In terms of service quality, information and the relationship with the public body etc., the 'consumer requirements' no longer differ depending on whether they are public or private. As a result, public bodies must also take these expectations and demands into account when conceiving and providing services. At the same time, citizens are increasingly insistent about their rights, and demand more 'individual' treatment of their needs. There are various reasons for this: although equal treatment can lead to wastage of resources and economic inefficiency the public sector must, in an increasingly difficult economic context, look for more rational approaches when providing services – and take other principles, such as opportunity, into account. One may also add that, given rising citizen participation, service beneficiaries are ever keener to be associated with the conception of public services, and this is liable to alter the relationship between the public body and citizens.

The State's responsibilities in economic activities are more and more extensive (financial sector, energy, tourism, transport, post, telecommunications, arms, etc.) and, even if the corresponding bodies enjoy considerable management autonomy and apply traditional marketing rules, they must also bear certain public service characteristics in mind.

Finally, public bodies are looking to improve their relationship with beneficiaries, either because they are judged through this relationship (satisfaction surveys), or because the beneficiaries' potential reactions (demonstrations, public support) may legitimize the organization's action and services, something which can prove decisive if funds are short. So they have good reason to develop marketing activities – in order to heighten the awareness of service beneficiaries and boost support for the organization's activities.

LIMITS OF PUBLIC MARKETING

If, as we have seen in the previous section, marketing tools – or even a thoroughgoing marketing approach – can be envisaged for public services, serious limits must be acknowledged about the use of marketing in the public sector in general.

Some of these limits are obvious enough, and follow on from characteristics mentioned earlier. Public bodies often act in the absence of a veritable market, and supply and demand can rarely be made to fit a traditional model. Nor is it easy to obtain a balanced exchange between the parties involved; and the relationship between information and power is greatly in favour of the public body. The administration's tasks are not restricted to providing services for beneficiaries, but also include developing public policies – for which marketing is of only limited use. Along with noting the absence of commercial aspects in the relationship between the public body and the beneficiary, other elements should be considered.

First, the functioning of the public sector is dependent above all on political considerations. Elections, changes of majority, specific political pressure linked to events, or the choices/inclinations of charismatic leaders, etc. may all decisively influence public action, and in no way derive from a coordinated marketing approach. Limited funding, a complex political agenda, citizens' opposition to a project, etc., may all make it difficult to carry out a marketing concept, when a city or region disposes of one. The pre-eminence of politics, with its own rationale and issues, must never be forgotten; a marketing approach here is subordinate to attaining political and public goals, not commercial ones. Box 2.4 gives an example of a political refusal to approve plans for re-organizing tourism marketing in a Swiss Canton (Valais).

■ BOX 2.4 VALAIS TOURISM LAW

Valais boasts such internationally famous resorts as Zermatt, Verbier and Crans-Montana, with tourism accounting for 25 per cent of the Canton's GDP. Over time, no fewer than 152 development organizations have been launched to promote tourism, usually with limited financial means.

In 2009 the Cantonal government proposed a new tourism law involving the creation of 8 to 12 tourist regions. To obtain the new status a region would need to have a touristic budget of CHF5 million or more, have an internationally recognized name and have at least 700,000 overnight stays per year. A federation of tourist regions (Promo Valais) would have been set up to coordinate touristic promotions. The total budget for Valais tourism would thus have been CHF80 million (compared to CHF55 million in 2011). This budget would have been financed by a new tourist accommodation tax, and an extra CHF10 million in annual investment by the Canton to promote the image of Valais.

Although this law was proposed by the government and adopted by the Cantonal parliament, it was rejected by the inhabitants of Valais on 29 November 2009, with around 75 per cent of those who voted saying no. One of the main reasons why this draft law – aiming to coordinate marketing activities and render them more efficient – was rejected by the population was the introduction of a tourist accommodation tax. Owners of second homes (including 20,000 Valais inhabitants) would have been more heavily taxed, as the tax would have been based not just on living space but also the number of nights spent in the Canton.

Sources: *Le Nouvelliste, Le Temps,* NZZ, Canton du Valais (http://www.vs.ch), Comité pour la Loi du Tourisme (www.oui-au-tourisme.ch).

The relationship between public bodies and beneficiaries is a complex one. Beneficiaries may need to play multiple, sometimes contradictory roles, such as calling for lower taxes while demanding improved services (e.g. wishing for closer post offices or hospitals, longer opening hours of a government office, etc.). It is difficult to take these expectations into account, especially as they vary over time and take various forms. For example, people who suddenly find themselves unemployed will have needs they would never have thought of, such as receiving benefit or an allowance while they seek a new job, advice about professional retraining and, no doubt, finding someone to listen to and empathize with them as they face up to a situation that is difficult to bear. The skills and knowledge required to respond to these needs often exceed what is available within a single public body.

Another problem is the absence of individual needs and satisfaction as regards collective entities. While it is certainly possible to measure people's satisfaction with a service or relationship (e.g. with the standard of welcome or a website's user-friendliness), it is almost impossible to study this same satisfaction from a marketing point of view as regards the overall set-up of public services grouped together in a public policy. How do you measure satisfaction with a fire brigade, schooling or justice? Partial measures for analysing needs or satisfaction cannot just be added together, and do not suffice to convey a public entity's contribution to the community (people may have a high opinion of the quality of the relationship with the organization providing a service, yet consider its services superfluous). It should be remembered that the sum of individual advantages or satisfactions does not necessarily correspond to collective satisfaction when it comes to collective entities.

Even if many public bodies tend to seek, and sometimes obtain, increased management autonomy, they do not necessarily seek to use every marketing tool to maximize the value of the exchange for both parties. Chapman and Cowdell (1998) compare public bodies to animals in a zoo: these bodies do not need to go looking for resources (food) as, come what may, they are regularly 'fed' by budgets voted in parliament. There is little to encourage them to seek to increase their revenue outside their budget, or reduce costs of their own accord. And, as many studies have clearly shown (Emery, 2006), the motivation of public agents lies outside a commercial framework (community service, ethics, etc.) and can even conflict with a more commercial approach.

More fundamentally, some criticism of the use of marketing in the public sector is due to the fact that marketing participates itself in creating the need (Marion, 2004): marketing tools serve not only to interpret signals from consumers, but clearly contribute to increasing them. Public action derives from a publicly defined issue (public conscience and demand) which receives a political response (voting the legal framework). In some cases public action may aim to limit consumption rather than stimulate it. So using marketing to define (individual) needs and promote services may come into conflict with the democratic process.

To conclude: there is no clear-cut answer as to the best use of marketing for public services. Some marketing tools, and sometimes integrated marketing approaches, may undeniably help improve services and the relationship with beneficiaries. However, from a methodological point of view, marketing presupposes a grasping and understanding of individual needs, expectations and behaviour (methodological individualism). Consequently, marketing is ill-equipped for the study of collective problems and practice, and its use can only serve to complement political, sociological, cultural and economic approaches.

EXERCISE 2.1

For a specific public service – issuing a passport – identify those elements that can and those that cannot be part of a marketing approach.

Identify what is exchanged and who are the partners to the exchange in the following situations:

- issuing a driver's licence
- providing electricity in a non-monopolistic system
- hospital care.

DISCUSSION QUESTIONS

1   What are the marketing-related initiatives present in your work place? What are the limits to applying public marketing in your own organization?
2   How does your organization envisage the relationship with the beneficiaries of your services?
3   Is the term 'marketing' officially used by your organization? Why do you believe this is the case?

NOTE

1   The Ministry of Transport test (usually abbreviated to MOT test).

REFERENCES

American Marketing Association (AMA) (2007) Definition of Marketing. Online at http://www.marketingpower.com/AboutAMA/Pages/DefinitionofMarketing.aspx (accessed 28 February 2011).
Ashworth, G. and Kavaratzis, M. (2009) Beyond the Logo: Brand Management for Cities, *Journal of Brand Management,* 18, 520–31.
Bagozzi, R. P. (1975) Marketing as Exchange, *Journal of Marketing,* 39, 32–9.

Beckman, T. N., Maynard, H. H. and Davidson, W. R. (1927) *Principles of Marketing*, New York, Ronald Press.

Berry, L. (1983) *Relationship Marketing*, Chicago, American Marketing Association.

Borden, N. H. (1965) The Concept of the Marketing Mix, in Schnertz, G. (ed.) *Science in Marketing*, Chichester, John Wiley & Sons.

Burton, S. (1999) Marketing for Public Organizations: New Ways, New Methods, *Public Management,* 1, 373–85.

Butler, P. and Collins, N. (1995) Marketing Public Sector Services: Concepts and Characteristics, *Journal of Marketing Management*, 11, 83–96.

Buurma, H. (2001) Public Policy Marketing: Marketing Exchange in the Public Sector, *European Journal of Marketing*, 35 (1), 287–300.

Chapman, D. and Cowdell, T. (1998) *New Public Sector Marketing*, London, Financial Times/Pitman.

Copeland, M. T. (1920) *Marketing Problems*, New York, A. W. Shaw.

Cousins, L. (1990) Marketing Planning in the Public and Non-profit Sectors, *European Journal of Marketing*, 24, 15–30.

Dean, J. (1950) Pricing Policies for New Products, *Harvard Business Review,* November, 45–53.

Emery, Y. (2006) *Réformes de la Gestion Publique, Nouvelles Pratiques de GRH et Motivation des Agents Publics. Personalpolitik im Spannungsfeld von Veränderung und Wissens-Management*, Berne: A. Hofmeister.

Gardner, B. B. and Levy, S. J. (1955) The Product and the Brand, *Harvard Business Review,* 33, 33–9.

Gilly, M. C. and Dean, D. L. (1984) A Market-oriented Taxonomy of Public Services: Implications for Marketing Management, in Bloch, T. M., Upah, G. D. and Zeithaml, V. A. (eds) *Services Marketing in a Changing Environment*, Chicago, American Marketing Association.

Godfrey, J. (1984) I Love New York, *Tourism Management*, 5, 148–9.

Greffe, X. (1999) *Gestion Publique*, Paris, Dalloz.

Grundlach, G. (2007) The American Marketing Association's 2004 Definition of Marketing: Perspectives on Its Implications for Scholarship and the Role and Responsibility of Marketing in Society, *Journal of Public Policy and Marketing*, 26 (2), 243–50.

Howard, J. A. and Sheth, N. J. (1969) *Theory of Buyer Behaviour*, New York, John Wiley & Sons.

Hoyt, C. W. (1912) *Scientific Sales Management*, New Haven, Woolson.

Jackson, B. (1985) *Winning and Keeping Customers: The Dynamics of Customer Relationships*, Massachusetts/Toronto, Lexington Books.

Kapferer, J. N. and Laurent, G. (1985) Consumer Involvement Profiles: A New Practical Approach to Consumer Involvement, *Journal of Advertising Research,* 25–26, 48–56.

Kearsey, A. and Varey, J. (1998) Managerialist Thinking on Marketing for Public Services, *Public Money & Management*, 51–60.

Kotler, P. (1967) *Marketing Management: Analysis, Planning, and Control*, Englewood Cliffs, New Jersey, Prentice-Hall.

—— (1972) A Generic Concept of Marketing, *Journal of Marketing*, 36, 46–54.

Kotler, P., Haider, D. H. and Rein, I. (1993) *Marketing Places*, New York, Free Press.

Kotler, P. and Levy, S. J. (1969) Broadening the Concept of Marketing, *Journal of Marketing*, 33, 10–15.

Kotler, P., Roberto, N. and Lee, N. (2002) *Social Marketing: Improving the Quality of Life*, Thousand Oaks, Sage.

Lazer, W. (1963) Life Style Concepts and Marketing, in Association, A. M. (ed.) *Toward Scientific Marketing*, Chicago, Stephen A. Greyser.

Levy, S. J. (1958) Symbols By Which We Buy, *Advancing Marketing Efficiency*, American Marketing Association, December, 409–16.

Marion, G. (2004) *Idéologie Marketing*, Paris, Eyrolles.

McCarthy, E. J. (1960) *Basic Marketing: A Managerial Approach*, Illinois, Irwin.

McKitterick, J. B. (1957) What Is the Marketing Management Concept? In *Proceedings of the American Marketing Association Conference* (pp. 71–81), Chicago, American Marketing Association.

Ries, A. and Trout, J. (1976) *Positioning: The Battle for Your Mind*, New York: McGraw-Hill.

Ringold, D. J. and Weitz, B. A. (2007) The American Marketing Association Definition of Marketing: Moving from Lagging to Leading Indicator, *Journal of Public Policy & Marketing,* 26, 251–60.

Rossiter, J., Percy, L. and Donovan, R. (1991) A Better Advertising Grid, *Journal of Advertising Research,* 31(5), 11–21.

Scrivens, E. (1991) Is There a Role for Marketing in the Public Sector? *Public Money & Management,* 17–23.

Shostack, G. L. (1977) Breaking Free from Product Marketing, *Journal of Marketing,* April, 73–80.

Smith, W. R. (1956) Product Differentiation and Market Segmentation as Alternative Marketing Strategies, *Journal of Marketing,* 21, 3–8.

Sparling, S. E. (1906) *Introduction to Business Organization*, New York, Kessinger.

Weld, L. D. H. (1916) *Studies in the Marketing of Farm Products*, New York, Macmillan.

White, P. (1921) *Market Analysis, Its Principles and Methods*, New York, McGraw-Hill.

Chapter 3

Organizations, citizens and consumers

LEARNING OBJECTIVES

By the end of this chapter you should be able to:

- Identify and describe the nature of the beneficiary of a public service.
- Identify the likely expectations of the 'actor'.
- Identify the organizational consequences of the relationship with the beneficiary.

KEY POINTS OF THIS CHAPTER

- Citizens are not simple consumers of public services.
- Citizens' expectations will be wider, encompassing elements taking place upstream and downstream from the moment of interaction with the organization, and will be fused with the notion of publicness.
- Interacting with the citizen entails, at all times, interacting as well with the elector, the member of the political whole, and not simply with the atomized consumer.
- The nature of the citizen, and the way in which organizations interact with them has greatly changed over the last 50 to 60 years and now encompasses the logics of the administered, the user, the consumer and the citizen-partner.

KEY TERMS

Actor – generic term used to refer in a neutral manner to the individual interacting with a public organization in an administrative manner.

continued . . .

KEY TERMS ... *continued*

Consumer – actor defining his role at the moment of the exchange, underlining the importance of the concept of choice over all others.

Citizen-partner – actor that is defined by his integration to the various processes of the state, underlining logics of transparency and participation.

Administered – most traditional form of the actor, defined by a logic of distance, hierarchy and relative powerlessness.

User – actor defined first and foremost by his right to services. Concept that evolved in the post-war period, especially used in France.

INTRODUCTION

The public sector, in democratic systems, has always had a close relationship with the population at large. It is a source of legitimacy (through elections), and a source of financing (through taxes). But, more than anything, it is the object of the action of the public sector.

In the field of public administration, the study of this relationship has developed along two relatively distinct lines. The first has been focusing on the relationship with the citizen as a political entity. In this category one finds opinion polls, electoral analyses or more conceptual discussion on the nature of the citizen and of democracy. The other strand of research is more recent and focuses on the study of the relationship with the citizen as an administrative entity; the study of the delivery of public services. As students of public marketing, it is to that second aspect of the relationship that we shall focus on.

In this relationship, the citizen as a political entity is of course not entirely forgotten. A citizen interacting with a public organization, no matter how transactional the relationship, will retain part of their political and even 'electoral' nature. It is, in part, that public nature that will qualify much of this discussion.

HISTORICAL EVOLUTION OF THE CITIZEN– PUBLIC-ADMINISTRATION RELATIONSHIP

Over the last decades, consumers and citizens have mutated: they are now better informed, more active and reactive and represent an increasingly enigmatic actor for businesses and public organisations. These new realities are rooted in economic, technological, social or political developments. They have opened new possibilities for the relationship between individuals and organizations – greater participation, choice, voice, etc.

35 ■

New possibilities are effectively re-shaping public sector organizations and the relationships they build with citizens. Citizens, in return, are adapting to these realities either by embracing, resisting or even initiating some of them. The different types of relationships and roles for citizens – through the development of terminologies of 'user', 'administered', 'consumer' or 'partner' – are now accepted by both citizens and administrations as possibilities even if not as concrete realities yet.

A first step to analyse the multiplication of roles and attributes is to look at the elements that made this very discussion possible: the movement away from the traditional or Weberian model through the emergence of the individual. This transformation of the role of the citizen away from uniformity and administrative imposition has created room for other approaches, and, in doing so, made possible our very own discussion on public marketing.

The evolution of a relationship

For a long time, the relationship between citizens and public administrations has been rooted in the traditional or bureaucratic model best presented by Max Weber (1921). This ideal-type model, even if not uniformly and entirely applied, gives a rather clear image of the main characteristics of public-sector organizations and the roles and attributes of citizens in Western liberal democracies. This particular image, still valid in many ways to this day, has been at the heart of most reflections on citizens and public organizations until the last few decades.

This model is rooted in a system giving pre-eminence to juridical notions and concepts. A high degree of legal formalism taints the internal structure of public administrations, the possibilities and realities of citizens, but also the modes of relation they develop between them. In this model, public administrations are characterized by the concepts of professionalism, hierarchy and unity while the citizen is in a relationship that is characterized by the notions of distance and authority.

The traditional role of citizens

Distance and authority are, in part, a consequence of the construction of organizations. Public administrations are in control of expert knowledge through their professionalism and mastery of administrative laws and present themselves as a unified organizational structure. The public administration is thus in a position of authority vis-à-vis the citizen.

The notion of distance between citizen and public administration in this traditional model is based on a rigid and unidirectional nature of the interaction. The citizen finds himself 'too far' from the organization to have any significant influence in the relationship. Power and control flow from the organization to the citizen, not the other way around. The rules of contact are solely developed and controlled by the administration. This distance marks the administration as being in a different sphere, being separate, exterior and superior to the 'mere' citizen.

This traditional model is therefore one in which the citizen has little control over the relationship and is in fact dominated by the organization. The definition that best encapsulates the reality of the citizen in such a system is probably that of Chevallier for whom citizens are placed in a situation of radical inferiority, in a situation of dependence and forced to submit to a mysterious, removed and omnipotent authority over which they have not power. But this particular construct, this particular role for the citizen, has been challenged.

The emergence of the individual

The current debate is moving us beyond this traditional model of the passive citizen. It is this passive attitude and the limited possibilities for citizens in a Weberian model that have for a long time restrained the demand for more accommodating and flexible types of relationships with public administrations; in a word, for marketing.

A central transformation has made the current debate on the role of the citizen both possible and important: the rise in influence of the individual in the considerations of public administrations (OECD, 2005b). The citizen has seen his position in the relationship with public organizations move from the periphery to the centre. This centrality has meant a focus on and by the citizen in defining, delivering and evaluating the various services provided by public organizations.

Various scholars have presented the drivers of this transformation of the citizen's role in the relationship with public organisations. Clarke (2004) has underlined three main vectors that pushed the individual to the fore: socio-political evolutions, technological change and social consumerism. Among the most significant socio-political movements that have influenced the centrality of the individual in the citizen–public administration nexus is what has been termed the 'decline of deference': a generalized trend away from hierarchical social relations towards more egalitarian relationships and distributions of power. Moving away from a 'professionals know best' approach, it has effectively opened the door to the voice of the citizen (Hirschman, 1970). The opinion of the citizen was now a contribution to be valued in itself.

These transformations occur in combination with the widespread development of communication technologies. Technological changes have created possibilities that were once impossible, namely in terms of information management and diffusion as well as more targeted and individualized interactions with citizens. The organization has more detailed information about its own activities (analytical accounting) and better and improved channels to interact with the citizen on an individual basis. Social consumerism has meant the development and diffusion of a particular model of interaction between individuals and private-sector organizations. The growth of consumption in the private sphere has had a spill-over effect to the public sector. The possibilities seen and experienced on an increasingly regular basis in the private sector led to demands, explicit or implicit, from citizens for similar possibilities in the public realm.

These possibilities have also been made possible by transformations affecting public administrations and the relationships themselves. Over the past decades, the perimeter of action of public administrations has greatly increased leading to the multiplication of interactions between citizens and public administrations. That extension has led to new types of relationships and new logics of interaction, often moving away from the traditional Weberian mould. Also the very employees of these public administrations have been changing and slowly moving away from more traditional Weberian conceptions of their organizations and of the relationships they have with citizens. Their willingness to face change and to further integrate the individual in their approaches is also important.

Many scholars and practitioners have studied and pushed forward the concept of a citizen-centred management of public organizations (Clinton and Gore, 1992; UNDP, 2002). Accordingly, the role of the citizen in the preoccupations of public-sector organizations can be structured in three distinct yet overlapping spheres of public management (Caron, 2006): governance, management and service provisions.

The governance aspect is characterized by the increased participation of citizens in policy making and by the role of trust as an important metric of organizational performance (Vigoda-Gadot and Yuval, 2003; Heintzman and Marson, 2005). The role of the citizen has been strengthened by the multiplication of official forums inviting the participation of individual citizens into the policy-making process. This system, defined at the individual level, has also been replicated at a more organized level with the growing involvement of non-governmental organizations.

The management aspect is characterized by the increasing integration of citizens within managerial oversight mechanisms and by the role of efficiency (and perceived efficiency) as an important metric of organizational performance. At the managerial level, the role of the citizen has thus been transformed by the development of these oversight mechanisms allowing organized groups, including journalists, civil society and individual citizens, to peer within the organization and take part in the discussions regarding issues of management and accountability. The traditional managerial objective – the strict respect of budgetary lines – is still central but it is no longer seen as an exclusively internal matter. Through this transformation, the efficiency of the organization and its perceived efficiency, seen and perceived by the citizen, represent a new obligation. This obligation is directly derived from the centrality given to citizens.

The service-provision aspect is characterized by the development of surveying techniques, an increasing responsiveness to citizens, and the role of satisfaction as an important metric of organizational performance (Parasuraman et al., 1985). At the service end, the citizen has developed (qualitatively and quantitatively) his role in the interaction with public administrations. Quantitatively, the opinion of the citizen is sought more and more often as a guide to the adequacy of the policies as well as the modalities of their delivery. Qualitatively, the opinions expressed carry an increasing amount of 'weight' in the management of organizations. The level of satisfaction of the citizen takes here an importance that 'percolates' upward in terms of management and governance.

Concrete examples of the development of this newfound centrality of the citizen, real or simply rhetorical, include the Citizen First surveys and the 1–800-O-Canada campaigns in Canada, Service Public in France, USAGov in the USA, DirectGov in the UK, the central Swiss administrations' website, etc.[1]

Two approaches to the role of the individual

Two movements have, at varying degrees, changed the dynamics and functioning of public administrations: New Public Management (Osborne and Gaebler, 1993; Hood, 1991) and the 'Democratic Governance' agenda (Vigoda, 2002; UNDP, 2003).

These two approaches hold different conceptions of public action and perceptions of the role of the citizen in his relation with administrations. These conceptions are, in many ways, antagonistic. Whereas the NPM literature has repositioned the citizen as a client or even a consumer, emphasizing the reactivity to his needs and desires by a managerial and economic logic, Democratic Governance has tried to underline the nature of a citizen, transforming him into an effective co-producer of policies and services. Both movements give an increasingly important role to the individual, but they do it in fairly different ways, emphasizing different roles.

A TYPOLOGY OF THE CITIZEN FOR PUBLIC MANAGERS

The transformations to the relationship between citizens and public administrations have had numerous consequences. One of the main consequences of this situation has been the vast increase in the vocabulary used to identify the beneficiary of public-sector-produced goods and services and his relationships with public administrations: citizen, patient, citizen-consumer, client, administered, partner, tax payer, etc. Out of this situation we find two organizational approaches to the structuring of these possibilities (dichotomy and amalgamation) and one overriding dynamic (organizational confusion).

Dichotomy

The dichotomous approach has been characterized by the specific attempt to contrast the various roles and underline the various ways in which these possibilities are mutually exclusive: citizens are consumers and not participants, clients but not users, etc. They are either rooted in the public or the private sphere. For many scholars, there is more than a simple divide between possibilities. This approach glosses over the increasing interpenetrations of these various spheres of activity. This dichotomous approach has the benefit of simplifying the current situation, but in so doing it creates a structure that is more of a pastiche than a useful analysis.

Amalgamation

Another approach has been the amalgamation of constructs in the shape of the 'citizen-consumer-user-administered-tax-payer'. While the dichotomous approach has divided roles, the amalgamation approach has simply abolished all division. Such amalgamation cannot, by definition, account for the various possibilities for the citizen. For example, the Conseil Économique et Social of the Languedoc-Roussillon Region in France speaks of the 'citoyen-consommateur-usager-contribuable' (2002) thus collating a large number of terminologies. But, many have simply joined two logics: the British National Health Service (NHS) has an exchange platform to discuss its services entitled the 'Patient-Citizen exchange', while the French health system speaks of the need to provide information to the 'consumer-user' of its services (2002). In all these cases, the analysis of the current situation is avoided by the direct accumulation of older and newer possibilities. Out of such an analysis, the ability to understand the current roles (especially at the managerial level) is reduced rather than augmented.

Confusion

The strategies adopted, ranging from the complete dichotomy to amalgamation, seem to imply that either the differentiation of terms has no important bearing on the situation or that these terms are too complex to be effectively sorted and understood. A large number of public organizations seem to be located at the crossroads of this confusion. Examples are numerous: the development of 'Citizen Charters' that mainly reflect consumerist aspects of the relationships (UNDP, 2002); the use of the term 'client' applied to such unwilling participants as prisoners and hospital patients (Sampieri-Teissier and Sauviat, 2001). While working in an area that has been traditionally defined by highly asymmetrical relationships, the Canada Customs and Revenue Agency (CCRA, 2003), the organization in charge, among other things, of collecting income tax, clearly mentions that its very structure is built according to 'client groups'. For any inquiry as to their various obligations under Canadian laws, citizens must contact the Directorate of Client Services (CCRA, 2003). The mention of the 'customer' is also found in the British Social Security and Inland Revenue Department (Cabinet Office, 1999), an institution that used to be highly structured around the imposition of control by the administration. This list of examples regarding the haphazard use of concepts to describe the current possible roles for citizens could be extended significantly both in terms of geography and types of public organization.

The situation has led to an increasing level of tension between confused administrations and confused citizens. For administrations, confusion as to the possibilities for the relationship, which approach to take and the way in which to enact it, and confusion for citizens as to the nature of these roles and their effectiveness. Ferlie, Lynn and Pollitt mention in their introduction to *The Oxford Handbook of Public Management* that 'the organization and management of public services is moving through an intriguing and even disorienting period across the world' (2005). The situation described so far in terms of the relationship between citizens and public organizations, does feel like 'an intriguing and even disorienting period'.

STRUCTURING ROLES

A typology is an analytical tool allowing the structuring of possibilities according to specific criterion. Table 3.1 introduces a typology of the roles of the actor in his relationships with public administrations. This typology uses five criteria – history, heteronomy/autonomy, uniformity/diversity, participation and directionality/ relationality – in addition to a key concept and type of service.

The first criterion selected refers to the historical origins of the various roles of the actor. There exists a presupposition linking the appearance of roles with specific historical and institutional eras, creating different possibilities of interaction by their very framework. The transformations of the roles of the actor have generally gone hand in hand with the transformation of public services themselves.

Heteronomy and autonomy represent the opposite ends of a continuum and are crucial to differentiating the internal logic of each role. The heteronymous actor is one with little to no influence on the relationship with public administrations, while the autonomous actor is one with a high level of influence on the decisions affecting him.

Table 3.1 Typology of the actor

	The actor			
	Administered	User	Consumer	Citizen–partner
History	The State	Welfare state	Regulatory State	Post-modern State
Key concepts	Obligation	Right to service	Choice	Participation
Types of service	Regalian	Public	Universal	Democratic
Heteronomy/ autonomy	Heteronomy	Restrained heteronomy	False autonomy	Autonomy
Uniformity/ diversity	Uniformity	Conditional diversity	Large diversity	Total diversity
Participation	Electoral	By the use made of the different services and the rights attached to them	Choice limited to the moment of consumption	Guiding administrative action by its involvement
Directionality and	Top-down	Top-down	Bottom-up	Inward–outward
reliability	Unilateral domination	Rights limit arbitrary decisions	Apparent supremacy but needs defined by the administration	Symbiosis

This distinction is to be understood as a matter of degree and not in absolute terms. One is more or less autonomous, exhibits more or less heteronomy in a relationship.

The concepts of uniformity and diversity also represent opposites along a continuum. They reflect the degree of pluralism in the actor as recognized by the organization: the differences between individual actors that the organization recognizes. Are actors all the same or is there a certain level differentiation between them to be introduced? This element conditions the degree of individualization of the relation and thereby modulates the potential roles of the actor.

Participation is the actor's ability to take part in the exchange. The actor's capabilities but also his participatory possibilities must be defined. Is the participation taken in the largest sense of the word, including the direct, potential and non-users, or is it limited to the precise moment of interaction between the individual actor and the organization?

Directionality and relationality centre on the focus of power – who effectively controls the relationship. It is crucial to the definition of the roles of the actor in his relationship with public administrations. The capability to control the relationship is the defining element, that which allows for the activation or deactivation of the possibilities of the exchange.

A typology of the actor

The typology is constructed from elements in the international literature about the possible roles of the actor and presents four phenotypes that are analysed according to the structuring elements presented above.

The roles presented – the administered, the user, the consumer and the citizen partner – emanate mainly from the analysis of the experiences of the United Kingdom, Canada, the United States and France.

The administered

The elements making up this definition of the actor (inferiority, dependence) and the organization (removed, omnipotent) are key to understanding this particular role of the actor. This actor represents the powerless and the dependent, the one that is spoken to but has no real voice in the relationship. This model of the actor is best exemplified in relationships with organizations such as fiscal administrations and justice.

The administered is generally linked with organizations such as the fiscal administration or the legal system, underlining a relationship that is not reciprocal and marked by a high level of obligation on his part; it is a monologue rather than a dialogue. What are emphasized in all these relationships are the actor's obligations to participate and to engage in the relationship with the organization. In this relationship the actor has a strong level of heteronomy because he is constrained by the organization, hence his 'radical inferiority'. The position of the administered in this particular spectrum would be nearly absolute if it were not for the rules and regulations framing the actions of the administration.

The administered is powerless and has no autonomy to define the relationship in his own terms, aside from the rules and regulations bounding the relationship. The administered has power only insofar as he defends the strict applications of administrative law. When within his rights, he can be a powerful foe to the organisation. But this power is defensive and mainly negative, and cannot be projected or used proactively. This lack of power in the administrative relationship is not to be confused with the real power the administered has in his political relationship with the public sector.

In a relationship defined by dependence and subjugation, he is perceived in an almost completely uniform manner by the organization. There is, for the organization, not a multitude of administered, but an administered in the singular that sits for all the others, powerlessly. The level of differentiation in the appreciation of the actor and the services to be provided is minimal and in fact some would even say contradicts the nature of the administered. The model is based on equality in front of the law and the numerous governmental organizations. So, any differentiation, any segmentation, is bound to be problematic.

There is no active participation on the part of the actor. The participation is happening at a higher level and in a limited way, in terms of the relationship with the political sphere, through the electoral process. It is as an elector that the administered comes into being. Only through this particular quality does the administered have a voice.

Obligation is the key construct to recognizing the administered. Without the mandatory nature of a relationship there is no administered. That obligation might be defined as the obligation to engage (taxes) or an obligation of provider (e.g. La Poste for letters under 50 grams in Europe).

The user

In France, the central locus of the development of the concept, the user is outlined first in the Civil Code of 1804 in which it is noted that the user has a real right of usage on goods belonging to others that cannot be loaned or ceded.[2] It is in his use of public services and the rights that are attached to it that the concept of the user takes its roots. It is this use of public services that defines the role of the actor. It was to boom in the post-war years with the development of the welfare state.

This conceptualization was in stark contrast to that of the administered's legal roots, aimed mainly at circumscribing governmental action; the idea of the user and of public services allowed for the almost unlimited extension of such services. But above and beyond the simple availability of public services, the universal nature of the various service provisions (health care, education, social services) were also aimed at achieving wider objectives.

According to Spanou (2003) the user has the right to choose and a certain critical distance. The possibilities afforded to the user were unknown by the administered. Hence, this new role gave the user wider autonomy. Despite the move away from the

43 ▪

high level of heteronomy experienced by the administered, the user is nonetheless also quite constrained. Even in this role, the actor is in a situation that has been characterized as 'administrative paternalism' (Chevallier, 1992). More autonomous, the user still does not have the power to make meaningful decisions. He has more rights, but the administration continues to define the structure and modalities of the relationship.

The recognition of the diversity of the actor is conditional. The little diversity accepted by the organization is seen from high above. The administration decides and segments the offers and thus recognizes the diversity of the user. It is a privilege granted by the administration. In this sense the actor has but little power in the relationship that is shaped and dictated by professionals within the organisation.

The level and type of participation the administration allows to the user are different and more varied than those for the administered. This new form allows the actor to exert pressure for increased autonomy and diversity. This voice has been made possible, first and foremost, by the multiplication of user associations and by the pressures for greater autonomy.

The relationship has changed with the user where the administration is not there to dominate but rather to serve. This represents a complete inversion of logic. It sees the emergence of the changes to come in the increasing centrality of the individual in the relationship.

One notable exception with the next model – the consumer – is the relative absence of choice for the user. The administration generally has a monopolistic role in the relationship. In such a situation voice or exit are possible, even if both carry a high price in terms of being denied service or not being able to afford the same service provided by a third party. In fact, on many levels, the user remains an administered.

The directionality of the relationship is thus clear: the actor is not at the centre of the relationship – he is in a top-down relationship where he has a limited amount of autonomy. He is captive, and has the power either to shape himself according to the wishes of the organization or to press for changes through channels defined by the organization.

The 'rights guaranteed to users' of Chevallier is the concept that accounts for all other aspects. It is by these rights that the user differentiates himself from the administered, even if the distance covered is not as important as might have been believed. The user defines himself by his usage of services and defines the relationship by the mandatory participation of the organization in these relationships.

The consumer

The appearance of the consumer as a possible role for the actor in public-sector relationships is relatively recent. Linked in part with the rise of New Public Management and the development of social consumerism, it now represents a generalized model being used by administrations and assumed by actors in most OECD countries (OECD, 2005a). The term is rooted in the concepts of choice, individuality and satisfaction, and it represents one of the two main challenges to the historical models of the administered and the user.

Born of the crisis of public finance, the increasing marketization of social interactions, and the rise in neo-liberal economics and rational choice theory, NPM sought to bring into the public sphere concepts and dynamics that were once the exclusive domain of the private sector. It has led governments to rethink some of their approaches, most notably in terms of strategic management and service delivery in part through the development of the regulatory State (Lane, 2000). This trend has been underway for more than a decade. First emerging in Anglo-Saxon countries (most notably in New Zealand) it has had a direct effect on most governments, through the application, in one way or another, of its basic premises: choice, subsidiarity, leadership and control. These dynamics have paved the way for a new understanding of the relationship between actors and public organizations, namely the focus on the actor as consumer. This approach, in a reversal of the traditional Weberian concept of the hierarchical public bureaucracy, positions the actor at the centre of the organization's preoccupations.

In the United States, the recognition of the consumer in the public sector was first noted in Al Gore's *From Red Tape to Results* (Gore, 1993) with his new customer service contract. It put official and high-ranking words on a reality that had appeared through the Total Quality movement almost two decades before (Fountain, 2001). The Putting People First initiative of 1992, stemming from similar sentiments, urged organizations to identify their 'clients' and to survey their attitudes and expectations (Clinton and Gore, 1992). This was followed by the 'setting customer service standards' executive order of 1993 that further pushed this idea on governmental departments and agencies to 'identify the customers who are, or should be, served by the agency' and 'survey customers to determine the kind and quality of services they want and their level of satisfaction with existing services' (The White House, 1993).

The actor as a consumer is considered to have a 'false' autonomy. As a consumer, one could believe that he is in an interaction framed along the lines of those in the private sector, which include, among other things, a large choice and the possibility of exit. The autonomy, presumably full and complete on the part of the actor, is qualified as 'false', given that the public nature of the encounter, and the particularities of specific encounters will, in many cases, limit the potential of exit and the nature of choices for the actor. The decisions regarding possibilities in terms of choice and exit are defined not by the actor but rather by the administration. The actor's autonomy depends on the good-will of the organization more than anything else. The difference with the user is in the apparent bottom-up situation of the consumer.

The consumer has, by definition, a large diversity since the concept entails a tailoring of services and goods offered to the smallest possible segments, and thus the multiplication of the possibilities at all levels for the actor. In a relationship with the actor as a consumer, the organization is faced with as many types of consumer as there are consumers. It represents the highest possible level of diversity. This position is, of course, more or less plausible depending on the specifics of the relationship in question. The idealized nature of the construct is here quite clear. The consumer participates insofar as he uses the services offered. This participation is self-interested, focused on the moment of exchange, and does not have a wider political or social component.

The actor is an abstraction without any social identity (Spanou, 2003). The actor is atomized and completely isolated in this relationship.

The transformation of the actor into a consumer effectively mutes his reactions and limits his capacity for voice to individual preferences. In this configuration the actor seeks above all satisfaction in his encounter with the public organisation. This is a situation in which the actor could theoretically have voice only insofar as he is also a member of the political whole. This voice is not linked with the actor as a consumer. In fact, he seems to mirror the administered more than any other model.

Given the characteristics mentioned above, the actor in this configuration does not have the collective power or the option to resist the administration. The asymmetry of power remains considerable despite all the empowering language used to describe the relationship. Consumers 'do not participate in decisions concerning the products they buy' (Elcock, 1996). This is, therefore, a false bottom-up situation. The actor is, in many cases, not shaping services by his preferences. Rather he sees them being dictated by the organization and this within the limits of their acceptability for him.

The key concern and the key concept connected to the rise of the idea of the consumer in the provision of public services is the notion of choice; thus empowering the actor to shape public service provisions. Potentially, choice is believed to offer a far more direct and precise influence for actors than voice.

For the Office of Public Service Reform in the United Kingdom, 'public services . . . have to be refocused around the needs of patients, the pupils, the passengers and the general public rather than those who provide the services' (Blair: preface to Office of Public Services Reform, 2002). What the government strives for are 'services personal to each and fair for all' and where 'choice puts the levers in the hands of parents and patients so that they as citizens and consumers can be a driving force for improvement in their public services' (White and Wintour, 2004). Choice in this sense is viewed as a tool to achieve wider objectives. It puts the levers of change firmly in the hands of the actor.

The concept of choice can apply to various aspects of the relationship. There is choice over the type of service, the level of service, the provider, the type of interaction, etc. The implicit assumption is that the actor is willing and able to actively use this tool, that he is able and willing to choose. This does not, however, address the basic asymmetry of information and power between the actor and the organization (Laing and Hogg, 2002).

In many ways, the notion of choice central to the role of the actor as a consumer, is presented more as a way to achieve wider political aims than in developing effective choice at all levels for actors (Clarke and Newman, 2005).

The citizen-partner

While advocates of NPM believe that greater efficiency and better management are the answer to the current woes of political cynicism (Kelly, 2005), supporters of Democratic Governance think that one solution is to make the citizen a more active and engaged participant in the politico-administrative system. This would in turn increase accountability, political and social participation and restore a greater level of trust and confidence in the mechanics and dynamics of public organisations.

This approach has had a direct impact on the conception of the citizen by public organisations. The proponents of Democratic Governance believe that the citizen should not be transformed into a simple consumer of public services, but rather the co-producer and main partner of public organizations. Public organizations are thus operating as part of a network, exchanging and redistributing tasks and responsibilities with the citizen-partner. Whereas NPM underlines the importance of efficiency, Democratic Governance has at its centre the concepts of accountability and democratic participation.

People are not only the simple end receivers of products and services but also co-producers in defining aspects of the interaction. However, many question the effective implementation of these Democratic Governance approaches in the actor–public-administration relationship (Moro, 2001). The relatively recent nature of the development of Democratic Governance in the administrative context has to be kept in mind when evaluating its impacts.

This approach has been linked to what some have called the post-modern State; a State that has fully integrated the actor and other stakeholders in its decisional mechanisms. Being in the system and shaping it by its choices and voices, the actor gains a high level of autonomy. In fact, similarly to other criteria, this one is positioned at an extreme end of the spectrum. The actor as citizen-partner exhibits a total diversity. This is the natural consequence of considering the actor as the embodiment of a singular and uniquely qualified individual not only as recipient of services but as shaper and creator of these services. The citizen-partner is in a system that is neither top-down or bottom-up but inward-outward. This is a symbiotic system between actor and administration. In such a system the level of responsibility on the shoulders of the actor is significantly increased.

At the centre of the concept of the citizen-partner is the idea of participation. That notion has been studied from a number of angles, but the main attempt at structuring it as a tool for interaction has been that of Arnstein (1969) that differentiates between at one end 'token participation' and at the other 'citizen control'.

The various steps on the ladder offer numerous strategies and techniques to involve the actor. These strategies can involve numerous tools:

> small-scale surveys of key informer groups; larger scale customer satisfaction surveys; local/regional/national opinion polls; referenda; surveys of geographic-ally defined populations where spatial factors are believed to be significant; feedback from the frontline experiences of service providers; user boards and suggestion boxes; customer complaints procedures; user advisory boards; repre-sentation of users on boards; focus groups; brainstorming groups; monitoring of news media reports; as well as public hearings or sounding board meetings.
>
> (Humphreys, 2002)

The variety of option is large and in constant evolution.

These procedures, while rooted in a relationship that puts the stress on the citizen-partner, can be the result of ulterior motives. According to Needham's study (2002), the consultation processes under way could benefit the actor as a consumer rather than as a citizen-partner because many of the procedures seek to 'institutionalise a network of passive individuals [rather] than create or empower active citizens' (Chandler, 2001, quoted in Needham, 2002). There is a clear distinction between voice used in the environment of the citizen-partner, allowing for discussion and debate, and the limited possibilities the actor has in his role as a consumer.

PUBLICNESS AND SCHIZOPHRENIA

The first challenge in using a typology of the roles of the actor is that the actor's roles are not homogeneous and consistent; they are constructed at the cross-roads of many overlapping concepts. It is for this reason that the idea of a certain 'schizophrenic' nature has been presented (Villeneuve, 2006). This schizophrenia has two distinct manifestations: one external, the other internal.

The external schizophrenia means that a given actor, when facing a given organization, will not necessarily be the same depending on the conditions of this particular encounter (environmental, temporal, economic, etc.). For example, when dealing with a specific organization providing a specific service, say the issuing of an official certificate, the actor might have different preoccupations than when he is in the same building, likely at the same counter facing the same employee, but this time for the payment of a licence. So, externally, the actor will be perceived as being schizophrenic from one encounter to the next.

The actor's role will also be a construct rather than represent a 'pure' model. This is what can be termed the internal schizophrenia. This schizophrenia therefore manifests itself in the hybrid nature of the actor's roles – not simply exhibiting a 'user' or a 'consumer' to the relationship, but rather a mix and match of the various possibilities. As Clarke (2004) points out, 'we need to take seriously the view that people occupy more than one identity. While this has a general applicability in the conception of multiple or plural subjectivities, it has a particular importance for relationships to public services.'

This hybridization will have to be taken into account as actors will effectively superimpose roles upon roles in their interactions with public administrations. This could either be done in the very construction of the typology, as some of the authors have done by allowing for flexible borders between classifications, or by making provision allowing for a differentiated and flexible use of the typology. The nature of the barriers between the various models in the typology and their relative rigidity or porousness might end up being more significant than their exact positioning. Pushing ahead towards the analytical implications that the challenge of schizophrenia represents lies the question of precedence, as the superimposition of models will also mean the eventual ordering and ranking of these possibilities.[3]

The other challenge is the publicness[4] of the environment of the relationship, as well as the nature of the actor as a member of the general political body. This particular situation has a fundamental role in delimiting the whole sphere of interactions possible and underpins the legitimacy of actions and the expectations of actors and organizations.

In each of the possible structurations of the actor there is a varying degree of this 'political citizen', a part of the collective political whole, present. Each structuration of the roles of the actor, each aspect of a typology, will possess a certain dose of citizenship for the actor and publicness for the relationship. This particularity will serve as a background for the categorization of the roles of the actor. That aspect has to be acknowledged and properly integrated as the challenge of understanding the possibilities for actors resides in great part in this specificity. This is one of the central challenges for the understanding of the current situation and not only for the construction of a typology of roles.

CONSEQUENCES FOR MARKETING

The role of actors has evolved over time to be represented today through a mix of various concepts defined in the typology presented in Table 3.1. These elements raise numerous questions in terms on the role of citizenship and the shape of democracy, on the nature of public interactions and on the objectives of proper public management. But these also raise fundamental questions and issues in terms of public marketing.

Marketing being the study of relationships, the proper understanding of who the organization is facing is crucial. It is a significant step in defining the proper shape to give the relationship in order to ensure a satisfactory outcome for all involved. Some of these specificities are presented in the next chapters, but here are some of the key elements.

It stands to reason that a poor adaptation between the expectation of the actor and the offer of the organization will lead to problems: problems in terms of satisfaction, but also, in the public sector, problems in terms of image and problems in terms of trust. The likely impact on the organization of a poor alignment between the way it defines the actor and the way this same actor defines himself raises numerous problems.

The nature of the various roles presented in the typology vary greatly. These aspects all underline different natures and different expectations. The ability of the organization to address these expectations is at the heart of its attempt at identifying them. Addressing a consumer can be problematic when that actor defines himself as a citizen focusing on issues of transparency and trust and not on issues of price and availability. What is at stake is the very foundation of an organization's marketing strategy.

The impact of this situation bears on all aspects of the organization. The type of role selected by the organization at the planning level, either focusing on a participatory or choice environment, will not target the same types of hires. The qualities sought in the staffing will greatly differ, as will the type of staff the organization is likely to attract. As well, the financial priorities are likely to be different. If price is the key, or the speed of service delivery versus a thorough consultation process, the sensitivity to the price of these options will likely vary as well. Something as simple as the location of the organization would also be affected. Open, transparent and central, or located at a busy intersection of two highways? Large and sunlit or small and dark? Other aspects of the execution will also be affected. The communication approach will need to be tailored to the expectations of the actor and to respect the logic identified and developed through the interaction model and the interactive environment of the organization.

MEASURING ROLES AND PERFORMANCES

The proper identification of the actor and the measuring of his evaluation of the relationship has led to the development, or should we say the adaptation, of various analytical tools. The identification of the actor is a complex affair, and rests as much upon a proper analysis as on the nature and structure of the organization delivering the service. The identification of the model, and more specifically the mix of models present in the relationship, can be achieved through qualitative approaches (interviews of actors) or quantitative approaches (surveys of attitudes). One approach focuses on the evaluation of the perceived performance of the relationship as a way to evaluate the appropriateness of the actor model selected by the organization.

Numerous studies have used the concept of performance as an analytical tool. Many have looked at the performance of the organization (Behn, 2003), focusing on the financial performance (Willoughby and Melkers, 2000; McGill, 2001), the performance of service delivery (Joyce, 1999; OECD, 1997; Kane, 1996) or the effectiveness and efficiency of the organization (Heinrich, 2003). Others have focused on the actor's evaluation of the performance of the organization and his evaluation of the performance of the relationships he has with it (van de Walle and Bouckaert, 2007).

In our case, the focus shall be on the actor's evaluation of the performance of the relationship. Table 3.2 presents some of the criteria used to evaluate the various elements of the relationship in the case of a student counselling organization. These criteria are somewhat removed from the more traditional satisfaction survey approach. They underline the fact that in understanding and evaluating the relationship in the public sector, the mere satisfaction of the actor is not a sufficient metric to evaluate the success of the relationship.

These elements raise the question of the drivers of the performance of the relationship in the public sector. There is no one exact and complete listing of all the drivers of the actor's evaluation of the performance of a public administration. Some scholars put the number of drivers at ten (Neilson et al., 1999) while others claim that there are only five (Parasuraman et al., 1985). The important element at this point of the analysis is simply to take into consideration the fact that there are a number of drivers making up the concept of performance.

These drivers do not all operate in the same way. They can be classified according to their impact in the overall logic of performance evaluation. Four logics are generally underlined (MORI, 2002):

Table 3.2 *Criteria for evaluation of a student counselling organization*

Tangible aspects	Information available for job hunt
	Opportunities available for a specific geographic area
	Large choice of resources for career planning
	Complete information provided by employees
Reliability	Fulfilling promises of service
	Showing a sincere interest in solving problems
	Transmitting the right information every time
	Admitting only flawless reports
Responsibility	Communicating clearly the waiting time
	Rapid service
Safety	Politeness
	Amiability
	Respect for students
Empathy	Having the student's best interest at heart
	Having convenient opening hours

Source: Adapted from Engelland *et al.* (2000).

■ A *dissatisfier* or *hygiene* factor is one that has little impact when present, but a large and negative impact when absent. This particular type of driver can be illustrated through the classical example of a dirty fork in a restaurant. Clean it makes no difference, but the tiniest speck of dirt can make a strongly negative impression on the customer.

■ *Satisfiers* have a positive effect on the overall evaluation when improved beyond a certain point. But when absent or not emphasized they have little to no impact. To continue with the restaurant metaphor: 'if a waiter does not remember you from your last visit to the restaurant you are unlikely to be dissatisfied, but if he does and also remembers your favourite wine, you are likely to be delighted' (MORI, 2002).

■ *Critical* factors will influence satisfaction both ways, positively and negatively. You are likely to be satisfied if service is rapid and dissatisfied when it is slow.

■ *Neutral* factors have little to no influence on one's overall evaluation of a situation.

Taking into account these four potential characteristics of performance drivers allows for a proper understanding of the dynamics. Performance scores can be low or high but depending on the nature of the driver in question they can lead to very different conclusions in terms of overall performance evaluation. Another key element in

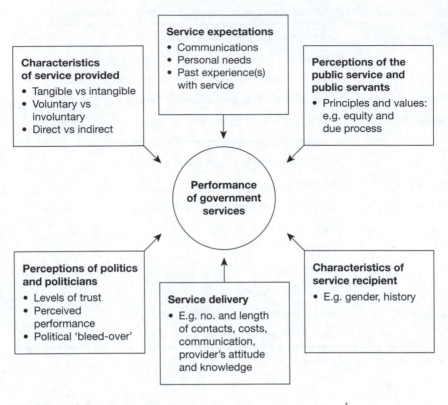

Figure 3.1 *Drivers of performance*

gauging the impact of drivers is the differentiated level of importance attributed to each driver by actors themselves.

Figure 3.1 shows some of the drivers that can be envisaged for the evaluation of the performance of government services.

These various drivers, and their evaluation, allow the organization to have a more subtle image of the relationship and hence to manage its marketing approach accordingly.

ADAPTING TO THE PLURAL NATURE OF THE ACTOR

The recognition of the plurality of roles played by the actor has to be acknowledged at three specific levels: 1) internally within the organization; 2) relationally in effectively shaping the relationship; and 3) at the end point, making it a reality for the actor.

At these three levels one first needs to be aware of the situation before acting on it. A necessary step before thinking about the actor's roles and performance evaluation should be to identify the actor. Who are the beneficiaries of the organisation? Administered, users, consumers, citizen-partners, etc.? Such strategies are presented in Chapter 4.

At the relational level the various modes of interaction should be analysed and categorized in terms of the roles they apply and make possible for the actor. At the organizational level a number of options are present ranging from an analysis of the vocabulary used in active and passive communication, to the analysis of the possible relationships. These elements would generate a mass of information regarding the plural nature of the actor in his relationship with the organization, as well as detailing the roles used in the relationship and in the organization.

Recognizing the plurality of the actor is but a means to an end; in this particular case, the end being a better evaluation by actors of their relations with public administrations. It is for that reason that this process must be made real to the actor.

Another step in recognising plurality would in effect be the development of measures of performance that do take into account these roles. A measure of performance should be introduced to capture the variety of roles the actor plays in the relationship. A more plural measure of the performance of the relationship would, by default, be a measure to recognize the plurality of the actor.

A first step is to clearly establish what these roles ought to be. Taking together the information regarding the actor and the organization, and fully accounting for items such as the type of goods and services the organization delivers, should help in defining the models to be favoured. Proper respect should also be given to the historical moorings of the organization. Just as an organization cannot transform itself overnight, managers should not expect actors to be able to do it. Having identified the model, or models, that best fit with the relationships between actor and public administration, a number of steps can then be taken to minimize the gaps that are likely to develop.

At the organizational level the various models used must be first and foremost homogenized. These models express themselves in predominantly two ways, rhetorical, the vocabulary used, and effective, the way of shaping relationships. The organization should homogenize the vocabulary used, inside and outside the organisation, and clearly posit who the actor is for the organization. The rhetorical should also be harmonized with the effective. There is no need to refer to the consumer if the actor has no choice in the relationship, as this can only lead to problems.

EXERCISE 3.1

In small groups, try to identify that type of actor your organization is serving and to link that with some of the internal marketing and/or managerial tools put in place. Are they developed in harmony or in a separate manner?

Question your co-workers, employees and superiors on the role they ascribe to the actor. Is that definition consistent across the organization? Does it vary according to the hierarchical level, specialization or age and experience?

DISCUSSION QUESTIONS

1   What is the impact of the language used in your communication/marketing on the perceptions of the actor and the organization?
2   In a public-sector setting, should an organization impose a role on the actor or should it be accommodating to his expectations and desires?

NOTES

1   See http://www.iccs-isac.org, http://www.canada.gc.ca, http://www.service-public.fr, http://www.usa.gov, http://www.direct.gov.uk, http://www.ch.ch.
2   Citing Titre III, 'De l'usufruit, de l'usage et de l'habitation'.
3   One can be simultaneously a user and a client, but is the actor more one than the other, and if so in what proportions?
4   Publicness refers here to the environment of the relationship, its location within the public sphere.

REFERENCES

Arnstein, S. R. (1969) A Ladder of Citizen Participation, *Journal of the American Insitute of Planners*, 35, 216–24.

Behn, R. D. (2003) Why Measure Performance? Different Purposes Require Different Measures, *Public Administration Review*, 63, 586–606.

Cabinet Office (1999) Modernising Government, London, HMSO.

Caron, D. J. (2006) Customer Satisfaction and Public Interest, *Optimum*, 36, 1–10.

CCRA (2003) General Income Tax and Benefit Guide, Ottawa, The Canada Customs and Revenue Agency.

Chandler, D. (2001) Active Citizens and the Therapeutic State: the Role of Democratic Participation in Local Government Reform, *Policy and Politics*, 29, 3–14.

Chevallier, J. (1992) Regards sur L'administré, in Chauvière, M. and Godbout, J. T. (eds.) *Les Usagers Entre Marché et Citoyenneté*, Paris: L'Harmattan.

Clarke, J. (2004) Creating Citizen-Consumers: the Trajectory of an Identity, CASCA Annual Conference, London, May.

Clarke, J. and Newman, J. (2005) What's in a Name? New Labour's Citizen-Consumers and the Remaking of Public Services, paper presented to CRESC conference Culture and Social Change: Disciplinary Exchanges, University of Manchester, July.

Clinton, B. and Gore, A. (1992) *Putting People First*, New York, Three Rivers Press.

Conseil Economique et Social du Languedoc-Roussillon (2002) Assises Régionales des Libertés locales, Montpellier: Conseil Economic et Social.

Elcock, H. (1996) What Price Citizenship? Public Management and the Citizen's Charter, in Chandler, J. A. (ed.) *The Citizen's Charter*, Dartmouth, Aldershot: Aldershot Publishers.

Engelland, B. T., Workman, L. and Singh, M. (2000) Ensuring Service Quality for Campus Career Services Centers: A Modified SERVQUAL Scale, *Journal of Marketing Education*, 22, 236–45.

Ferlie, E., Lynn, L. E. and Pollitt, C. (2005) *The Oxford Handbook of Public Management*, Oxford, Oxford University Press.

Fountain, J. E. (2001) Paradoxes of Public Sector Customer Service, *Governance*, 14, 55–73.

Gore, A. (1993) *From Red Tape to Results: Creating a Government that Works Better and Costs Less. Report of the National Performance Reviews*, New York, Times Books and Random House.

Heinrich, C. J. (2003) Measuring Public Sector Performance and Effectiveness, in Peters, B. G. and Pierre, J. (eds) *Handbook of Public Administration*, London, Sage Publications.

Heintzman, R. and Marson, B. (2005) People, Service and Trust: Is There a Public Sector Value Chain? *International Review of Administrative Sciences,* 71, 549–75.

Hirschman, A. O. (1970) *Exit Voice and Loyalty: Responses to Decline in Firms, Organizations, and States*, Cambridge, Harvard University Press.

Hood, C. (1991) A Public Management for All Seasons? *Public Administration,* 69, 3–19.

Humphreys, P. C. (2002) *Effective Consultation With The External Customer*, Dublin, Institute of Public Administration.

Joyce, P. (1999) *Strategic Management for the Public Services*, Buckingham, Open University Press.

Kane, J. (1996) Services de Qualité: Guide des Gestionnaires pour la Prestation de Services de Qualité, Ottawa, Secrétariat du Conseil du Trésor du Canada.

Kelly, J. M. (2005) The Dilemma of the Unsatisfied Customer in a Market model of Public Administration, *Public Administrative Review,* 65, 76–84.

Laing, A. W. and Hogg, G. (2002) Political Exhortation, Patient Expectation and Professional Execution: Perspectives on the Consumerisation of Health Care, *British Journal of Management,* 13, 173–88.

Lane, J. E. (2000) *New Public Management*, London, Routledge.

McGill, R. (2001) Performance Budgeting, *The International Journal of Public Sector Management,* 14, 376–90.

MORI (2002) Public Service Reform, Measuring and Understanding Customer Satisfaction, London, The Prime Minister's Office of Public Service Reform.

Moro, G. (2001) The Citizen's Side of Governance, *The Journal of Corporate Citizenship,* 7, 18–30.

Needham, C. (2002) Empowering Citizens, Consumers, Councillors or Cabinets? The Impact of Consultation on Local Government in the United Kingdom, ECPR Joint Workshop Session, Turin, March.

Neilson, A., Mcgriffen, D., Stewart, D. and Wisniewski, M. (1999) Can't Get No Satisfaction? Using a Gap Approach to Measure Service Quality, Edinburgh, Accounts Commission for Scotland.

Organisation for Economic Co-operation and Development (OECD) (1997) Contracting Out Government Services: Best Practice Guidelines and Case Studies, Paris, OECD.

—— (2005a) Public Sector Modernization: Open Government, *Policy Brief*, Paris, OECD.

—— (2005b) Services to Citizens, Paris, OECD.

55

Office of Public Services Reform (2002) *Reforming Our Public Services,* London, OPSR.

Osborne, D. and Gaebler, T. (1993) *Reinventing Government: How the Entrepreneurial Spirit is Transforming the Public Sector,* New York, Penguin.

Parasuraman, A., Zeithaml, V. A. and Berry, L. L. (1985) A Conceptual Model of Service Quality and Its Implications for Future Research, *Journal of Marketing,* 49, 41–50.

Sampieri-Teissier, N. and Sauviat, I. (2001) Les Évolutions du Positionnement des Acteurs du Système Hospitalier: le Cas de la Situation du Patient-Usager-Client, conference held in RECEMAP seminar, October, Limoges, Laboratoire du CRETLOG.

Spanou, C. (2003) *Citoyens et Administration: les Enjeux de L'autonomie et du Pluralisme,* Paris, L'Harmattan.

The White House (1993) Executive Order 12862: Setting Customer Service Standards.

United Nations Development Programme (UNDP) (2002) *Citizen's Charters,* New York, UNDP.

—— (2003) Access to Information: Practice Note, New York, UNDP.

van de Walle, S. and Bouckaert, G. (2007) Perceptions of Productivity and Performance in Europe and the USA, *International Journal of Public Administration,* 30, 1,123–40.

Vigoda, E. (2002) From Responsiveness to Collaboration: Governance, Citizens, and the Next Generation of Public Administration, *Public Administration Review,* 62, 527–40.

Vigoda-Gadot, E. and Yuval, F. (2003) Managerial Quality, Administrative Performance and Trust in Government Revisited, *The International Journal of Public Sector Management,* 16, 502–22.

Villeneuve, J. P. (2006) Citoyen-Clients et Administrations: Acteurs Confus et Organisations Entêtées. Typologie et Analyse des Rôles. *Revue Économique et Sociale,* March, 81–90.

Weber, M. (1921) *Wirtschaft und Gesellschaft. Grundriss der Sozialökonomik,* Tübingen, Mohr.

White, M. and Wintour, P. (2004) Public Services: the Choice, *The Guardian,* London, 24 June.

Willoughby, K. G. and Melkers, J. E. (2000) Implementing PBB: Conflicting Views of Success, *Public Budgeting and Finance,* 20, 105–20.

Part II

Chapter 4

Basic marketing concepts

LEARNING OBJECTIVES

By the end of this chapter you should be able to:

- Identify the various actors in the marketing system of your organization and their impact/role.
- Classify market orientations, either product- or client-oriented, and identify the pitfalls of each.
- Identify the market orientation of your organization and competitors.
- Understand the nuances of the marketing mix.

KEY POINTS OF THIS CHAPTER

- There are four main concepts in marketing: the market system, market orientation, marketing management and marketing instruments.
- Among marketing instruments, the marketing mix – with its concepts of product, price, promotion and place – is a central tool for structuring a marketing initiative.

KEY TERMS

Systemic analysis – analytical tool of an organization's market environment, including the organization, its competitors, marketing activities, intermediaries, prescriptors, final users and environmental factors. It allows the proper understanding of relationships between actors.

continued . . .

KEY TERMS ... *continued*

Market orientation – helps identify an organization's basic approach to its marketing functions; it can be either product-oriented (focused on a product's technical development and overall presentation to the client) or client-oriented (first assess client's needs, then design the product accordingly).

Marketing management – tools and processes of marketing which facilitate the relationship and exchange between partners – a cycle composed of marketing analysis; marketing strategy; marketing planning and organization; marketing resources; and marketing control.

Marketing instruments – instruments (e.g. marketing mix) designed to reach and convince target groups.

CONCEPT OVERVIEW

Over time, marketing has developed numerous concepts – as presented in detail by the leading works on marketing (McDonald, 2007; Kotler and Armstrong, 2009). Without seeking to be exhaustive, this chapter develops the main basic concepts which continue to serve as marketing references and are important for understanding the following chapters.

Figure 4.1 regroups these concepts synthetically. They are:

■ The *marketing system*, taking into account all the parties involved in the exchange and explaining the inter-relationships between them. Only the integration and understanding of what is at stake for partners in the exchange makes it possible to understand, and if possible anticipate, their behaviour.

■ *Marketing orientation*, which, put simply, means the culture adopted by an organization in its relationship with clients. Various orientations are possible, and may affect both how the organization is run, and how its clients behave.

■ *Marketing management*, involving all the decisions, processes and activities (from strategy to control of marketing activities) that an organization takes and sets in motion to attain its marketing goals.

■ *Marketing instruments*, consisting of the visible part of an organization's marketing, concerning elements addressed to clients (concrete offer of products and services, prices, communication, agents or distributors proposing products and services, etc.).

A SYSTEMIC, ANALYTICAL APPROACH

Since the emergence of the systems theory (Bertalanffy, 1968), numerous systemic approaches have been developed – in biology, neuroscience, sociology and psychology,

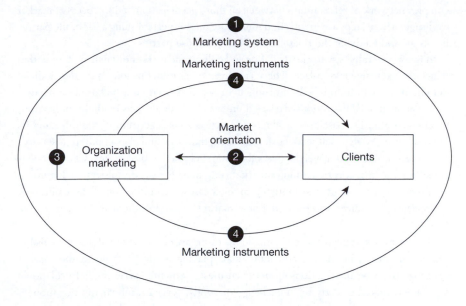

Figure 4.1 *Main marketing concepts*

but also in economics, management and marketing. Systemic analysis is based on the principle that the study of a causal relationship between two elements is often not suited to conveying the functioning of an ensemble – whether this is a living being or a group of people, organizations or electronic systems. It is therefore worth looking more closely at the exchanges between the parties in the system (rather than analysing them individually) and studying the system's checks and balances.

As an organization permanently interacts with other organizations (competitors, suppliers, distributors) and individuals (clients, influencers) within a market frame-work, a systemic approach can be used to list and prioritize the components of the organization's environment (market); study the relationships between these components (competitors, distributors, clients, etc.); and, above all, analyse the effects of decisions or actions taken by one of the components on the system as a whole (how the parties will react when a new service is announced, and what might be the potential consequences on the system's equilibrium). Marketing becomes a sub-system of the organization, which has its own sub-systems like distribution circuits and channels.

From a more practical point of view (Kühn *et al.*, 2006) a systemic approach to marketing can be used to analyse the organization's market environment. Many marketing decisions (launching a new product, changing price strategy, aggressive communication against a competitor, etc.) can spell failure for organizations that are unable to anticipate or understand the actions of the other parties involved and, above all, the corresponding interactions. So it is vital to organize and understand the complex network of relationships between all those participating in the process of market exchange. Three steps are involved: defining the market; establishing a list of the parties involved; and studying the relationship between these parties.

It is not generally easy to clearly define and delimit the market or environment within which the exchange takes place. There are three types of definition: a) legal or judicial definition; b) definition based on products or services; c) definition based on needs.

Legal or judicial definitions are based on laws and regulations or their application, whereas a definition based on products and services takes account of the offer and its various forms. With postal services, for instance, the speed and class of different services (e.g. a second-class letter weighing less than 50g) help define the market. Clients' needs constitute the final way of defining a market (e.g. need for an administrative document to travel from one country to another). In most cases, a combination of these different approaches is required to clearly define a market or environment for exchange (see Box 4.1).

The market system is therefore made up of organizations, individuals responsible for groups of organizations, and individuals playing a specific role in the market exchange process; the relationship between these elements corresponds to relational acts or acts linked directly to an exchange of goods, services, information or money. Figure 4.2 presents a synthesis of the various partners in the exchange process.

Apart from the organization proposing an offer, and its actual and potential competitors, one should remember all the intermediaries which sell products or services using their own marketing measures, as distinct from those of the company producing them. Product users or beneficiaries naturally constitute a major partner in this exchange. Users should nevertheless be defined in the broad sense of the term, often include indirect product- or service-beneficiaries like family members or even friends and relatives (e.g. anyone hospitalized after an accident benefits directly from the service; but their family, and perhaps relatives and/or employer, are indirect beneficiaries). The final major partner consists of external prescriptors or individuals already mentioned:

■ BOX 4.1 PRINCIPAL CRITERIA FOR DEFINING A MARKET

- ■ nature of service (characteristics of offer)
- ■ orientation of transaction (before or after)
- ■ place of transaction
- ■ regulatory elements
- ■ ability to access market (barriers)
- ■ number and size of participants (structure of market)

Source: Adapted from Meffert, Burmann and Kirchgeorg (2008a, pp.49–51).

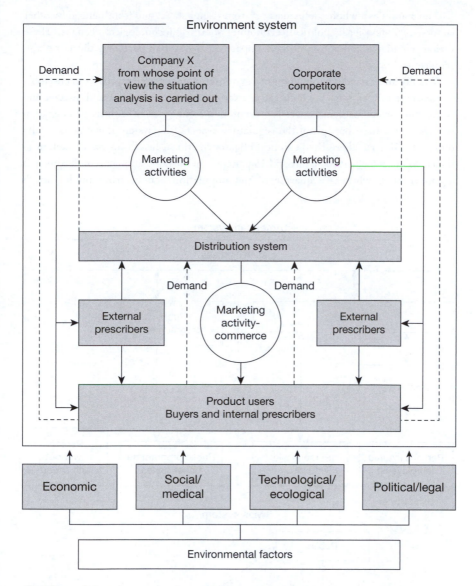

Figure 4.2 *Components of a market viewed as a system*

Source: Kühn and Pasquier (2000).

in many cases, decisions are largely influenced by persons who do not take part directly in the exchange (the nurse influences the choice of milk for an infant, the architect influences the choice of building materials, journalists influence choice of software, etc.). Although they are not buying or selling services, these persons or organizations usually have a decisive impact on decisions taken by other exchange partners.

The market as a whole, defined as a system, is not static, and is influenced by other factors, including legal, political, economic, social or technological changes. These various elements, and above all their impact on the system partners, therefore also require study.

To fully understand the usefulness of a systemic approach with regard to an ensemble of exchange relationships, a comparative example between the USA and Switzerland concerning health insurance cover is presented in Figure 4.3. In both cases the system is largely privatized but, given the regulatory aspects, the system dynamic is totally different. Hitherto there has been no obligatory national health insurance system in the USA,[1] meaning that some (around 15 per cent) of the population have no protection against illness, whereas a quarter of the population benefit from public health

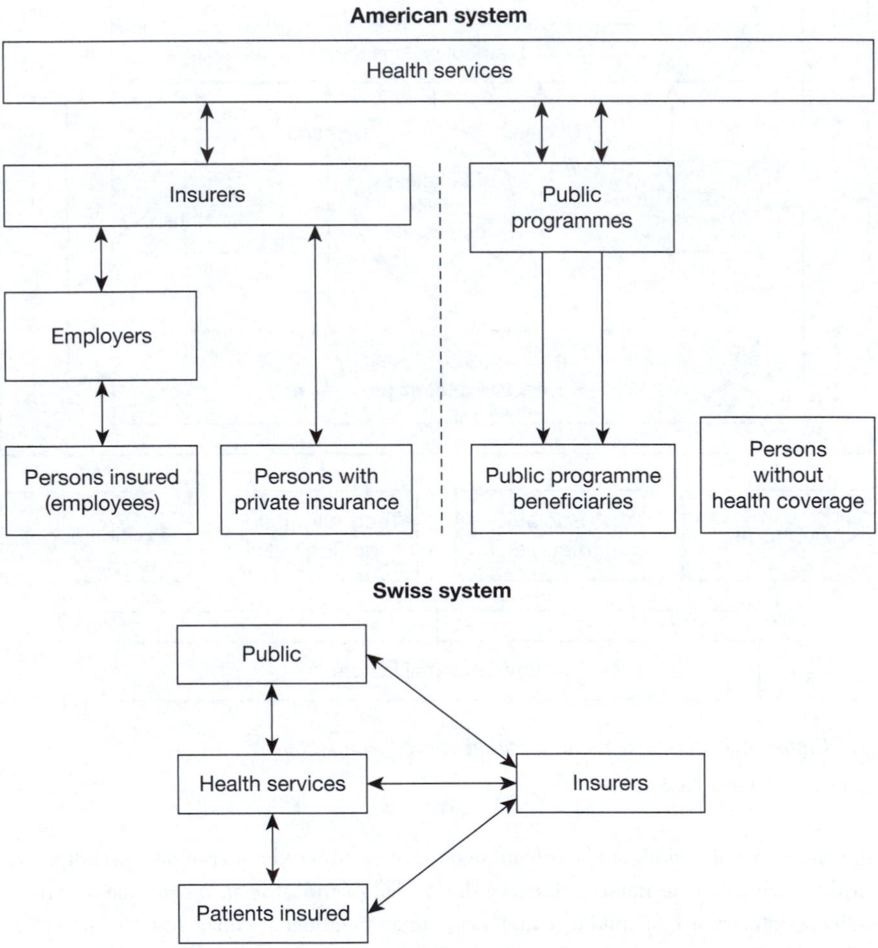

Figure 4.3 *Comparison of American and Swiss health insurance systems*

programmes (Medicaid for poor families, Medicare mainly for the elderly). Health coverage for the active population is largely linked to their job. So, for health insurers, the direct client is not the beneficiary of the service but rather their employers with whom they agree overall contracts with offer and types of cover subject to negotiation. Insurance companies also sign contracts with service suppliers (medical centres, hospitals, etc.) and may or may not include them in offers made to companies. Employees and beneficiaries have a limited choice of offers and, for many, the cover available constitutes a major share of the company's social services, to which they no longer have access if they lose their job (nearly 80 per cent of premiums are paid by employers).

The situation in Switzerland is different. Health insurance is mandatory for all residents, but they have a free choice of insurer. The minimal cover that insurers must provide is defined by the State – but prices are mainly set by the insurers, who may also offer extra cover. There is competition between insurers to attract clients but, as any health service providers recognized by the State may propose and charge an agreed rate for their services, insurers have virtually no effect on the latter, as the obligation to contract exists.

Without going into the political and social aspects of these systems, it should be stressed that the existence of a strongly privatized market, with a large number of offerers, means that the relationship between the various parties should be understood in very different ways – otherwise it is impossible to understand these markets appropriately.

MARKETING ORIENTATION

Types of orientation

Marketing orientation corresponds to the philosophy of reference adopted by an organization in conducting its marketing activities. Several types of marketing orientation have been identified (Meffert *et al.*, 2008; Kotler and Keller, 2006). See Figure 4.4.

Production orientation emphasizes a product's or service's availability. The organization's priority lies in being able to produce and distribute the goods concerned. The recent H1N1 flu epidemic tellingly illustrates such a situation. To the authorities, it was essential to organize and support the production of vaccines, then ensure their availability throughout the area they were in charge of. Product orientation is based on the principle that the beneficiary will buy a service according to its objective characteristics (purchase of best service). This situation is increasingly rare in the private sector, but typical of public markets, where the public body is obliged to choose the offerer who comes closest to fulfilling the criteria defined in the invitation to tender. Such an orientation is also generally common in the public and tertiary sectors.

Sales orientation requires an organization to make great efforts to stimulate buyers' interest in a product: clients need to be convinced that such a purchase is worth their

65

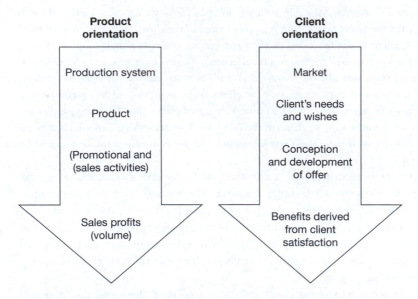

Figure 4.4 *Comparison of an organization's product and client orientations*

while. To some, such an orientation can also be found in politics, when candidates try to 'sell' their ideas by committing themselves (and vast sums of money) to persuading voters to adopt their ideas.

Finally, market or client orientation requires an organization to satisfy previously identified needs (as the saying goes – it's not a drill that's needed, but a hole in the wall). By using knowledge of clients and their needs, an organization can develop services that will suit them as closely as possible. If the service really does meet a need, clients will buy it anyway, without the organization having to make much effort to promote it. This orientation – the one most frequently recommended for private bodies – was conceptualized by Narver and Slater (1990) and Kohli *et al.* (1993) who have shown that an active and positive attitude in the collection, analysis and internal transmission of data concerning clients and other parties to the exchange allows the organization to better serve its market and improve its own performance.

It is rare to find an absolute form of marketing orientation in an organization; it is not easy for a company to be strictly product-oriented without taking clients' needs at least partially/occasionally into account. Conversely, client orientation often presents great dangers, as clients are not always able to express their needs clearly, and it is not certain that the offer corresponding to those needs will continue to be bought or used by these same clients. In fact, marketing orientation depends on the branch and market on the one hand; and on the organization's history, culture and goals on the other. Lees-Marshment (2001) presents the various types of marketing orientation as applied to political parties.

Symptoms of marketing orientation

Although strict forms of marketing orientation are quite rare, we can still analyse the type of marketing orientation an organization is leaning towards. Kühn, Reimer and Fasnacht (2006) suggest studying the symptoms which shed light on the marketing orientation favoured within an organization. Table 4.1 contains a list of these symptoms for product and client orientations.

The public sector and orientation marketing

As a rule, the marketing philosophy of public-sector bodies is geared towards production or product. Given legal constraints and monopolistic market structures, organizations do not need to promote their services; often they are not responsible for identifying and determining needs, given that these are theoretically the fruit of political debate and decisions. However, with the arrival of New Public Management and the development of public bodies, the latter are increasingly inclined to modify their marketing orientation to be more and more market- or client-oriented, for several reasons.

First, with the introduction of competition to various public-sector activities (postal service, telecommunications, hospitals, security, education, etc.), public bodies must show greater interest in clients, and provide services better suited to their needs. If clients have a choice, even one limited to using a service or not, they will evaluate it according to their needs, so public bodies cannot disregard existing needs.

A second reason can be found in pressure from service beneficiaries. They or their families have become increasingly used to voicing their opinion about the services on offer, and to complaining – or even taking action/demonstrating – in order to oblige an organization to do things as they wish. Public-sector agents, on the other hand, are also keen to satisfy collective and even individual needs, and incite the organization to adapt the service offer as necessary.

Then, the introduction of the norms and processes of quality management has (not always intentionally) encouraged consideration of beneficiaries' needs. These processes nearly always require beneficiaries' needs, and/or degree of satisfaction, to be assessed. So, public bodies must systematically take beneficiaries' needs into account in order to obtain certificates of conformity to quality norms.

Finally, in the wake of New Public Management, client orientation now counts among the priorities of public administration reform programmes. Considering public administration primarily as an entity responsible for making services available to citizen-clients, advocates of NPM (and the reforms it has inspired) have stressed the need for these bodies to alter their approach by placing the beneficiary at the heart of their concerns.

MARKETING MANAGEMENT

As outlined in Chapter 2, the concept of marketing is based on the notions of exchange, relationship, and the processes for carrying out these exchanges and the corresponding

Table 4.1 *Symptoms of product orientation and client orientation*

Elements or function	Symptoms of products orientation	Symptoms of market orientation
Direction	Organizational aspects are dominating: production specialists lead the organization	Client aspects are dominating: marketing specialists lead the organization
Programme of products/services	Narrow: selling what we produce	Large: producing what we can sell
Organization	Centralized: organizational structure based on a staff and line approach; strong on accounting and financial controls	Decentralized: few hierarchical levels; generally organized by division rather than by function
Objectives	Internal influences: short-term objectives; importance of methods	External influences: long-term objectives; importance of strategic planning
Research	Advanced technical research	Advanced market analysis
Further development	Proposition for functional improvements or costs reductions: technical tests	Based on client proposals (needs): market tests
Production	Production is not flexible: everything is based on production capabilities	Production is flexible: everything is based on market opportunities
Welcoming clients	No parking for clients; cold welcome; the client is almost a burden	Parking spaces available and clearly indicated; welcoming hall; phone service; the client is king
Data regarding clients and market	Little to none; must nevertheless make sure to know the clients and their needs	Development of market studies; qualitative and quantitative data; tendency to believe that market surveys have all the answers
Marketing/ communication	Technical arguments dominate	After-sales service and client's needs dominate
After-sales service	Only if absolutely necessary; complaints are seen as distractions	Development of after-sales service as the main relationship with the client; complaints are seen as opportunities

relationships. Marketing management concerns the process and activities facilitating the relationship and exchange between partners (see Figure 4.5). This is the most highly developed aspect of marketing – and also the most practical one, in that it offers organizations tools for planning and undertaking marketing activities.

Like generic management tasks, marketing management involves analysing the situation, taking strategic decisions, planning and organizing activities in detail, carrying them out, and controlling them – which, in conjunction with a situation analysis, makes it possible to confirm, correct or adapt subsequent tasks and decisions.

The first task of a managerial process involves analysing the market and environment situation (marketing analysis). In most cases a systemic approach helps define the market, identify and analyse the leading actors, and study the relationship between them. The goal here lies in assessing chances and overall risks, and the organization's strengths and weaknesses compared to other actors (SWOT analysis). Many tools linked to analysis of buying and consumer behaviour, competition, distribution systems and, more generally, to marketing analysis, have been developed, making it possible to establish a basic diagnosis of the situation, based on data obtained.

The next task, after situation analysis, is to determine the main marketing goals and the strategy needed to achieve them (marketing strategy). This phase involves defining which groups of clients (segments) to target with which offer; fixing quantitative goals in terms of turnover figures, market share or profit margin; and the qualitative or

Figure 4.5 *Main tasks of marketing management*

psychographic goals corresponding essentially to the positioning the company is seeking among target groups with its offer. Selecting the circuits and channels of distribution complete these strategic choices.

Based on these strategic decisions, the company identifies the instruments it will use to reach its targets (marketing planning). The marketing instruments or marketing mix (see the following section) are the tools available to the company to attain the goals targeted, and are visible to both clients and other market actors. They are traditionally know as the 'four Ps' (product, price, promotion and place). Other instruments have since been proposed as additions to this list, as we shall see.

To instigate and accomplish the actions planned, a company should dispose of and activate internal resources (marketing implementation); financial resources (budget); human resources; I.T. resources (marketing information systems); and behaviour and process systems. Coordinated use of these resources helps the company attain the goals it has set.

Finally, the conformity and completion of decisions and actions must be studied within the framework of a marketing control system. This involves collecting and structuring the relevant information, then submitting it to marketing executives so they can evaluate the decisions made and actions carried out before taking any necessary corrective measures.

In the public sector, given that the market system is generally very different (no competitors, same offer for all beneficiaries, price set by a political authority, etc.), the organization's room for manoeuvre is often reduced to activities of communication and distribution, and to the resources used by the organization for developing and introducing the service. Aspects linked to the search for information, and strategic considerations, will be examined in more detail in Chapters 5 and 6.

MARKETING INSTRUMENTS

A central element in marketing is the marketing mix, or the range of instruments used to attain and convince an organization's target groups. The concept was first used by Borden (1965), and is based on an analogy between a 'cake-mix' and marketing activities. Borden metaphorically compared marketing tools to the ingredients needed to bake a cake, suggesting that only the right mix of known ingredients can yield a satisfactory result; and it is not so much a basic knowledge of the ingredients that ensures their success as their appropriate use together in the right proportions.

McCarthy (1960) systematized the marketing mix concept in 1960 by introducing the 'four Ps', corresponding to the basic instruments available: product, price, promotion and place (see Figure 4.6).

Let us apply these elements to a service provided by the public sector: issuing an identity document for foreign travel.

The product or offer consists of the number and range of products/services available; their characteristics; possible options; guarantees; after-sales service etc. For identity documents these may (according to country) include an I.D. card, passport

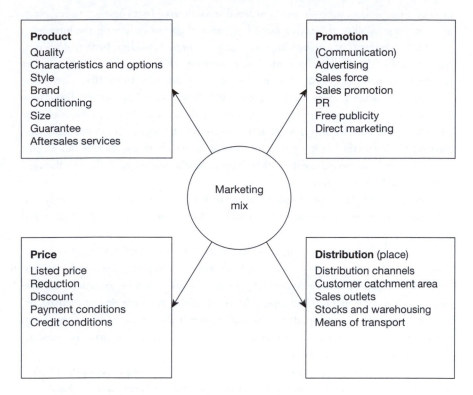

Figure 4.6 *Ingredients in the marketing mix*

or temporary passport (issued, say, if a passport is lost or stolen). The time needed to obtain the document can also be added here.

The price naturally includes the cost of the service and its different forms (cost, stated price, remuneration, etc.), and also any reduction or discount, along with the conditions of payment or credit. The price of an identity document is fixed by the government (according, say, to the number of pages in a passport, or how quickly it is issued), but the administration may accept various methods of payment (cash, credit or debit cards, bank transfer, etc.).

Promotion consists of all the communication activities which present, and seek to promote, the offer as a whole. Leading communication tools include advertising, public relations, the persons forming the sales team, promotional activities, etc. For an identity document, the main communication activities might include an information brochure explaining the procedure involved, updating the relevant website, etc.

The final group of instruments is formed by distribution (place): the systems which help the organization convey the offer to its beneficiary (logistics, storage and warehousing, distribution channels, etc. for goods; direct relations, website, etc. for services). The principal elements of distribution for an identity document include the places the document can be physically ordered and delivered (with opening times, etc.), or even the possibility of carrying out all or some of the procedure on the internet.

Although this way of categorizing marketing instruments has long been widespread, many authors (Van Waterschoot and Van den Bulte, 1992) have criticized its rather simplistic nature, suggesting it is no longer fully adapted to reality. Given the development of services marketing, Bitner and Booms (1981) proposed three new instruments: people (personnel in charge of supplying the service); processes (the procedure, mechanisms and flow of activities by which services are consumed); and physical facilities (the ability and environment in which the service is delivered). Other academic proposals combine these various tools, usually according to the type of market and service offered.

Irrespective of the number and structure of marketing instruments, a number of rules must be observed as regards their combined use (Kühn *et al.*, 2006; Kotler and Keller, 2006).

The first rule lies in adapting the instruments to the market situation. Target groups' habits when it comes to services, how they react to price, the communication supports with which they are in contact, etc. may all vary, and organizations must be careful to use instruments which reach the required targets according to their needs, expectations and behaviour patterns. Nowadays hardly any organization, for instance, can afford to neglect internet communication – whereas this tool was virtually unknown for such purposes a few years ago.

The second rule concerns long-term harmony and consistency. As in the original sense of 'mix', marketing instruments must be combined harmoniously. Success in marketing often comes from a subtle blend of instruments which lend the offer overall coherence (avoiding an aggressive price strategy for a luxury product, for instance, or seeking to reach a broad target group with a product only available in a few retail outlets). Similarly, this mix should stand the test of time and avoid sudden changes which are unpopular with buyers. (Who has never been surprised or annoyed by a simple change to a product's packaging, causing doubt or even a change in attitude?)

The final rule to respect is the need for marketing instruments to be used in a concerted fashion. Organizations often use too many instruments at once (advertising, public relations, promotion at the point of sale, etc.), without having the means to ensure that each instrument attains a minimum efficiency threshold. A waste of resources is the result. So it is usually better to concentrate on a limited number of instruments, and ensure they are effective with target groups.

Marketing instruments applied to the public sector are outlined in Chapter 7.

EXERCISE 4.1

Using a process or product you have good knowledge of, can you identify the various steps of marketing management shown in Figure 4.5?

DISCUSSION QUESTIONS

1   Based on the definition of a systemic analysis provided in this chapter, discuss the limits and potential of such an approach. Is it realistic to talk of market system in the public sector? What are the limits of this particular model in the case of your own organization?

2   The marketing mix is like baking a cake. What are the most important ingredients, in your opinion? In your experience, is one of them more likely to ruin the cake if there is too much/too little of it?

NOTE

1   This may (or may not) change with the health care reform of President Obama.

REFERENCES

Bertalanffy, K. L. (1968) *General System Theory: Foundations, Development, Applications*, New York, George Braziller.

Bitner, J. and Booms, B. (1981) Marketing Strategies and Organizational Structures for Service Firms, in Donnelly, J. and George, W. (eds) *Marketing of Services*, Chicago, American Marketing Association.

Borden, N. H. (1965) The Concept of the Marketing Mix, in Schnertz, G. *Science in Marketing*, Chichester, John Wiley & Sons.

Kohli A.K, J. B. and Kumar, A. (1993) MARKOR: A Measure of Market Orientation, *Journal of Marketing Research*, 30, 467–77.

Kotler, P. and Amstrong, G. (2009) *Principles of Marketing*, New York, Pearson Education.

Kotler, P. and Keller, K. L. (2006) *Marketing Management*, New Jersey, Prentice Hall.

Kotler, P., Roberto, N. and Lee, N. (2002) *Social Marketing: Improving the Quality of Life,* Thousand Oaks, Sage.

Kühn, R. and Pasquier, M. (2000) *Marketing: Analyse et Stratégie,* Fribourg, Editions Universitaires.

Kühn, R., Reimer, A. and Fasnacht, R. (2006) *Marketing: System, Strategie und Instrumente*, Bern: Haupt Verlag Ag.

Lees-Marshment, J. (2001) The Marriage of Politics and Marketing, *Political Studies,* 49, 692–713.

McCarthy, E. J. (1960) *Basic Marketing: A Managerial Approach*, Illinois, Irwin.

McDonald, M. (2007) *Marketing Plans*, Oxford, Elsevier.

Meffert, H., Burman, C. and Kirchgeorg, M. (2008) *Marketing: Grundlagen Marketorientierter Unternehmensführung*, Wiesbaden, Gabler Verlag.

Narver, J. C. and Slater, S. F. (1990) The Effect of a Market Orientation on Business Profitability, *Journal of Marketing*, 54, 20–35.

van Waterschoot, W. and van den Bulte, C. (1992) The 4P Classification of the Marketing Mix Revisited, *Journal of Marketing*, 56, 83–93.

Chapter 5

Marketing information research

LEARNING OBJECTIVES

By the end of this chapter you should be able to:

- Identify the information needs of your organization.
- Select the appropriate information-gathering strategies and tools.
- Integrate the information gathered into the organization's managerial framework.

KEY POINTS OF THIS CHAPTER

- The objectives of organizations in seeking information can be: 1) descriptive; 2) exploratory; or 3) explanatory. One's strategy must be in line with the objectives of the information-gathering operation.
- Studies may be either primary or secondary: in primary studies, information is collected specifically for the objective defined by the organization, while secondary studies use information already collected and available.
- Data collected must be integrated into a coherent organizational information system if they are to be used effectively either for policy purposes or managerial objectives.

KEY TERMS

Survey – the most widely used form of primary information gathering, entailing directly asking respondents for information on themselves, their habits and opinions.

continued . . .

KEY TERMS ... *continued*

Observations – information-gathering approach that seeks to observe the behaviour of individuals without questioning them directly.

Tests – recreation of life-like conditions in a controlled environment and analysis of the information obtained.

Sample – representative group from a given population.

MARKETING INFORMATION IN THE PUBLIC SECTOR

All organizations need information in order to take decisions, understand aspects of the behaviour of people or organizations, ensure that measures are implemented correctly or evaluate such measures. Although businesses in the private sector have been conducting market research and mandating specialized research institutes for a long time, public-sector organizations have adopted such practices much more recently. Box 5.1 gives some examples of situations in which administrations may seek to obtain 'marketing' data in the way that private companies do.

There are a number of reasons to explain the increasing use[1] by public-sector organizations of studies to gather data on stakeholders. First, there is a substantial imbalance between the tasks that the public sector has to perform and the resources available to it. Because political authorities often give few concrete indications regarding priorities for

■ BOX 5.1 EXAMPLES OF SITUATIONS IN WHICH 'MARKETING' INFORMATION MUST BE GATHERED

- Determining the expectations of the beneficiaries of services and comparing them with the way in which the organization perceives and defines them
- Assessing the quality of services provided to beneficiaries, and beneficiaries' satisfaction with these services
- Understanding the behaviour of those who use services and their attitude towards the organization
- Assessing the effectiveness of measures (e.g. communications measures)
- Assessing priorities in the light of available resources and reducing or eliminating superfluous services
- Testing and validating new services or measures for beneficiaries

services that should be developed, restricted or even abolished, such decisions are often left to the discretion of public-sector organizations. One source of information that can help public-sector organizations arrive at and validate such decisions is beneficiary surveys (what are the best opening hours? what procedures require simplifying?). A second reason is growing demand for accountability from public-sector organizations and the spread of concepts such as 'customer', 'customer orientation' and 'customer satisfaction' in the New Public Management approach. Detailed information must be provided on services, the manner in which they are delivered, their beneficiaries and so on, and this information has to be gathered. Because relations between public-sector organizations and beneficiaries have been 'marketized' and to some extent individualized, organizations are forced to gather specific data on 'customers' to adapt services to different groups of customers as needed, and to regularly check both the quality of the services delivered and users' satisfaction with these services. To obtain information of this kind, organizations use classic techniques such as polls and qualitative surveys.

Other reasons have to do with the economic significance, complexity and costs of activities deployed by public organizations. In such situations it is wise to make certain that the services developed are well thought-out, economical and, naturally, well matched to the needs they have to satisfy. Otherwise there is a risk that much greater costs will be incurred to remedy mistakes made. Figure 5.1 illustrates the various costs of a service, particularly those resulting from a bad match between the service and expectations or needs.

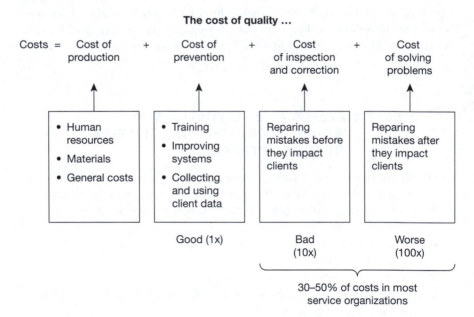

Figure 5.1 *The various types of costs involved in producing a service and making it available*

Source: Schmidt (2000, 4).

A final explanation of increased use of marketing studies lies in the information needed to develop public policies. Faced with the complexity of the world, and as part of their function of assisting political authorities to prepare public policies, public-sector organizations must gather information to reduce uncertainty and allow political authorities to take enlightened decisions. This task is partially devolved to government statistics departments, which carry out large numbers of studies every year, but is increasingly performed by departments that are in direct charge of the public policy concerned, for reasons both of knowledge of the subject matter and time. Many study techniques are used, ranging from surveys and electronic behaviour-observation methods to focus groups, perhaps as part of participatory initiatives.

Generally, studies made by organizations of their marketing environment are aimed at three types of objectives:

- *Descriptive:* in these cases, the need is for information that will provide a description of the situation and enable strategic decisions to be taken and measures to be planned or adjusted; for example, in preparing for world fairs that are held at intervals in various countries (Seville, 1992; Hanover, 2000; Shanghai, 2010; Milan, 2015), some countries conduct studies to gauge their image in the host nation or the corresponding region to help them develop concepts for the pavilions that will represent them. Studies of user satisfaction with a service, or tests of a communications campaign, also build better descriptive knowledge of measures deployed.
- *Objective:* when a public organization has to study, for example, various possibilities for the construction of a bypass, the placing of stops on a new bus route, or the building of a new school, it can survey the residents of a district or town so that needs and evaluation criteria for submitted projects can be better taken into account.
- *Explanatory:* in situations where a public organization is out of phase with citizens or groups of beneficiaries (services not being used, recurrent criticisms, etc.), the reasons why people reject a proposal or a service can be investigated. In 2008, the people of the Canton of Vaud, Switzerland, voted to reject a proposed municipal museum. Perplexed as to why the majority of the population should oppose the project, the administration conducted a survey. The results showed that the public were not opposed to support for culture or to the idea of a museum, but to the planned location on the shores of a lake and the architectural concept that had been chosen. The authorities then relaunched the project taking the information gathered into account.

The following sections begin with an overview of the main methods used for gathering information. Because of their widespread use, surveys are discussed in detail, followed by a summary presentation of other methods. The two subsequent sections deal with selecting samples and the process of planning a study. In conclusion, the chapter briefly looks at integrating marketing studies and opinion polls into a broader marketing information system.

77

INFORMATION-GATHERING METHODS

Marketing studies and opinion polls are systematic, empirical methods of gathering objective and subjective information for the purpose of increasing the transparency of the field concerned and improving both decision taking and the development of corresponding measures (Malhotra, 2009; Kühn and Kreuzer, 2006). This definition highlights the goal of this type of research: to increase knowledge of a specific subject and the attendant decisional capacity. All too frequently, studies are developed and carried out with no link to a clearly defined problem area, or without being used for decision making. When no consensus can be reached on the orientation to be taken regarding a particular subject or on a decision to be taken, a study is often commissioned – either as a play for time or to prevent a conflict – in the knowledge that the information gathered will probably or certainly do nothing to improve the basis for taking a decision (the uncertainty may well be the same before and after the study). In this situation, the study risks being used as an alibi or a second-best solution – and one that often ties up many internal resources to boot. For this reason it is very important, before conducting a study, to make certain there is a real need for new information, and that the new information will definitely be put to use in taking a decision, and indeed that it will improve the quality of the decision. In the negative, it may be advisable to drop the idea of planning and conducting the study, for the time being at least, unless the study itself constitutes an objective independently of the results obtained.

The methods used to collect and analyse data are many and varied; Figure 5.2 sets out the main methods in summary fashion.

The first methodological question to be asked is whether data that can meet the information need already exist. Here lies the distinction between primary and secondary studies.

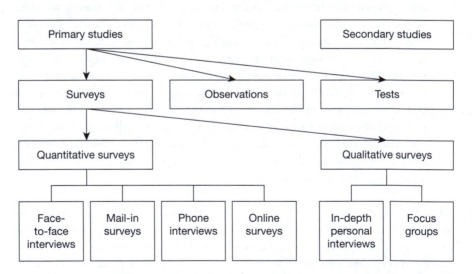

Figure 5.2 *Summary of the main marketing study and opinion survey methods*
Source: Kühn and Kreuzer (2006).

Primary studies involve the gathering and analysis of data, collected directly from information carriers, that are conducted specifically in connection with the defined object of study. In other words, these are new studies carried out to obtain information that does not already exist. Secondary studies involve identifying and using existing, available data (documentary sources) that often require reinterpretation in the light of the particular information need. This is a matter of making use of information that already exists but was not originally gathered in relation to the object of study.

Before committing substantial resources to the gathering of new data, it is important to check whether these data or similar data that will cover the information need already exist. Currently there are increasing amounts of information, both inside or outside an organization, that are largely unused. Table 5.1 shows possible information sources to be consulted. Very often, combining several sets of existing data can bring useful answers, limiting the need for new information, and thereby saving time and resources.

When an organization has to gather new information to cover needs identified, three groups of methods can be considered: surveys, observations and tests.

Surveys are the most widespread form of study and consist of asking people for information about themselves, their habits, their opinions, their attitudes or their behaviour with regard to a particular subject. In rare cases, people may also be asked

Table 5.1 *Secondary or documentary sources*

Public or para-public sources (data often available at no cost)	Data and reports from statistical departments
	Data and reports from various public organizations (customs, government departments, central bank, etc.)
	Research conducted by universities
Private sources (data may or may not be available free of charge)	Publications and reports by marketing study institutes
	Reports and documents of professional associations
	Publications in newspapers and journals
Internal sources (data available at no cost)	Previous market studies
	Accounting and financial data
	Data on customers and beneficiaries of services
	Data resulting from the study of existing measures

to give their opinions about other people (e.g. members of their family). It is important to bear in mind that this type of study is based on people's statements, and hence their capacity or willingness to express their opinions about past, present and future facts or subjects. It is easy enough to ask somebody whether they smoke cigarettes, when they started smoking, and how many cigarettes they smoke a day; but there is an obvious difficulty in asking similar questions about the use of illegal substances (narcotics or performance-enhancing drugs) or products whose consumption is a private matter or socially problematic (medication, alcohol, etc.). Surveys are generally divided into two types: quantitative and qualitative (see next section). Quantitative surveys are generally used to obtain representative information from the public surveyed (what is the opinion of the public about a planned museum? what is the satisfaction level of those working on or using a service? what percentage of people have seen the prevention campaign ads?). Since it is neither possible nor reasonable to question the entire segment of the population concerned, very often only a representative sample is surveyed. Qualitative surveys, on the other hand, normally involving a limited number of respondents, are designed to explore deep-seated motivations, discover complex reasons underlying behaviour, identifying possible changes, etc. Here it is not the representativeness of opinions expressed that counts but their quality and diversity.

Different methods can be used to conduct surveys. While people are generally required to be physically present for qualitative surveys (in-depth individual interview or focus groups), quantitative surveys can be conducted not only face to face but also by telephone, using a questionnaire sent by mail or, in recent years, over the internet (online surveys).

The second possible method of study is observation. Studies are aimed at observing people's behaviour without their having to express their opinion. For example, the number and possibly the type of people who decide to vote electronically during elections can be observed. While observation techniques obviously do not allow opinions to be gathered, in general they are much more reliable than surveys for studying people's behaviour in that the filters that may come into play when people make statements are absent. Box 5.2 shows an example in which the study methodology, originally based on a survey, was changed for a behavioural observation system. Although observation techniques have not been widely used until now, recent technological and computing developments (digital information, internet, GPS, electronic cameras, etc.) have sparked a considerable rise in interest, and specific new techniques have been developed in recent years.

The third type of study method is the test. This involves testing, either under laboratory conditions or real-life conditions, people's reactions to concrete proposals for marketing measures (new design for a community newspaper, new service, new communications campaign on prevention, etc.). Combined with either a survey or an observation study, this technique makes it possible to gather data on concrete rather than hypothetical elements and thus to test the relevance, reliability or potential success of proposed measures. 'Mystery shopping', involving sending a trained person to play a specific role (customer, partner, etc.) in order to test an organization's attitudes and behaviours, integrates both test and observation techniques.

■ BOX 5.2 ELECTRONIC OBSERVATION OF PEOPLE'S MOVEMENTS

The study of a population's movements is of interest both to the public sector (for example, in the planning and management of transport infrastructures) and the private sector (geomarketing applications where territorial and travel-related data are used to target marketing activities). For close to half a century, and still today using improved methodologies, analysis of movements was mainly carried out using personal surveys followed by telephone surveys of a sample of the population. These surveys consisted in asking people what movements they had made on the day before the interview. These movements (together with the reasons and modes of transport) are then transferred onto digital mapping systems.

Since the early 2000s, methods for recording movements based on GPS (global positioning system) technology have been developed. Instead of being asked about the movements they made in a day, people in the sample are given a specially developed GPS device and all their movements for the duration of the study (generally one week) are recorded by the device and transferred onto digital mapping systems.

For a study of the public's mobility behaviour in major Swiss cities, over 10,000 people were recruited and fitted with a GPS device.

This method of observation using electronic data collection brings a number of advantages. First, all the movements of participants in a week are gathered; this is significant because mobility behaviour is not the same during the week and at weekends, for example. Second, all movements – not just main movements – are collected. In a telephone survey, many movements such as walking the dog, visiting a friend, a spontaneous trip to a neighbourhood store, etc. are often not reported. Lastly, the information gathered is much more accurate with an observation survey because one is no longer relying on people's memories, since their behaviour is recorded by an electronic system.

Surveys

Types of surveys

As mentioned previously, surveys may be either quantitative or qualitative. Although in practice the two types are sometimes combined to create a kind of hybrid, each type is aimed at specific objectives and has different characteristics.

Quantitative surveys are designed to measure or evaluate phenomena in such a way that the results can be extrapolated to the whole target population (e.g. polling a sample of citizens in order to gauge the opinion of the entire population). Surveys of this type canvass a large number of people (representative sample) and it must be possible to aggregate the data gathered easily. A structured questionnaire containing a limited number of closed questions (i.e. questions having a set list of possible answers) is used. Results are analysed using statistical tools.

Qualitative surveys are designed to investigate, in order to anticipate or explain, phenomena without it necessarily being possible to extrapolate the results to the entire population. A limited number of people are involved (often less than 30), who are asked a large number of open questions in order to elicit detailed information. The discussions involved are generally quite long (up to one hour) and loosely structured. Since the analysis will focus on remarks made by interviewees, methods such as content analysis will be used (user-friendly specialist software is available for some analyses, such as word frequency, whether words used form part of specialized lexicons, word association maps, etc.).

Choosing the survey type may not always be straightforward: sometimes it is first necessary to conduct a qualitative survey to identify problems or hypotheses and then a quantitative study to validate these hypotheses using a representative sample of the population. However, it is always important to determine the purpose of the study, what type of answers are sought, whether it is necessary for the results to be representative of the entire population, and whether the quality of the data gathered will be sufficient to enable decisions to be made. Box 5.3 lists typical objectives for quantitative and qualitative surveys in the public sector and Box 5.4 lists the types of quantitative and qualitative surveys conducted by the European Commission.

■ BOX 5.3 TYPICAL OBJECTIVES FOR QUANTITATIVE AND QUALITATIVE SURVEYS IN THE PUBLIC SECTOR

Quantitative survey objectives

- Test a communications campaign while it is running or afterwards (post-test)
- Study how a service is being used by its direct or indirect beneficiaries
- Study the attitudes, opinions or behaviour of the population or certain segments of it with regard to a topical subject
- Measure the satisfaction of users or customers
- Gather data for use in developing public policy measures (public transport, etc.)

Qualitative survey objectives

- Test the understanding and objectives of a communications campaign (pre-test)
- Anticipate potential reactions to a new policy, new service, etc.
- Identify and analyse critical user experiences (positive or negative) of a service
- Verify the content and comprehension of documents (e.g. a website)
- Generate ideas for improving the service or relations with the public

■ BOX 5.4 EUROBAROMETER SURVEYS CONDUCTED BY THE EUROPEAN COMMISSION

The European Commission (EC) conducts a series of surveys to analyse public opinion in member countries. This system of surveys is known as the Eurobarometer (http://ec.europa.eu/public_opinion/index_en.htm). It includes four main types of surveys:

The *Standard Eurobarometer* was established in 1973. Each survey consists of approximately 1,000 face-to-face interviews per member state (except Germany: 2,000, Luxembourg: 600; United Kingdom 1,300 including 300 in Northern Ireland). Reports are published twice yearly.

Special Eurobarometer reports are based on in-depth thematic studies carried out for various services of the EC or other EU institutions and integrated in Standard Eurobarometer's polling waves. In 2009, for example, the EC carried out a special study on Europeans' attitudes to corruption. This survey highlighted differences between countries, with 95 per cent of respondents in Greece stating that corruption was a major problem in their country whereas in Denmark the figure was only 22 per cent (Attitudes of Europeans towards Corruption 2009, conducted by TNS Opinion and Social at the request of Directorate-General for Justice, Freedom and Security).

Flash Eurobarometers are ad hoc, thematic telephone interviews conducted at the request of any service of the EC. Flash surveys enable the EC to obtain results relatively quickly and to focus on specific target groups as and when required. In 2009, a study was conducted in Ireland following the referendum in which the population of the country approved the Lisbon Treaty (67 per cent positive votes). Two thousand people were polled in order to explore the reasons for the Irish vote and to understand why the result was different after an initial failure in June 2008 (Lisbon Treaty Post-Referendum Survey Ireland 2009).

Qualitative Studies investigate in depth the motivations, feelings and reactions of selected social groups towards a given subject or concept, by listening and analysing their way of expressing themselves in discussion groups or non-directed interviews. In 2007, the EC commissioned a research institute to carry out a qualitative study on the subject of a safer internet for children. This study covered 27 countries and involved children (boys and girls aged 9 to 14 years). It was aimed at improving knowledge about internet usage by children, their online behaviour and their perception of risks and safety-related questions (Safer Internet for Children 2007, conducted by Optem at the request of Directorate-General for Information, Society and Media).

Quantitative surveys

Quantitative surveys can be conducted in various ways: interviews in person (face-to-face), by telephone, by mail or, in the past few years, by internet (online). In most countries, the most widely used method is the telephone survey, for reasons of both speed and cost. However, depending on the survey's objective, the other forms should also be considered.

Telephone surveys (also known as CATI, for Computer-Assisted Telephone Interview) are favoured because they can be carried out quickly, provide a degree of flexibility in how the questionnaire is handled depending on answers already obtained, make it possible to control the structure of the sample and avoid possible bias caused by the presence of the interviewer. In addition, they can be monitored to ensure their quality. On the other hand, because telephone surveys have multiplied, a decreasing rate of response is being observed and, if a list of the entire target population is not obtained beforehand, it is increasingly difficult to be certain of having a representative sample (e.g., people with unlisted numbers, people on 'do not call' registers, people having only a mobile telephone, people with no telephone). Telephone surveys can be used for simple questions (complex subjects cannot be addressed over the telephone) which should be limited in number (to last no longer than 10–15 minutes).

If the purpose of the survey is more complex (e.g. if the subject matter is delicate, or there are many possible answers) or requires documents to be shown (layout sketch, logos, etc.), personal interviews will be preferred. Normally conducted after making an appointment, this type of survey requires time and is expensive (interviewer's travel and duration of the interview). In addition, the fact that certain segments of the population are difficult to reach (young people, ethnic communities, etc.), and that experienced interviewers are required, should be taken into account.

Postal or correspondence surveys are relatively rarely used because of low response rates, but are useful when those surveyed have a proximity relationship with the organization commissioning the survey (satisfaction survey of employees of an organization, survey of members of an association, etc.). This form of survey is very economical when the addresses of the target population are known, and is also of benefit to respondents because they can choose when to complete the survey and take the time to provide well-thought-out answers (no pressure from the interviewer). However, because no control is possible (one cannot know who actually completed the questionnaire or whether the respondent completed some unrelated fields), this form of survey can only be used to canvass people who are sufficiently literate and are able to complete the questionnaire completely independently.

Online surveys are very easy to plan and construct (software applications make it easy to prepare online questionnaires), but quite complex to conduct in a professional manner. First, unless one has a list of people in the target population and can provide advance information by e-mail (with a link to the questionnaire), it is very difficult to obtain representative samples that are chosen in a truly random manner – all the more so because a significant part of the population does not have private access to the internet.

Second, although putting together a questionnaire is easy, it is equally easy to complete one without giving much thought to the questions asked (clicking on answers without having read or understood the questions) and respondents can easily abandon the questionnaire without having answered all questions. Provided that information about the target population is available, online surveys can easily replace postal surveys and, in some cases, telephone surveys. This is because, in spite of the difficulties mentioned, the advantages of the online survey, combined with its speed of execution, the instant capture of answers, the possibility of presenting a variety of elements to be tested and its low cost, make it a form of survey that is bound to develop further.

As part of a study on the images of countries in preparation for the Shanghai World Expo (2010), a survey was conducted in 2006 of a sample of 2,000 people in China (representative sample of the urban population having a medium to high standard of living). The results in Figure 5.3 were obtained in response to the question on spontaneous associations that people made on hearing the name of various countries.

These graphics show us that the Chinese public associates the United States with the economy, recent wars, terrorism and American presidents. For Germany, World War II, the economy, product quality and German brands were most often mentioned. Finally, Switzerland is associated with watchmaking, landscapes, banks and skiing.

Qualitative surveys

Qualitative surveys generally deal with complex problems that require a high level of interaction between the respondent and the interviewer (who needs to establish trust, adapt questions to the answers already received, etc.), and are generally conducted person-to-person (in rare cases, such as when the people surveyed are experts in a field living in different countries, a telephone quantitative survey can be envisaged). There are two forms of qualitative survey: in-depth personal interviews and focus groups.

The basic premise of in-depth personal interviews is that what is said in the interview contains or hides deep meaning. By allowing the person surveyed to talk as much as possible, the whole of his or her discourse, both verbal and nonverbal (gestures, silences, etc.), provides information which, using specific analysis methods, allows better understanding of behaviours, opinions or intentions. In the most widespread form (semi-directed/directed interview), the interviewer uses an interview guide listing the main topics to be addressed. However, he or she will bring up these topics depending on the flow of the discussion, allowing the respondent time to respond (avoiding direct questions, avoiding closed questions, reviving the interview if necessary using the words spoken by the respondent, etc.). For reasons of completeness, these interviews are normally recorded, with the interviewer rounding out the information by taking notes on non-verbal aspects. Box 5.5 gives an example of this type of survey.

Focus groups or group meetings are based on the principle that interactions between several people on a specific topic will produce results that are superior to the sum total of information that would be collected from each person individually. The difference lies in the group dynamics that develop during the discussion.

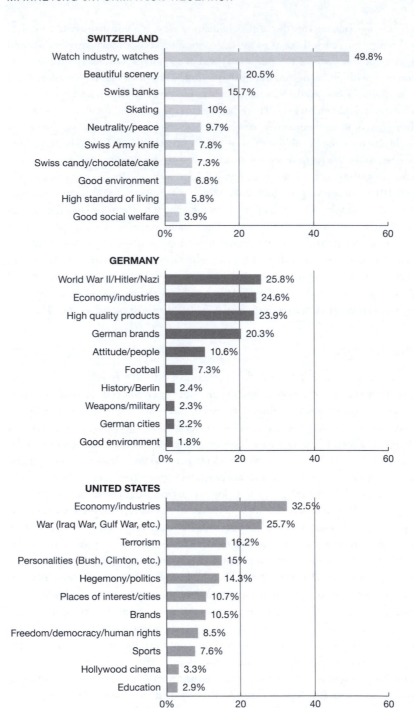

SWITZERLAND

Watch industry, watches	49.8%
Beautiful scenery	20.5%
Swiss banks	15.7%
Skating	10%
Neutrality/peace	9.7%
Swiss Army knife	7.8%
Swiss candy/chocolate/cake	7.3%
Good environment	6.8%
High standard of living	5.8%
Good social welfare	3.9%

GERMANY

World War II/Hitler/Nazi	25.8%
Economy/industries	24.6%
High quality products	23.9%
German brands	20.3%
Attitude/people	10.6%
Football	7.3%
History/Berlin	2.4%
Weapons/military	2.3%
German cities	2.2%
Good environment	1.8%

UNITED STATES

Economy/industries	32.5%
War (Iraq War, Gulf War, etc.)	25.7%
Terrorism	16.2%
Personalities (Bush, Clinton, etc.)	15%
Hegemony/politics	14.3%
Places of interest/cities	10.7%
Brands	10.5%
Freedom/democracy/human rights	8.5%
Sports	7.6%
Hollywood cinema	3.3%
Education	2.9%

Figure 5.3 *The images of Germany, the USA and Switzerland in China*

■ BOX 5.5 QUALITATIVE STUDY ON EU CITIZENS AND THE EURO

This qualitative study, commissioned by the European Commission's Directorate-General for Health and Consumer Protection and conducted in 2002, was mainly aimed at analysing attitudes to the euro and assessing difficulties encountered by the elderly (those aged over 70) and those in an insecure economic situation. In addition to these two target groups, a control sample was also surveyed. In each of the three groups, seven people were surveyed in each country, making a total of 263 persons. Each personal interview lasted an average of 60 minutes. This survey highlighted, among other things, the fact the elderly found it difficult to establish a value scale for the euro and that they had to convert prices in euros into their former national currency almost systematically in order to be able to establish such a value scale.

Source: Directorate-General for Health and Consumer Protection (2002)

Focus groups are normally composed of eight to ten persons and hosted by a trained moderator. They are often recorded so that guidance can be given to the moderator and so that the discussions can be transcribed. Although it is important to have a reasonably homogeneous group, the people recruited must not know each other and the amount of information given about the topic to be discussed must be restricted. Depending on the topic and the commissioning body, a small compensation is paid to each participant at the end of the meeting. Because the composition of the group can affect the results (one member may exert a strong influence, several participants may be passive, etc.), generally at least two groups are formed so that the results can be compared.

Other methods

An omnibus survey is one conducted on behalf of several organizations, each of which can include a limited number of questions. Organizations can thus benefit from a representative survey even when their need for information is limited (answers being required to only two or three questions, for example). In addition, this type of survey allows the costs to be spread over several organizations, each paying on the basis of the number and complexity of the questions asked. This aspect is important, because it allows smaller organizations or those with a limited budget to gain access to this type of survey. Omnibus surveys are frequently designed and conducted by market research firms that announce their intention to conduct a study and give organizations an opportunity to include their questions.

Panels involve questioning or observing the same group of people at regular intervals on opinions, attitudes or behaviours. The make-up and representativity of the panel are very important. Panels of the following types are used:

- *Household panel:* gathers information on all purchases of consumer goods in a household; in Switzerland, the household panel comprises 5,074 households (12,031 persons).
- *Media panel (television or internet):* in Germany, 5,000 households have agreed to have a device connected to their television sets that transmits information on channels watched and the characteristics of those watching (number, sociodemographic criteria, etc.).

Because of the constraints involved in this type of survey and the risk that people will rationalize their behaviour after being questioned on several occasions (people become aware of their behaviour as they complete questionnaires), those in charge of a panel will ensure that panel members are renewed regularly (20–25 per cent per year).

SELECTING A SAMPLE

Regardless of the method used, it is rare that every member of the target population is surveyed, for two main reasons. First, the costs of doing so are extremely high and the benefit is marginal compared with data provided by a sample (sufficient approximation for decision taking). Second, the technical and legal difficulties of obtaining a list of every member of the target population would be enormous (for example, nobody has a list of all smokers, or all HIV-positive persons, should a study wish to focus on these target groups). In fact, all members of a population are surveyed in only two cases: during censuses (such as population censuses) and, provided that the population is known, when its size is small (satisfaction survey of all employees in an organization). In other cases, a representative sample of the target population is taken.

Allowing for a margin of error which is fixed at the outset, the results obtained with a sample can be generalized to the entire population under study. Consequently, depending on the desired accuracy and the complexity of the questions, the size of samples will vary between 50 and 2,000. It is important to note that the accuracy of the results obtained in a survey depend on the size of the sample and not the percentage of the population studied (there is no relationship between the size of the population and the size of the sample). Since methods for selecting a sample are many, only a general overview of these methods is given here, while the two most widely used methods – random sampling and quota sampling – will be compared in greater detail. To complete this discussion, information will be given about the size of samples.

Overview of sampling methods

Generally, sampling methods fall into two categories: probability (or random) methods and nonprobability (or empirical) methods.

The principle of probability methods is that the sample is constituted by a random draw from a list of the target population. This means that every person theoretically has the same chance of being included in the sample. Practically, there are three variants (Malhotra, 2009; Vernette, 2002):

- *Simple random sampling:* members of the sample are drawn at random using computer algorithms or a table of random numbers if the sample is small.
- *Stratified random sampling:* the target population is first divided into strata or groups (for example, by age range or depending on the district of residence) and random sampling is then applied. This method is very useful when, for example, a higher survey rate is wanted for certain groups (e.g. populations in urban areas) than others (populations in rural areas).
- *Cluster random sampling:* the population is divided into clusters (e.g. streets, schools, factories, hospitals); elements from each cluster are then drawn at random and all individuals belonging to the selected elements are surveyed. Let us take a study on the vocational training of young people as an example: one might first draw up a list of all existing training establishments (or all existing classes), draw a number of them, or a number of classes in these establishments, at random, and then survey every member of the establishment or class who meets the study criteria.

Nonprobability methods are based on a reasoned selection of individuals for the sample, when complete files are unavailable, when funding is very limited, or when it is relatively difficult to obtain a random sample containing a certain number of individuals who meet various criteria that are important for the study. A number of variants exist:

- *Quota sampling:* the sample is determined on the basis of characteristics or quotas of the target population (depending on the survey, these quotas might be professional activity, age, income bracket, social status, etc.). Figure 5.4 shows an example of the use of the quota method.
- *Convenience sampling:* information is gathered from people who are conveniently available – for example, all passengers in a train at a particular time. This solution is very useful for testing hypotheses or carrying out an exploratory study.

Take as an example a study designed to find out whether and under what conditions home owners would be prepared to invest in measures designed to reduce their building's energy consumption.

Since we do not have a complete list of all owners and all heating systems, we can proceed by quota to determine the sample. Two quotas could be used: ownership type (house or unit in a multi-occupancy building) and the main type of heating in use (electricity, heating oil, gas, renewable energy sources). If we know the national distribution of the number and type of owners (in this case, 60 per cent of non-owners and 40 per cent of owners divided between 18 per cent house owners and 22 per cent

	Own an individual house 18%	Own a unit in a building 22%	Total owners 40%	Renters 60%
	45%	55%	←100%	
Electricity	10% 50	10% 50	20%	
Oil	20% 100	35% 175	55%	
Natural gas	10% 50	8% 40	10%	
Renewable energies	5% 25	2% 10	7%	

Figure 5.4 *Example of quota sampling study*

owners of units in buildings) and the main types of heating in these categories, we can initially determine the basic structure of the target population. Thus, if we take owners with oil heating (55 per cent of all owners), 20 per cent are house owners while 35 per cent are owners of units in larger buildings.

If we chose a sample of 500 persons, we could then determine the number of owners to survey for the eight groups arising out of the two defined quotas. In this way, 40 condominium owners who have gas heating should be part of the sample. These people could then be recruited in various ways (by telephone, by ringing doorbells in blocks of flats, etc.).

Leaving aside professional surveys conducted by statistics departments that make use of multiple forms of sampling methods, the two main methods used to conduct market studies in the public sector are random sampling and quota sampling. Table 5.2 presents these two methods comparatively.

Sample size

As mentioned above, the size of the sample does not depend on the size of the target population but on statistical rules and, inevitably, on budgetary constraints: available funds often strongly influence the maximum size of the sample.

Since the objective of a sample is to make it possible to generalize results to the target population, the acceptable risk threshold regarding results needs to be determined. For example, if a 5 per cent risk is tolerated, there will be a 95 per cent

■ **Table 5.2** *Comparison of random sampling and quota sampling*

Characteristics	Random sampling	Quota sampling
Representation	Use processes that guarantee that each individual has the same chances of being drawn at random	If the characteristics of the population are available, the sample representing the population can be constructed
Difficulties	Databases nonexistent or out of date Individuals difficult to reach or fail to respond to the questionnaire (risk of certain groups being underrepresented)	Difficult to guarantee good representation of the population using quotas Data regarding certain quotas missing Risk of easy-to-reach groups being overrepresented
Application of probability theory	In principle, yes	In principle, no
Choice influenced by the interviewer	In principle, no (no choice over people to be interviewed)	Yes, but it is possible to control the choices made
Costs	Relatively high	Limited

Source: adapted from Kühn and Kreuzer (2006).

chance that the result will lie within a defined range (95 per cent chance that the percentage of people who vote 'yes' at the next referendum will be 51–55 per cent). The narrower the level of confidence, the more accurate the survey. Thus, if the sample is large, accuracy will be good and the results can be generalized without too much risk. Box 5.6 shows how to calculate the sample.

Take the following example: it is estimated that 30 per cent of the people in a town of 20,000 inhabitants are dissatisfied with the services of the roads and highways department and the municipality wishes to verify this information and better understand the reasons for satisfaction and dissatisfaction. Suppose that those responsible for the study accept a margin of error of +/−3 per cent and a 5 per cent level of risk. The size of the sample is calculated as follows:

n = sample size
1.96 is the level of confidence (95 per cent)
0.3 stands for the 30 per cent of the population who are dissatisfied
0.7 stands for the 70 per cent of the population who are satisfied (1–0.3)
0.03 stands for the confidence interval

■ BOX 5.6 FORMULA TO CALCULATE SAMPLES

$$n = \frac{t^2 pq}{e^2}$$

n = size of sample
t = confidence coefficient (very often 95% = 1.96)

     t = 1 (probability of 68.3%)
     t = 2 (probability of 95.5%)
     t = 3 (probability of 99.7%)
     t = 4 (probability of 95%)

e = level of precision judged sufficient to generalize results (confidence interval)
p = percentage of a given characteristic inside the sample
q = (100 − p)

$$n = \frac{(1.96)^2 . (0.3) . (0.7)}{(0.03)^2} = 896$$

Thus, for this study, the recommended sample size will be 896 individuals. The size of the sample can be calculated using the formula in Box 5.6. Independently of the possibilities available for determining the sample size and for selecting the individuals that will make it up, one must bear in mind the risks of error in the representativity of the sample. These risks are of two types:

■ Statistical sampling error: to limit this risk, it is recommended that, before analysing the results, various characteristics of the sample be compared with those of the population (sociodemographic characteristics, for example).

■ Errors arising out of the fact that certain groups are overrepresented or underrepresented in the sample. In the example given above of a survey on the roads and highways department in a town, it is possible that all the dissatisfied people polled and all those close to people who work in the department will respond to the questionnaire, whereas those with no definite opinion will take little interest in the study and not respond. Errors such as these can be identified using various statistical tests.

PLANNING A STUDY

Given the complexity and cost of market research, it is important to plan very carefully. The process can be divided into six phases, set out in summary fashion in Box 5.7.

■ BOX 5.7 PHASES OF A MARKET RESEARCH STUDY

1 Define the problem and decide whether to conduct the study

- ■ Define the purpose of the research
- ■ Determine the research objectives (the information to be obtained)
- ■ Conduct a documentary analysis (secondary study)
- ■ Evaluate the main research parameters
- ■ Decide whether or not to carry out the study

2 Study plan

- ■ Research design: population(s) observed, survey techniques, nature and size of the sample
- ■ Develop data-collection tools (questionnaire, observation system)
- ■ Design analysis plan

3 Data collection

- ■ Detailed information on the sample and individuals to be recruited
- ■ Training of interviewers
- ■ Data gathering

4 Data analysis

- ■ Coding of responses
- ■ Data entry and processing
- ■ Statistical data analysis

5 Presentation of results

- ■ Highlight the main results
- ■ Draft study report (with interpretation of results)
- ■ Presentation

6 Contribution to the decision taking

Source: adapted from Kühn and Kreuzer (2000).

The first phase is to delimit the problem and decide whether or not to conduct research. This involves defining the purpose of the research and determining the corresponding objectives. This phase is very constraining because it necessitates accurately identifying the concrete need for information that will allow a decision to be taken. This will entail finding out whether secondary data are available and evaluating the main research parameters (target populations, possible study techniques, sample sizes, budget and timetable). On these bases, a decision can be taken on the timeliness and usefulness of conducting primary research.

The second phase is the design of the research plan. This involves, first, the design of the study, which must identify the target population and choose the survey technique and nature and size of the sample(s). It is not always easy to identify the people to be surveyed with precision. For example, in a study of the satisfaction of the residents of a nursing home, should the survey canvass residents themselves, their family members, their visitors or outside professionals working on their case (physicians, social workers, etc.)? All carry some of the information, and detailed guidelines about those needing to be surveyed will be required. Next, the data-gathering tools (questionnaire, observation system, etc.) must be developed. Box 5.8 sets out the main rules to follow in developing a questionnaire for a quantitative study. Lastly, this phase must also specify how the results will be analysed. It is important to avoid first collecting the data and only afterwards addressing the issue of how they are to be analysed. At this point it is still possible to refine the collection tool (questionnaire) to make sure that the information needs are covered.

■ BOX 5.8 RULES FOR DESIGNING A QUESTIONNAIRE

Recommendations on the structure of the questionnaire

- The introduction to the questionnaire must be short, precise and generally contain the following points: the name of the institution, the purpose of the study, a guarantee of anonymity and the time required. Depending on the objective of the survey, indications on the commissioning body might or might not be given. If the commissioning body's name is liable to influence responses, it could be stated at the outset that the commissioning body will be disclosed at the end of the questionnaire (not possible if the questionnaire is mailed).
- At the start of the questionnaire, questions must be easy and interesting and must avoid sensitive topics.
- Sensitive topics and more complex questions should, if possible, be placed at the end of the questionnaire.
- Questions on the socio-demographic profile (age, gender, income, ethnic origin, etc.) are placed at the end of the questionnaire.
- Topical questions must be asked before those referring to the past. It is easier to remember a current or very recent fact than one from the distant past.
- Questions regarding behaviour must be asked before those related to opinions, expectations or motivations.
- Sudden changes of topic must be avoided, as must be long lists of very similar questions. If many questions are monotonous, intervening questions that will reawaken participants' interest should be inserted.

continued . . .

■ BOX 5.8 RULES FOR DESIGNING A QUESTIONNAIRE
... continued

■ Put one or two open questions at the end of the questionnaire if no questions of this type have yet been asked.

■ Thank the participants in the survey at the end of the questionnaire.

Recommendations regarding the formulation of questions

■ Questions must be concrete, short and unambiguous. Abstract questions, complicated definitions and technical jargon must be avoided. If necessary, questions must be adapted in the light of the experience of those polled (young people, the elderly, foreigners, etc.).

■ Questions must be asked in a neutral manner (no suggestive questions and none containing value judgments).

■ Each question must contain only one element requiring an answer (avoid double questions that cover several ideas).

■ Because respondents have a tendency to be positive in order to please the interviewer or to avoid having to justify a negative answer, it is a good idea to vary the manner in which questions are formulated.

■ When the same scale is used throughout a questionnaire, respondents tend to give the same answers and to use the same parts of the scale. For this reason it is a good idea to vary the scales.

■ In closed questions, it is advisable to add an alternative response category such as 'Other' or 'Don't know'. A 'don't know' answer is preferable to a forced response which does not reflect reality.

Sources: Hague and Jackson (1999); Freudiger and Stihl, (1996).

The third phase is data collection. Details regarding the recruitment of individuals and the sample will be decided upon, interviewers trained and, lastly, the data actually gathered. This phase will be followed by data entry and then data analysis. Before entering the information collected into a computer system, all responses must be coded (for example, if the questionnaire includes a question such as 'What do you spontaneously associate with the Netherlands?', it must be determined whether the responses 'flowers', 'floristry', 'roses', 'tulips', etc. should be grouped into a single category or whether a category should be opened for every association, which would make analysis and interpretation very difficult).

The last two phases involve the presentation of results (formatting of the main results, study reports, oral presentations to deciders) and, lastly, decision taking.

MANAGING INFORMATION IN AN INFORMATION SYSTEM

Many studies are carried out in organizations where information is gathered in an ad-hoc manner. Often they respond to a one-time need for information in connection with a decision that needs to be taken or a particular requirement of an authority (what percentage of smokers are aged under 18? what is the satisfaction level of beneficiaries of a service? etc.). Although these studies can resolve the information problem at a particular moment, the designers and producers of the studies often fail to consider how the data can be integrated into an information system. As a result, a great deal of information is gathered with no possibility of subsequently comparing it with information gathered during other studies (different samples, variables defined differently, etc.) because the information is not integrated into the system (a few years later on, nobody knows where the data are, the data are no longer available in electronic format, or they cannot be imported into a compatible system). In order to prevent wastage of resources and to improve the organization's efficiency, when carrying out a study it is important to consider and plan the integration of the data to be gathered into an information system.

An information system is an organized set of elements that allows the collection, storage, processing and above all structured dissemination of information on a given phenomenon (products, customers, competition, the organization's processes, etc.). It is principally comprised of:

- a set of resources (data, personnel, equipment, procedures, etc.) that make it possible to acquire, store, structure and communicate information in various forms (texts, tables, images, etc.)
- the computer system enabling all the data to be linked and managed.

In marketing, with the recent realization of the importance of relationships in attracting and keeping customers that are of value to a business, the construction, management and use of systems to manage mass quantities of customer-related information (data on persons, their purchases and purchase frequency, on claims and services rendered, on corporate hospitality events, etc.) have become vitally important for business success. In many sectors, the cost of securing the fidelity of an existing customer is considerably lower than the cost of acquiring a new one, which means it is worth investing in the management of relations with existing customers. This field is generally known as Customer Relationship Management (CRM).

Systems for managing data on users or beneficiaries of services are not limited to the private sector. The public sector also has an interest in developing such systems for the purposes of gaining better knowledge and optimizing the use of services. Take the example of the school system. In very many countries, every time a pupil or student changes from one level or institution to another, he or she (or a parent) has to complete new forms, provide transcripts or examination results from previous levels, etc., which involves the use of specific resources (staff assigned to the task, forms developed by schools, computerized tools, etc.), possible loss of information and the introduction of errors in the completion of questionnaires or their entry into the computer system. Consequently, an integrated system that would track the student's progress independently of his or her study level and the institution attended would make it possible to economize on resources, avoid the pitfalls mentioned, and above all deliver information that often cannot be obtained in a complete manner without such a system (such as the percentage of students who repeat a year during their education, the effect of support and integration measures on results, or the relationship between marks obtained in early educational levels and the choice of academic or vocational training).

In summary, the analysis of existing data and the gathering of new data in ad-hoc studies must as far as possible be carried out using information systems that allow these data to be used over time (for monitoring purposes) and make them available to people who could use them for authorized purposes.

EXERCISE 5.1

Define an information research strategy for the following hypothetical situations and identify the possible pitfalls.

- satisfaction of patients in a local hospital
- identification of potential users of a new sport complex
- citizens' perception of an environmental policy regarding traffic lanes to be reserved for cars carrying more than two people.

DISCUSSION QUESTIONS

This chapter addresses the collection of information by the State.

1 How justified is the State in seeking information, especially for exploratory reasons?
2 Is it not the role of parliamentarians to anticipate the needs of citizens?
3 What is the role of the State, and more specifically of its administrative and political branches in this situation?

NOTE

1 The government of Canada lists all market studies carried out each year (see http://dsp-psd.pwgsc.gc.ca/Collection-R/Statcan/63–224-XIB/63–224-XIB-e.html, accessed on 15 February 2010).

REFERENCES

Directorate-General for Health and Consumer Protection (2002) Qualitative Study on EU Citizens and the Euro in the Months Following its Introduction, Brussels, European Commission.

Freudiger, P. and Stihl, S. (1996) Methodische Handlungsregeln zur Gestaltung von Fragebogen und zur Formulierung von Fragen, Bern, Institut für Marketing und Unternehmungsführung der Universität Bern.

Hague, P. and Jackson, P. (1999) *Market Research: A Guide to Planning and Evaluation*, London, Kogan Page.

Insititute for Citizen Centered Services (1998) Citizen First – Common Measurement Tool, Ottawa, Institute for Citizen Centered Services.

Kühn, R. and Kreuzer, M. (2006) *Marktforschung: Best Practices für Marketingverantwortliche*, Bern, Stuttgart, Vienna, Haupt Verlag.

Malhotra, N. (2009) *Marketing Research: An Applied Orientation*, New York, Pearson Education.

Pasquier, M. and Weiss Richard, M. (2006) *Das Image der Schweiz in China: Ergebnisse der Länderstudie China*, Berne, Presence Switzerland.

Schmidt, F. (2000) Sondages sur la Satisfaction des Clients: Guide du Gestionnaire, Centre Canadien de Gestion.

Vernette, E. (2002) *Techniques D'études de Marché*, Paris, Vuibert.

Chapter 6

Marketing strategy

LEARNING OBJECTIVES

By the end of this chapter you should be able to:

- Understand the various steps in the strategic planning process.
- Identify and select the appropriate elements and tools of marketing analysis.
- Understand the process leading to the determination of marketing strategy, taking into account implementation dynamics and the inherent limitations of this approach.

KEY POINTS OF THIS CHAPTER

- The structuring of strategic processes differs significantly between public and private organizations, notably in terms of translating political objectives into managerial action.
- Marking strategy is divided into analytical (information-gathering) and decisional phases – the analytical phase may focus on the market, the demand side, the supply side and/or the organization's marketing resources.
- To develop a marketing strategy, the following issues must be addressed:

  (a) choice of market and target group priorities
  (b) competitive strategy
  (c) positioning of the organization
  (d) market exploitation strategy.

KEY TERMS

Marketing strategy – the frame of reference for the means and objectives used by an organization in its marketing activities.

continued . . .

KEY TERMS ... *continued*

Translation – the passage from political objectives to managerial action.

Segmentation strategy – when an organization focuses on a specific sub-group, based on specific needs or demographic criteria.

Differentiation strategy – when an organization's strategy is focused on the specificities of its products and services as a competitive advantage versus other organizations.

Price strategy – when an organization's strategy is focused on the lower prices of its products and services as a competitive advantage versus other organizations.

STRATEGIC PLANNING PROCESS

Marketing strategy provides an organization with a framework for carrying out its marketing activities. 'Strategy' is originally a military concept, basically aiming to determine goals and how best to obtain them. More precisely, Mintzberg (1992, pp.12–19) defines strategy on five different levels (the five Ps):

- *Plan:* a purposive course of action or guideline to deal with a given situation (the actions are developed consciously and purposefully).
- *Ploy:* designed to gain competitive advantage (e.g. pose a threat to a competitor).
- *Pattern:* more than just a plan – the actions needed to accomplish it.
- *Position:* where an organization wants to be on a given market (characterizing the relationship between the organization and its environment).
- *Perspective:* the shared vision of how an organization's personnel see the world (common values) as shown by their intentions and actions.

Before outlining the process for developing a marketing strategy, we shall first look at how marketing strategy can be applied to a public organization – insofar as the institutional, organizational and market contexts are very different for a private company than for a traditional public body.

Strategy within a public organization

Figure 6.1 presents a comparative overview of how strategic processes are structured in private and public organizations. For major organizations, four strategic levels can be identified: the general level, not linked to any specific time-frame; the overall strategic level, defining the main priorities; the strategic level, within which – in the narrow sense of the term – the organization pursues its development, notably as regards its competitors; and, lastly, the functional level.

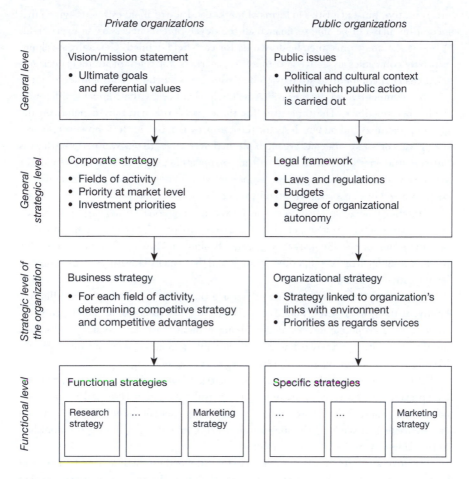

Private organizations   *Public organizations*

General level

Vision/mission statement
- Ultimate goals and referential values

Public issues
- Political and cultural context within which public action is carried out

General strategic level

Corporate strategy
- Fields of activity
- Priority at market level
- Investment priorities

Legal framework
- Laws and regulations
- Budgets
- Degree of organizational autonomy

Strategic level of the organization

Business strategy
- For each field of activity, determining competitive strategy and competitive advantages

Organizational strategy
- Strategy linked to organization's links with environment
- Priorities as regards services

Functional level

Functional strategies

| Research strategy | ... | Marketing strategy |

Specific strategies

| ... | ... | Marketing strategy |

Figure 6.1 *Strategic development processes: comparison between private and public organizations*

In private companies, the general level involves the corporate mission ('We are a bank involved in international wealth management' or 'We are a security firm involved in protecting goods and people') and the values which its staff should respect in their attitudes, decisions and behaviour ('in total confidence', 'respect for the hierarchy', 'high degree of confidence accorded to staff', etc.). Unless a major event occurs that implies significant change (e.g. a merger with another company or investing in a totally new field), these elements are likely to remain for the long term, and change or evolve only gradually (Grünig and Kühn, 2008).

The next level is corporate strategy. For major companies active in a number of fields and/or different markets, these fields need to be defined (e.g. investment banking, private wealth management, corporate wealth management, retail banking etc.). So, too, must priorities in terms of market and above all investment – given that a company may not be able to finance all the developments necessary in every field. A business strategy must then be drawn up for each field defined. Generally speaking, as private companies are active in competitive markets, the relevant strategic decisions must enable a competitive strategy to be defined (see Porter, 1985) and identify the effective competitive advantages which will help clients view the company differently from its competitors. The time-scale for these two levels naturally depends on the economic context and on which sector the company is active in. It is, however, worth noting that corporate strategies are often planned over a five- to ten-year period, whereas business strategies sometimes need revising or updating every three to five years. For small or medium-sized companies – whose activity is concentrated in a single field – corporate and business strategies tend to be one and the same.

Marketing strategy is one of a company's various functional strategies (e.g. research strategy, production strategy, etc.) and must identify priority target groups in a field of activity and/or specific market (e.g. retail banking in France) – with a competitive position resulting from a competitive strategy and the principal measures at instrumental level (marketing mix).

The rationale for establishing strategy for a public organization is very different. Firstly, at the general level, public action takes place in response to public problems (there can be no public intervention without a 'public' problem to start with). The political and cultural framework within which public action is carried out varies greatly from country to country, and even from region to region.

Let us take the example of police action as regards road safety. National priorities and preventive/repressive measures vary considerably in nature and scope from country to country. They may evolve over time, but depend largely on political and cultural criteria (exceeding the speed limit by 20 kilometres per hour is not punished in the same way in the USA as in Italy).

At an overall strategic level, public activity is defined on the one hand by laws and regulations (aspects of public policy) and, on the other, by arrangements concerning the organizations responsible for carrying out these tasks (degree of organizational and decision-making autonomy). Matters are affected by whether an organization is a legal entity or not, with its own budget, right to hire personnel, etc. Organizational strategy only occurs at the following level, and must take account of both the context previously mentioned, and the organization's environment. These are both discussed in more detail below.

In private organizations the passage from corporate to business level is relatively straightforward. But, at the public level, the relationship between the legal framework and organizational strategy is more complex – given that the legal framework has a political base, while organizational strategy depends on an economic and managerial rationale. Figure 6.2 illustrates the interplay between these two levels.

One of the problems for an official in a public organization is to 'translate' decisions that result from political rationale and debate into objectives and practical measures that can be implemented. To take road safety: laws and regulations voted by parliament

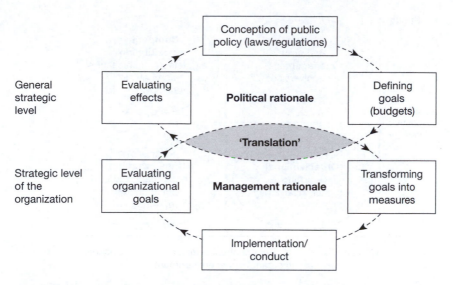

Figure 6.2 *Interaction between an organization's political and strategic levels*
Source: adapted from Schedler and Proeller (2003).

require road users to respect the law so that fewer accidents occur. No political decision-maker would dare assert that an annual threshold of, say, 5,000 deaths on the roads is acceptable. In theory, a politician's approach and activity will target a fall in the number of deaths (objective: zero deaths). The police need to translate political intentions into practical measures – based on the (budgetary) means at their disposal, and also on more technical criteria (greater presence at 'accident-prone areas' or outside schools, more speed-checks and breathalyser tests, installing new radars, etc.). The police cannot prevent every type of accident or dangerous behaviour, and also have other duties (ensuring the safety of goods and persons, crime-fighting, emergency services, etc.); so they must choose what to prioritize, ensure measures are implemented in a structured and coordinated fashion, and evaluate results not just in terms of public policy goals but also with respect to available resources.

The environmental context also needs to be taken into account when defining an organization's strategy. Unlike private companies, the overwhelming majority of public organizations do not face competition, so they cannot develop competitive strategies. Another reference framework must therefore be found for public organization strategies. Two criteria help establish a typology of a public organization's possible strategic orientation: the degree of competitive intensity; and the degree of uncertainty in the organizational environment. Figure 6.3 looks at these two criteria and suggests strategies that result from combining them.

Should an organization find itself in a relatively stable environment (no likely change to its public mission, budgetary stability, etc.) and without any direct competition, strategy will basically consist of achieving constant improvement (organizational

103

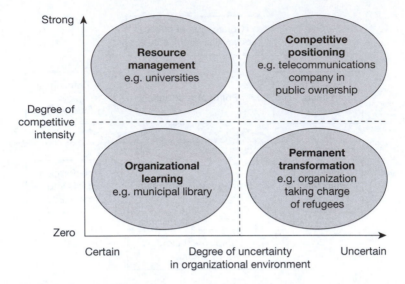

Figure 6.3 *Possible public organization strategies*

learning) – through staff training, establishing a dialogue with consumers (if possible), paying attention to outside criticism, and making comparisons with similar organizations in other regions to improve procedures (benchmarking), etc.

The situation is different if, despite a relatively stable environment, there is a high degree of competitive intensity. Direct or indirect competition cannot be ignored; but, rather than seeking to position itself vis-à-vis its competitors, an organization needs to have its own – preferably unique – resources, which similar organizations cannot emulate. Some universities, facing competition from other learning institutions, have perfected such high-level teaching and research capabilities that they have to focus on and reinforce these specific resources to maintain their pre-eminent position, reputation and status.

The third, less frequent scenario concerns a relatively unstable context and an absence of competition. An organization's mission (or some of its major aspects) may change rapidly, so it must maintain the flexibility needed to respond to unexpected tasks. For example, an organization whose mission is to house and feed asylum-seekers, and deal with the relevant administrative tasks, should be able to react quickly to a sudden influx of refugees in the wake of political conflict; have the language skills needed to communicate with them; and have staff able to understand the refugees' socio-cultural habits.

The final scenario has similarities with the private sector, involving intense competition and an unstable environment (technological developments, market liberalization, etc.). In these circumstances, strategies tend to be the same as those adopted by private companies, as described by Porter (1985). Organizations basically have a choice between three types of strategy:

■ *Segmentation strategy:* concentrating on a segment or niche (i.e. a set of clients with specific, identifiable needs distinct from those of other segments).

■ *Differentiation strategy:* the organization wishes to exploit the market as a whole, and offers specific competitive advantage(s) which other organizations lack (high level of service, level of quality, products adapted to client's needs, etc.).

■ *Price strategy:* the organization's prices are the most attractive on the market, and help it stand out from its competitors.

This final scenario is relatively infrequent in the public sector, and mainly concerns public enterprises active in liberalized markets (telecommunications, postal services, electricity, etc.).

MARKETING STRATEGY PLANNING PROCESS

Marketing strategy is a functional strategy which must answer the following questions, especially in the public sector:

■ Who does the service offer target? Can the offer be differentiated to target specific groups?

■ What is the effective offer being addressed to these persons?

■ What is the offer's image and profile?

■ What are the quantitative and qualitative objectives?

■ How will the offer be proposed on the market (price? means of communication? where available? etc.)?

To answer these questions requires a planning process that includes an analysis phase, then a decision-making phase. Both phases must then be presented in detail (see Figure 6.4). The analysis phase integrates market analysis and an analysis of the

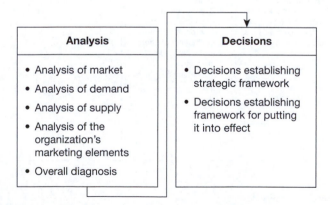

Figure 6.4 *Phases of marketing strategy*

demand, offer and organization; the decision-making phase differentiates between decisions fixing the strategic framework, and those fixing the framework for putting the strategy into effect. The next two sections deal first with the analysis phase, then the decision-making phase.

ELEMENTS OF ANALYSIS

A situation analysis helps obtain and structure the information needed for decision taking – leading to an overall diagnosis highlighting an organization's strengths and weaknesses; what it has to offer; and the risks and opportunities it faces on the market. Figure 6.5 shows the different analysis phases, comprising (1) a general market analysis, (2, 3) specific analyses of the market's twin components (demand and offer), and (4) an analysis of the organization's own marketing elements. A diagnosis based on a synthesis of the information obtained (5) completes the analytical stage.

Before looking at these phases in more detail, it should be pointed out that the elements mentioned in Figure 6.5 are the subject of more or less detailed studies, depending on the market context and on their relevance: some points warrant detailed analysis, while the response to others may be obvious or irrelevant. These limitations must therefore be used with flexibility and adapted to the context.

Analysing the market

The first phase aims to study the 'market' and its principal actors. The tools linked to constructing the market system (see Chapter 4) can be used, as they help identify the

1. Analysis of market	2. Analysis of demand	3. Analysis of offer	4. Analysis of organization's marketing elements
– Definition of market – Constitution of market system – Description of leading actors and how they inter-relate – Description of auxiliary elements – Study of development potential – Analysis of intensity of competition	– Structuring of clients and potential clients (segmentation) – Analysis of major segments (direct and indirect beneficiaries, etc.)	– Description of current competing offers – Description of organization's offer – Comparative positioning of offers (objective and subjective advantages)	– Resources – Conduct system – Information system

5. Overall diagnosis
– Market risks and opportunities – Strengths and weaknesses of organization's offer

Figure 6.5 *Stages of marketing analysis*

106

leading participants and the links between them. Along with an analysis of all the elements liable to influence market development (technological changes, modifications to the legal framework, economic situation, etc.), the overall development potential should also be assessed, to make it easier to reply to demand as and when necessary. Finally, depending on the market context, the intensity of the competition is analysed; obviously, in the absence of competition, such analysis is pointless.

Analysis of the demand

Structuring and analysing demand – known as market segmentation – is at the heart of the marketing strategy planning process. Most authors agree that segmentation is one of the most important marketing concepts. It first appeared in specialist literature in 1956, in an article published by Smith (1956), who described it as follows: 'Segmentation is based upon the development of the demand side of the market. . . . It is attributable to the desires of consumers or users for more precise satisfaction of their varying wants.'

The basic rationale behind this type of structure is that a competitive relationship between products can be treated directly through consumer characteristics. Different needs and expectations help create homogenous consumer groups (segments) likely to behave in similar fashion, and which can be targeted by specific measures. It follows that, for segmentation to be used, demand needs to be heterogeneous (different purchase criteria), and the types of market which result must be sufficiently interesting for a company's profitability to be assured.

There are two ways of distinguishing between all the various segmentation criteria. The first centres on the relationship between the person and product or service desired (direct and objective relationship, or indirect relationship). The second concerns general consumer properties or product-specific consumer properties (see Table 6.1). Combining these two approaches yields the following groups of criteria:

- *Socio-demographic, socio-economic and socio-geographic criteria:* gender, age, size of household, religion, domicile, geographic criteria, revenue, profession, etc. These are the oldest criteria, corresponding to the general characteristics of the various parties, and are often used as the information is easy to obtain and understand; but their relationship with market purchasing behaviour can be tenuous.
- *Behavioural criteria linked to products:* choice of product, intensity of purchase or use, price sensitivity, preferences as regards the distribution system, etc. These behaviour-linked criteria may vary, and do not concern individuals as such, but rather how they react to a range of marketing activities or stimuli.
- *General psychographic criteria:* reasons for purchasing, or personality. These criteria are of an introspective nature and cannot be directly obtained. Motivation is a construct, involving both a need and how to satisfy it. Segmentation linking behaviour to personality criteria is open to criticism given that it attempts to explain consumers' behaviour by their traits of personality (obsessions, degree of introversion, etc.).

107

- *Mixed psychographic criteria:* attitudes, lifestyles. Attitudes have special importance in consumer research. This concept simultaneously integrates a product, person and situation on which a judgment is made. The use of variables describing lifestyle involves measuring the activity of those questioned in terms of interests, basic socio-demographic variables, their opinions, etc., and derives from the hypothesis that, by better understanding consumers, it is easier to communicate with them.
- *Psychographic criteria linked to products:* advantages or profits obtained. These criteria are based on the advantages consumers derive when buying and/or using a product. The benefits consumers seek from using a product are supposed to be the fundamental reasons for the existence of market segments.

In his segmentation case-study of high-speed train users in Germany, Perrey (1998) used mainly behavioural criteria linked to the product, like price or the service offered; and psychographic criteria linked to products, like social utility, ecological aspects, etc. Box 6.1 shows the results of the study, made from a sample of over 5,000 users.

A variety of methods can be used to carry out a segmentation study. The most frequent is the intuitive or empirical method, based on experience and general observation of the market and its actors. If, for instance, one wishes to segment demand for training in the medical field, criteria may include participants' needs (professional improvement or career-guidance, general knowledge, etc.) and/or availability (e.g. evening classes, full days, weekdays or Saturdays) to structure demand.

The other possible approach involves using statistical methods (hierarchical analysis). Such methods are commonly used in the fields of medicine, biology or archaeology, and aim to structure observed data into explicit groups, allowing taxonomies to develop. Technically speaking, such methods rely on separating objects into groups so that each object in a group is more similar to other objects in the same group than any object in another group. Box 6.1 reflects a hierarchical analysis of personal data. An alternative to constructing a specific typology for a market involves taking an existing general typology whose lessons can be used with the help of complementary information.

Table 6.1 Typology – segmentation criteria

	General consumer properties	Product-specific consumer properties	
Direct and objective relationship	Socio-demographic and socio-economic characteristics	Observable criteria of consumer behaviour	
Indirect relationship	Psychographic characteristics		
	General criteria	Mixed criteria	Product-specific criteria

■ BOX 6.1 SEGMENTATION OF HIGH-SPEED TRAIN USERS IN GERMANY

Price-conscious clients

This market segment accounts for 51 per cent of rail users, and is the largest in numerical terms. The main criterion when choosing a means of transport is the price – followed, at some distance, by journey time. Such train users view the study's other criteria – service, facilities and social usefulness – as secondary. Because of its relative unimportance to users, service offers railway companies little scope to stand out. Compared to the other two segments, price-conscious clients are younger, and include men and women in roughly equal numbers. A large proportion of these users are still in training (24 per cent), and their average disposable income is comparatively modest.

Clients in a hurry

This market segment concerns users for whom journey time is the main criterion when choosing their means of transport. Price is less important, although not irrelevant; other criteria are not decisive. This segment represents 31 per cent of users. Clients in a hurry are aged 27–55 and predominantly male (just over two-thirds). They are employed in the private and public sectors, with a monthly income of over €3,000, and describe their journeys as business trips or shuttles. They tend to buy their tickets at sales points other than train stations. Price-conscious clients in a hurry represent over 80 per cent of total demand.

Comfort-lovers

This is the smallest market segment (18 per cent of users). Journey time and price are of secondary importance to such clients, who attach over-riding importance to service and facilities, with the former outweighing the latter. This segment therefore offers railway companies the opportunity to stand out by providing a better level of service. The scant importance of price shows that customers in this market segment are prepared to pay more for good service and facilities, which suggests that there is an unexploited margin potential at a corresponding level of cost. The majority of comfort lovers are aged 27–59, male and salaried or retired with above-average disposable income.

Source: Perrey (1998).

Whether intuitively or ideologically, it soon becomes apparent that market segmentation can create problems in the public sector – especially when the results produced are liable to distort principles of fairness and equality. However, for reasons of both economy and efficiency, segmentation may help in identifying bias in the distribution and utilization of public services – or help more effective public policies to be introduced, if there are significant differences regarding users' potential access to services. For instance: a segmentation of the population according to the use they make (or could be make) of a municipal library could help to adapt the offer to these various groups, and pay closer attention to groups who are unaware of, or do not use, these services. Likewise, bodies responsible for activities of prevention are obliged to structure all the persons liable to be affected by their offer and message. In the field of AIDS prevention, such activities and information will obviously vary, depending on which group is addressed: persons carrying the virus; members of their family; high-risk groups (prostitutes, prisoners, etc.); or adolescents. Structuring groups in the most homogenous way possible helps the corresponding measures be targeted more efficiently.

Once the structures are obtained, it is still necessary to analyse and describe the most important segments, notably to ascertain what affects their importance, stability and relevance in helping target specific offers.

Analysis of the offer

Structuring the offer involves identifying and grouping together differences between offers that are considered substitutable. A distinction may be made between structures based on a product's objective characteristics (technical criteria, physical or chemical components, etc.) and those based on people's perception of a product or service depending on their judgment or preferences (for an example of how these two types of structure can be applied, see Box 6.2). While the first type of structure is relatively simple to understand and apply, the second – called 'positioning' in marketing terms – is far more complex.

Structuring the offer in this way derives from psychology (Spiegel, 1961) and advertising (Reeves, 1960), and was made famous by Ries and Trout (1976), who asserted that 'positioning is not attached to what one does with the product, but rather to what the product represents in the head of the prospect'. The result of positioning is therefore what allows one offer to be distinguished from another.

The principal instruments for measuring positioning occur in consumers' minds; they are impressions, attitudes. These 'constructs' that may be measured in various ways:

■ *Associations:* the most direct approach consists of asking people to evaluate the dimensions associated with an offer (e.g. on a scale of one to ten). The main advantage of this form of operationalization is that many of the offer's objective characteristics can be reduced to a limited number of dimensions associated with

■ **BOX 6.2 EXAMPLE OF STRUCTURATION**

Let us take the offer of a city's museums. Structuring the museum offer on the basis of objective criteria could, for instance, yield the following results:

- ■ art museums (traditional, contemporary, tribal, etc.)
- ■ art museums devoted to a single artist
- ■ history museums
- ■ natural history museums
- ■ special interest museums (dolls, toys, cars, etc.)
- ■ technical museums

The other possibility would involve positioning these museums according to criteria linked to the image we have of them. This would mean creating groups of, say, prestige museums; museums of a strongly didactic character (for schools, say); museums of a conservationist or historical nature; museums that stage lots of different events, etc. The museums' positioning would no longer depend on what they offer, but on how they were perceived.

the product, perceived by consumers subjectively. Box 6.3 presents a typical example of association between economic sectors and countries to measure the potential difference of the countries' image.

- ■ *Perceived similarity:* this concept, linked to the analysis of similarities, is the most widely used in positioning studies. Perceived similarity between two products is defined as a combination of the number of their mutual and distinct characteristics. The results obtained make it possible to draw up representative charts of the offers available on the market, based on criteria which differentiate the alternatives or offers proposed from a perception point of view. Perceived similarity prompts a cognitive type of judgement, as those questioned will be judging the offers' attributes.

- ■ *Substitutability:* with the two previous instruments, the measure of positioning is essentially at a cognitive level; but perceived substitutability involves evaluating the offer in terms of attitudes or preferences. In marketing terms this concept is defined as the ability of two alternatives to satisfy the same needs within a market. Substitutability covers the concept of preference, and results from evaluating an offer's attributes in a consumer context.

- ■ *Competition:* this is linked to consumer behaviour, and can be defined as the relationship between two alternatives in a world of choice. This concept differs from that of perceived similarity, in that two offers perceived as similar may not

111 ■

necessarily be in competition (e.g. in the event of strong brand loyalty). Likewise, two brands can be differentiated at a perceptual level while remaining in competition.

This brief description of the instruments used for measuring positioning highlights the fact that the relationship between offers is not measured systematically. So it is fundamental to determine the nature of the positioning issue (Who are the competitors I need to position myself against? How is my offer perceived by consumers compared to other substitutable or competing offers? etc.), before choosing the type of measure and a method for treating the data obtained. The most widely used methods are: factorial analysis; multidimensional analysis of similarities; and joint analysis.

■ BOX 6.3 IMAGE DIFFERENTIAL BETWEEN ECONOMIC SECTORS

Research carried out in six countries in 1997 studied the image of different branches of the economy. The chart below presents the 'international' image of each branch in the six countries concerned. For instance, if one takes the machine industry, Germany is the country most closely associated with this economic sector.

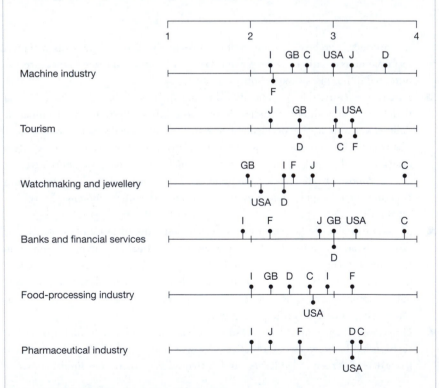

■ **Figure 6.6** *Image differential between economic sectors*

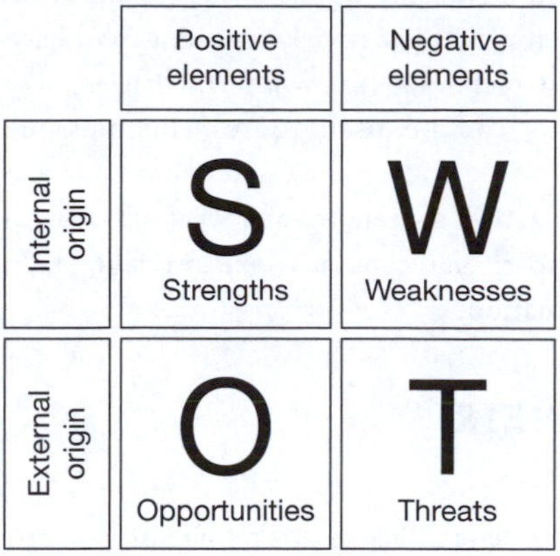

Figure 6.7 *SWOT diagnosis*
Source: Kühn (1993)

The organization's new or existing offer must be compared with others on the market so that the organization may develop alternatives as to the positioning it seeks.

Analysis of organizations' marketing elements

Implementing marketing activities requires skills and resources within an organization. So it is important to be sure of their internal or external availability before taking decisions. There are three main types:

- financial resources in personnel, and the specific skills needed for activities to be carried out (number of staff, their knowledge and skills, etc.)
- system for applying marketing instruments: staff's attitude or state of mind as regards marketing tasks, marketing organization, training, pay, etc.
- information system: indicators and information, databases and how to use them, etc.

The analysis phase should not be underestimated: it is crucial that the resources and skills available correspond to the goals an organization sets itself. Otherwise there is a strong risk of failure.

Overall diagnosis

In theory, market analysis culminates in an overall SWOT-type diagnosis (see Figure 6.7) aiming to provide a synthetic overview of strengths, weaknesses, opportunities and threats. An external and internal diagnosis are produced:

■ The external diagnosis looks at opportunities and threats: the organization must identify which elements within its environment (market system) will have an impact on all the actors concerned (new technology, new intermediaries, new competition, etc.) – different scenarios can be used to test the possible consequences of these developments.

■ The internal diagnosis concerns the organization's strengths and weaknesses with respect to its environment: systematic comparison techniques (benchmarking) help identify and outline the organization's situation.

STRATEGIC DECISIONS AND THEIR IMPLEMENTATION

Determining a marketing strategy, and the consequent choice of marketing instruments, is often associated with problems of optimization. Solutions require operational research methods but, in practice, such methods can create various problems:

■ There are too many strategic choices and instruments available for all of them to be reviewed systematically without entailing excessive financial outlay.

■ The information obtained about the consequences of these choices often lacks the quality required to apply these methods.

■ The methods proposed are based partly on fictitious conditions, and limited to quantitative aspects of marketing (e.g. size of advertising budget, or price) – neglecting qualitative factors of at least equal importance (e.g. the product's required characteristics, or the content of the advertising message).

The very limited field of application of the quantitative methods proposed in literature leads, in practical terms, to the process of defining strategy being broken down into a series of smaller problems to be resolved one at a time. Similar processes also occur in other fields of management and organization, notably as regards planning. Such 'heuristic' methods systematically simplify a complex problem to facilitate swifter progress towards an acceptable – if not always ideal – solution. Heuristic methods for determining a marketing strategy usually make a distinction between:

■ Decision-making problems of a conceptual nature – resolving these problems helps determine and articulate programmes for implementing marketing instruments in the form of a master-plan.

■ Operational decisions connected to the use of the marketing instruments, and serving to put the previously defined strategy into effect in 'everyday corporate routines'.

The listing below presents a synthetic overview of the principal stages and corresponding decisions – distinguishing between those decisions that establish an organization's strategic framework, and those that affect the strategy's implementation, especially as regards marketing instruments.

Decisions regarding the strategic framework:

- Market strategy and market segmentation: what offer for what target groups?
- Competitive strategy: what difference with other offers?
- Positioning of the offer: what image with target groups?
- Elaborating the market strategy: what relations with the partners of the exchange?

Decisions regarding implementation:

- defining the instruments of the marketing mix
- necessary changes and adaptations to the marketing infrastructure
- establishment of the marketing budget.

Description of decisions

The first decision concerns market choice, and priorities in terms of target groups or segments. The main issue for a public organization, given that its 'market' or scope of action is generally fixed by law, concerns which target groups to prioritize. Some areas of the public sector cannot (or may only with great difficulty) prioritize their actions according to target group (e.g. emergency services, providing ID cards, etc.). Most, however, retain the possibility of establishing differences − not as regards the essence of public action (legal tasks or basic missions), but as regards aspects often termed peripheral, yet which are essential in evaluating the service concerned. For example:

The law differentiates between at least two of the parties[1] with which it is in contact: the parties standing trial (citizens, residents, companies) and their representatives (usually lawyers or specialist bodies). The intensity of the law's relationship with these two groups − and the needs in terms of information and how to communicate, etc. − can, or even must, be adapted to circumstance. Some countries even hold 'legal information' days for citizens, involving detailed explanations about how the law operates, mock trials, etc.; they also develop information management tools for professionals (electronic data management, access to all jurisprudence, etc.). Without questioning the principle of equality in how cases are treated, priorities can be established in how to treat the law's relationship with its environment, and appropriate marketing activities introduced.

In many countries, car-owners are required to have their vehicle tested regularly (MOT in England, *contrôle technique* in France). In some countries this task is assigned to private operators (officially-approved garages), but usually a public organization is responsible. The latter can easily vary its offer according to whether they are targeting private car owners having their vehicle tested every three years or whenever; or professionals who come to have their own (or their clients') vehicles tested several times a week. The test itself, of course, needs to be the same whatever the vehicle or person presenting it; but all the auxiliary services (opening times, billing methods, etc.) can be adapted according to the target group.

115

In both cases the organization must decide whether the distinction between the target groups is relevant, and if it is better to establish priorities for handling them in order to develop marketing activities. Otherwise it will need to identify which specific offers it wishes to address to each of the defined target groups. Table 6.2 presents a similar situation for career guidance.

The second decision concerns competitive strategy. If there is no competition, this stage is clearly irrelevant. But, if the organization does have competitors, a competitive strategy must be defined. Public organizations involved in postal activities, telecommunications, transport, energy, etc. are increasingly subject to competitive pressure, and can no longer ignore the strategic approach of others. This competitive strategy derives from the generic strategies outlined in Figure 6.1. There are two main choices: differentiation strategy or price strategy. Generally speaking, the organization has to decide whether it wishes to profile its offer in the eyes of clients through an advantage linked to the service offered, or through lower prices. If the service-linked option is chosen, we speak of a differentiation strategy; if the advantage centres on lower prices, we speak of price strategy.

Advantages linked to service vary greatly in nature in the context of a differentiation strategy. One thinks first of differences in quality, or some particularly innovative aspect to the offer; but it must not be forgotten that many differences correspond to differences of image, created by using instruments of marketing communication. In any case, a differentiation strategy involves a wide range of marketing instruments, which all help profile the offer.

Price strategy, on the other hand, clearly stresses the instrument of price. The profile then becomes one-dimensional, and far more easily substitutable. All it takes is for another organization to propose a better-value offer to no longer have a veritable profile. So price strategy is only possible if the organization enjoys a long-term advantage in

Table 6.2 *Marketing strategy*

Segments	Young people completing their education	Other young people	Adults
Priority	1	2	3
Offers/services	Visiting classes at the beginning of the year	Visiting classes during the school year (timing upon availability)	
	Individual meetings with students (10–15 days delay)	Individual meetings upon request (1 month delay)	Individual meetings upon request (3 month delay)
	Free	Free	First session free, then fee-based

terms of cost structure, so that it can always offer better value than its competitors. The success of such a strategy also implies that buyers are price sensitive, and that price elasticity is important.

Another situation concerns new markets, where no organization is yet in a position to make an actual offer. In this case it is best to contribute to, and benefit from, the market's overall development, rather than concentrate on competitive strategies which may be inopportune in the circumstances.

The third stage is an important one for all organizations, irrespective of what is decided for the first two stages. It involves consolidating the organization's positioning and offer among selected target groups. Even if the offer is unique and competition totally absent, the image which the organization wishes to give of itself, and its offer to the outside world, must be established not just among beneficiaries, but among all other actors, too. If the organization's offer is specific and clearly distinct from others', it should seek to shore up its positioning through these relatively objective differences (what in marketing parlance is referred to as USP or Unique Selling Proposition). If, on the contrary, an organization's offer is interchangeable with others (no obvious difference), it should seek to use means of communication to construct what target groups will perceive as a difference. What universities have to offer may scarcely differ from one to the next, so they attempt to create a different image in other ways (special ambiance on campus, international character, close ties with alumni, etc.).

At the end of this stage, it is also recommended to establish the quantitative and qualitative aims targeted (number of services among target groups, image and attitude sought among beneficiaries, etc.). Box 6.4 shows an example of overlap between segmentation decisions and defining the service offer.

The final stage of the strategic framework concerns the strategy for exploiting the market. The corresponding decisions depend largely on the existing market system; the question is whether the organization should target beneficiaries directly, or via

BOX 6.4 MARKETING STRATEGY FOR A PROFESSIONAL CAREER-GUIDANCE SERVICE

Many countries have professional State career-guidance and -information services, with specialists offering help and advice about career choices and professional reorientation (skills appraisal, helping women return to work after spending several years at home bringing up children, etc.).

Given the reduced resources available, and above all the increased demand, some services – with the backing of political authorities – have segmented service beneficiaries and delimited the corresponding offer.

intermediaries. When it comes to consumer goods (drinks, washing powder, etc.), buyers are hardly ever in direct contact with producers, and buy via intermediaries. On the other hand, when it comes to services (banks, doctors, hairdressers, etc.), such intermediaries are rarer and the organization provides the service directly.

In the public sector, when it comes to services, it is usually the organization which takes charge of supplying the offer to beneficiaries, and handles relations with them directly; intermediaries tend to be rare. But there are other fields where the public organization has a merely regulatory role, and services are provided by a third party. This often applies, say, to places available at kindergarten (see Figure 6.8). Using rules, norms and financial incentives, public organizations can stimulate the creation of extra kindergarten places without having to provide or make available the corresponding offer themselves: a private third party proposes and manages the offer within the legal and financial framework. In the context of the overall system, private actors have a vital role as intermediaries; public organizations must manage their relationship with both service beneficiaries (families with young children) and the private organizations offering places in their kindergartens.

As well as dealing with intermediaries, an organization must also consider the measures it wishes to take as regards other market actors (influencers, suppliers, etc.). In the case presented above, keeping the media regularly informed may lead to articles in the press, as part of the goal of improving the flow of information to the parties concerned.

The decisions that ensue derive from strategic decisions and establish a framework for putting the strategy into effect. This means determining which marketing instruments to use, and to what extent; defining the necessary adjustments to the marketing infrastructure; and drawing up the necessary budget. Only then can the decisions' overall coherence be assessed, and modified if necessary (the budget could, for instance, prompt a review of target group priorities, or which instruments to use).

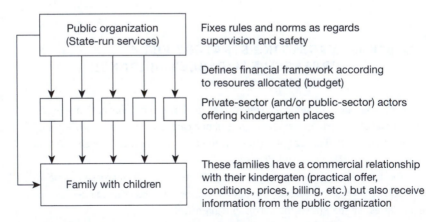

Figure 6.8 *Example of intermediation in market exploitation*

One should first decide which marketing instruments to use in order to put the defined strategy into effect, and to what extent they should be used. It is vital to ensure homogeneity when choosing these instruments, and also to ensure that their use is effective. For instance, there is a very strong risk of engaging in extensive promotional activity for a service (e.g. kindergartens) for which the organization (or its partners) is unable to satisfy the demand. Sometimes the budget available does not allow a minimum level of effectiveness to be obtained, leading to a waste of resources.

Then, the organization must verify its ability to attain the goals and implement the measures which derive from the decisions taken. This is not just a question of financial wherewithal: it is equally vital that the skills and attitude of personnel are in keeping with the organization's ambitions. Likewise, some adjustments to the organization's information and operational systems may well be necessary.

Finally, the decisions and measures taken will need to be put into effect on a financial level by drawing up a budget. It is this last phase which may or may not oblige the marketing's strategic planning to be reviewed. It is better to delay taking budgetary constraints into account during the planning process, so as not to limit creativity or put a brake on innovative ideas.

Problems in implementing strategy

Given the number of measures liable to play a role in the success of a marketing strategy, and the wide range of market elements (competition, environmental factors, product users, intermediaries, etc.), it is not surprising that putting instruments into effect is a complex task, and mastering it can cause organizations problems.

One problem comes from the fact that 'markets' (or target groups) are not compartmentalized. It is easy to forget that measures taken as regards one target group may impact on other groups, so it is all the more important to suitably define the market or commercial environment of the service offered.

The need for marketing instruments to be used in the long term also needs to be taken into account. Borden's call for a balanced dose of externally geared marketing instruments is no longer under dispute. Various behavioural studies have confirmed that product users and other marketing targets do not record or evaluate each message separately, but that all messages are considered as a whole. So a product's quality is not judged individually and 'objectively', but in relation to the price and the advertising message.

Nor can marketing instruments be coordinated harmoniously on an ad hoc basis. Changes over time, especially if too sudden or frequent, can hinder this constructive process. In general one needs to start from the premise that all marketing activity produces impulses which, in the eyes of individual targets, may mutually boost one another or cancel each other out. Hence the importance of keeping the same marketing approach in the eyes of product users and other market participants, so that images and preferences may be freely formed over time.

A common error observed in this implementation is the use of insufficient means. Empirical experience, and many studies, have highlighted a link between the degree of commitment to a marketing instrument (e.g. as measured in monetary units) and its impact. Each marketing instrument has a sort of inferior effectiveness threshold that must be exceeded to justify use of the instrument concerned. But, if the means are inadequate or scattered (sprinkler principle), they are highly unlikely to attain this minimum effectiveness threshold. For budgetary reasons, many communication activities in the public sector are not implemented with sufficient intensity to be properly perceived or have the required effectiveness.

LIMITATIONS

Developing marketing strategies poses a host of problems to public organizations and services, and the principal limitations involved need to be considered.

First, the process outlined above, and the principles of application, are difficult to implement given the constraints imposed on public organizations (laws, rules, etc.); the reduced leeway for decision making (absence of autonomy, an organizational culture that does not encourage risk taking or a corporate ethos); and an overall context enabling services to be introduced despite the absence of a coherent strategy (the legal framework and absence of competition mean public organizations can use resources to less than full effect without risking sanction).

Another important limitation lies in the difficulty of ensuring continuity in the application of strategic decisions. Whereas a private company may set aside reserves, and anticipate long-term investment, to attain its marketing goals (e.g. investments in the brand or in creating a distribution network), a public organization depends on an annual budget voted by politicians. It is not rare for PR campaigns, or projects linked to developing or promoting a service, to be halted or seriously scaled down due to a drop in annual funding. It then becomes difficult to ensure a correlation between the objectives targeted and the measures taken.

Finally, one should never forget the scale of values that guides public organizations in their decision making and activity – with principles of equality and fairness often prevailing over criteria of efficiency and effectiveness. Although the principle of opportunity is increasingly taken into account, it is not always easy to apply marketing rules and processes; intelligent adjustment, on a case-by-case basis, is often needed to 'remain within the confines of legality' and ensure public action remains legitimate.

EXERCISE 6.1

Using the SWOT approach, offer a general diagnosis on your organization.

DISCUSSION QUESTIONS

1   Is it the role of civil servants and public-sector employees to define an organization's strategy? Shouldn't that be left to politicians?
2   How fundamental is the difference between a public-sector and a private-sector organizational strategy?

NOTE

1   In fact, there are more – the media, political institutions etc. should also be mentioned.

REFERENCES

Grünig, R. and Kühn, R. (2008) *Process-based Strategic Planning*, Berlin, Springer.

Kühn, R. (1993) Das Image Ausgewählter Bereiche der Schweizer Wirtschaft im Internationalen Vergleich, *Die Volkswirtschaft,* 3, 14–22.

Mintzberg, H. (1992) *Five Ps for Strategy in the Strategy Process*, Englewood Cliffs, Prentice Hall International Editions.

Perrey, J. (1998) *Nutzenorientierte Marktsegmentierung*, Wiesbaden, Gabler.

Porter, M. E. (1985) *Competitive Advantage: Creating and Sustaining Superior Performance*, New York, Free Press.

Reeves, R. (1960) *Reality in Advertising*, New York, Knopf.

Ries, A. and Trout, J. (1976) *Positioning: The Battle for Your Mind*, New York, McGraw-Hill.

Schedler, K. and Proeller, I. (2003) *New Public Management*, Bern, Stuttgart, P. Haupt.

Smith, W. R. (1956) Product Differentiation and Market Segmentation as Alternative Marketing Strategies, *Journal of Marketing*, 21, 3–8.

Spiegel, B. (1961) *Die Struktur der Meinungsverteilung im Sozialen Feld*, Bern, Verlag Hans Huber.

Chapter 7

Marketing instruments

LEARNING OBJECTIVES

By the end of this chapter you should be able to:

- Understand the specificities of marketing instruments in the public sector structure public services, notably by taking into account their intangible nature.
- Differentiate the various approaches to pricing in the public sector.
- Understand the implications of various distribution models in the public sector.

KEY POINTS OF THIS CHAPTER

- The instruments of marketing, or marketing mix, are the means of action that an organization has to attain its marketing objectives.
- Many public services are intangible: this situation has numerous consequences, among them the impossibility of making stocks, the central role of human interaction, and the indivisibility of product and production.
- There are three types of approach to pricing in the public sector – free service, taxes and licence fee. The choice of which to use is based on the concepts of non-rivalry and non-exclusion. Each of these approaches puts the burden of the total payment of the service on different actors – be they the user, the government or a third party.
- The distribution model of public services is based on the legal and structural make-up of a country's specific institutional arrangement, and can consist of both direct delivery (with no intermediary between government and user) or an indirect one (where a third party plays a role in the delivery).

KEY TERMS

Four Ps – main instruments of the marketing mix: product, price, promotion and place.

Services of general interest – concept used by the European Union to identify core functions of the State's service provision.

Distribution channels – ways by which a service is made available to the user.

INTRODUCTION

Marketing instruments, also known as the marketing mix, represent an organization's means of action to attain the marketing goals it has set itself. This involves defining the terms of the exchange (what services and at what cost); how and where the exchange can take place (distribution or accessibility of the service, persons in charge of making the service available); and the means used to promote what the service has to offer (communication and 'branding').

As outlined in Chapter 4, Borden (1965) was the first to use the marketing mix concept, while McCarthy (1960) provided a basic structure for all the instruments available by introducing the four Ps (product, price, place, promotion). Subsequently, new proposals were made for structuring the instruments, including a further three Ps (people, process, physical facilities), as coined by Bitner and Booms (1981), linked mainly to the development of services marketing and since adopted by many other authors. Figure 7.1 presents the structure of marketing instruments.

While the first four Ps still remain a marketing reference, especially for the marketing of consumer goods, the last three Ps have become more important, given that a service is intangible by definition, and cannot be produced independently of the persons who are producing it (there is no school without a teacher to transmit knowledge, no justice without judges to make decisions, etc.).

This chapter seeks to present basic elements regarding marketing instruments used in the public sector, and will concentrate on the definition and structuring of public services, their pricing and the possibilities of using them. As the communication of organizations and public services is the subject of several other chapters in this book, it will not be dealt with in this chapter.

PRODUCT/PUBLIC SERVICES

The definition and analysis of public services is a political, managerial and marketing issue. At a political level, in a context of mounting public debt, analysing services helps to establish priorities; differentiate between basic and complementary services (e.g. with price differentiation); and link the allocation of resources to tangible results.

	Content of the offer	**Product:**	Goods and services, size of the offer (depth and breadth), level of quality
		Price:	Base price, reductions, modes of payment
Original structure	Diffusion of information on the offer	**Promotion:**	Publicity, promotional activities, personal relations
	Accessibility	**Place:**	Channels of distribution (points of access), opening hours
Complementary structure	Aspects of quality in the production of the service	**People:**	Abilities, knowledge and capabilities of staff in delivering the service
		Process:	Processes leading to the delivery of service
		Physical facilities	Physical aspects (tangibles) linked to service delivery (building, waiting room, parking)

■ **Figure 7.1** *Basic structures of marketing instruments*
Source: adapted from McCarthy (1960) and Bitner and Booms (1981).

At managerial level, analysing services can affect the organization's plans, or oblige it to determine more precisely which form the service should take. Finally, at marketing level, and in line with principles of New Public Management, a service must be linked to expectations, notably in terms of quality (as expected/perceived by beneficiaries).

Even though we often talk about public services, a distinction should be made between services provided by public bodies for external parties, and public policy services (planning for, putting into effect and monitoring public policies) destined for political institutions. Without neglecting the latter type of service (far more complex and difficult to systematize), this section will concentrate mainly on services destined for beneficiaries external to the administration.

DEFINITIONS OF A PUBLIC SERVICE

Politico-legal sense

Public services are provided by an administrative entity or delegated to a private body. They have a legal basis specifying the nature of the service and the basic ways in which it is provided.

The concept of public services derives from an older concept: service to the public or service of general interest, with both judicial and political scope. The notion of public service comes from French law, and serves to distinguish administrative law from private law. There are two distinct types of public service task: tasks linked to State sovereignty (justice, police, diplomacy, army, currency); and tasks concerning the administrative sector, i.e. looking to satisfy a general or social need which cannot be satisfied by the private sector (transport, teaching, social services, etc.). Given the general interest of these activities, they are required to come under a public authority and the corresponding jurisdiction (administrative law).

The term public service is hardly used by the EU[1] which, however, makes a distinction between services of general interest and services of general economic interest (Commission of the European Communities, 2003). Services of general interest are government services for citizens that are subject to the specific requirements of public service. Services of general economic interest form a sub-category of services of general interest, and refer to services of an economic nature which EU member States submit to specific public service requirements via the criterion of public interest. Whereas services of general interest remain under the sway of member states, services of general economic interest (energy, transport, postal services, telecommunications) come under the remit of the EU, which ensures that the principle of free competition is applied with respect to public service missions. These services are the subject of liberalizing policy, although they remain relatively strongly regulated (principle of separation of the functions of owner and regulator).

Whether the notion of 'public service' or the more neutral one of 'service of general interest' is used it is important to specify that what is concerned is an authority's decision to define and propose services in a non-exclusive way to beneficiaries who fulfil predefined conditions. Such services can, however, be provided either by a public body or delegated to a private concern (in some regions of Denmark, for instance, fire-fighting is ceded to private security firms).

A more managerial definition of public services

It is hard to use the notions of public service or service of general interest with regard to an organization, for two reasons: first, these notions have a strong political connotation, and are therefore often subject to intense debate; and, second, they remain vague, and do not suffice for organizing and establishing services for the population. For instance, legally stipulating that the State is responsible for maintaining the roads under its authority provides scant indication of the quality and frequency of upkeep, the means to be used or the possibility of delegating the task to a third party. The actual definition of the service to be provided and its organization requires a more managerial approach, hence the use of the private-sector term 'service provider'.

Although public-sector activities mainly involve services, it should first be specified that these are far from homogenous (there is nothing comparable about teaching and clearing snow off the road); and the tangible part of the service varies considerably

125

from one service to the next (the proportion is high for, say, issuing a passport, when a tangible document is delivered, or for a municipal library lending books and magazines; but very limited when it comes to police checks or medical treatment). Figure 7.2 gives some examples of tangible and intangible areas of public services.

There are several reasons to study the intangible aspect of services. First the number, and above all variety, of services provided by the public sector have considerably increased over the last 50 years. Then, the intangible aspect of these services has also grown, notably because the exchange's relational aspects (welcome, friendliness, empathy, etc.) have assumed greater importance, often serving as elements of reference when evaluating service quality. Finally – due to the development of both service activities in society and the principles of New Public Management – relations between a public administration and beneficiaries have become far more individualized, obliging the administration to clarify the services it can provide, and the level of differentiation acceptable within these services.

Services can be defined as follows at a marketing level (see Kotler, 2009; Kühn *et al.*, 2006):

■ *Intangible:* services which cannot be seen, touched or felt, let alone heard, before being bought. The offer is abstract, and it is only after 'buying' it that a person

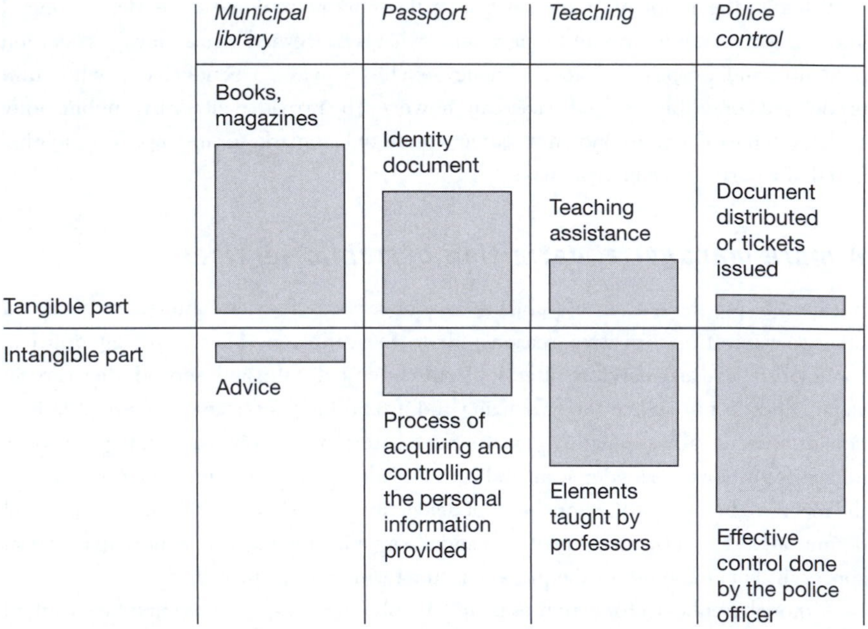

Figure 7.2 *Tangible versus intangible proportion of public services*

can really evaluate it (it is only after attending a class that one can judge the quality of the teaching). As a result, the offerer's credibility and confidence in their ability to deliver the service are particularly important.

- *Indivisible:* whereas material goods are produced before being sold, a service is produced at the same time as it is consumed. As the presence of both the persons buying and supplying the service is necessary, their proximity to one another is highly relevant (a beneficiary based far away from the service provider needs facilitated access to a certain number of services, such as long-distance teaching). Despite the development of electronic communication, notably the internet, the problem of service accessibility at public sector level remains crucial, given the administration's territorial scope.

- *Unable to store services:* an empty bus costs as much to run as one full of passengers. If demand for a service is stable and known in advance, the organization's offer (number of buses and drivers) can be adapted to the demand. The problem for many services is that the offer fluctuates and the administration – given the resources at its disposal and the constraints on their use – has great difficulties in flexibly adapting offer to demand.

- *Key role of personnel:* the quality of a service can vary considerably according to the persons in charge (the same lesson given by two different teachers can be exciting or tedious).

Three ways of improving service quality are explored: the search for qualified personnel; the codifying processes for conceiving the service and harmonizing the approach of those involved, in order to minimize variations in standards; and involving beneficiaries in producing the service as much as possible (and taking note of their criticism and comments) to help the organization reduce the difference between the level of service expected and the level perceived.

The greater the intangible part of a public service, the more public bodies need to take account of the above mentioned characteristics in defining and implementing their services.

Structuring public services

Although New Public Management has received some severe criticism, the structuring and analysing of public services is rarely questioned, and retained even if other aspects are rejected. Public services are usually structured according to their components or the necessary tasks involved.

Structuring according to components

A service can be divided into three parts (Kotler, 2009): central, secondary and peripheral elements – as shown in Figure 7.3, taking the issue of a passport as an example. The central elements of a service concern the principal benefit it provides.

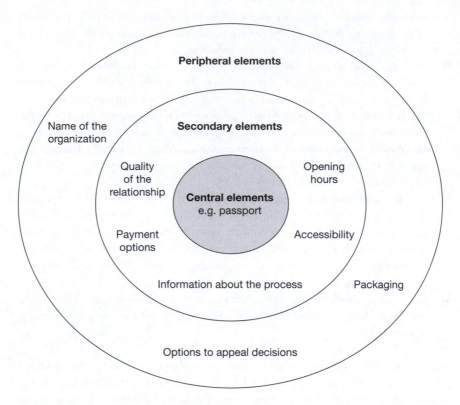

Figure 7.3 *Components of a public service (for issuing a passport)*

In Figure 7.3 the essence of the service is a passport. In the public sector, the essence of a service often concerns elements stipulated by law.

Secondary elements are not usually defined by law, but directly linked to producing the service, and naturally vary according to the service itself. In the case of issuing an identity document, the information prior to the process (documents and forms to provide), access to the service (physical accessibility, opening times, etc.) and methods of payment available (bank transfer, cash, cheque, debit or credit card) are elements which can facilitate the service or make it costlier and more complicated. Although a public service's quality is often assessed according to its peripheral elements (an identity document like a passport is strictly defined; no differentiation in the essence of the service is possible – a passport being the same for every citizen), it is the secondary elements which determine if the service is provided diligently, and whether citizens are satisfied with it or not.

Finally come elements peripheral to a service. In theory these have only limited importance to how the service is appreciated, while potentially offering a little plus. In Figure 7.3 a small wallet provided with the passport, and special facilities for contacting the organization in case of problems, count as peripheral elements.

Structuring in groups of services, services and activities

The idea of structuring government activities into services, like firms providing and commercializing services, has been little challenged. While it may seem obvious that tasks carried out by a public administration exceed the mere framework of producing and delivering services, such a concept of an administration's activities offers several advantages. First, the activities are grouped together and defined in the same way, according to service beneficiaries. Then the services can be analysed according to their cost and the income they generate. Finally, the services constitute a reasonably objective unit of analysis to help political authorities make choices linking political priorities to available resources and services delivered (or not). Increasing resources for a public task, say, not only indicates that a number of posts will be created, but also indicates an increase in the number of services provided or an improvement in their quality (e.g. reduced waiting time to obtain a document).

A service counts as a 'tangible output' of an administrative unit. To recap: an administrative unit is an entity responsible for carrying out a task defined by law or in official documents. Depending on how public communities are organized, these entities may vary greatly in size and autonomy; the main thing is that they can be attributed responsibility for carrying out a task. If, as we saw at the start of this chapter, administration services are invariably of an intangible nature, one should be able to make a service correspond to quantities (number of controls, classes, pupils, decisions taken, etc.); quality level (length, success rate etc.); goals; indicators; and costs. Several services provided by the same administrative body constitute a group of services; a service can be broken down into sub-services or partial services, depending on its level of complexity.

A service has the following characteristics:

- Its beneficiaries must be external to the administrative unit: they may be external to the administration (an individual, company, other body, etc.) or internal (other administrative entities, as with an IT service that supplies services to the other units within the administration). When appropriate, these internal services can be defined (support services). The same applies for important projects, or mandates that need to respect a deadline.
- It derives from laws and regulations. Sometimes, if these legal bases are too vague, the administrative entity has to issue precise guidelines about the services required as regards the legally defined goal.
- It may either be free, subject to tax (partially covering costs) or available only if all the costs are paid for.
- It consists of tasks which the administrative unit either supplies or purchases from other units or external bodies – tasks for which it is possible to specify a time of work or a cost (invoice). The process combining all these tasks enables the service to be provided.

The process for structuring services in an administrative unit is outlined in Box 7.1; an example of how the process is applied is shown in Box 7.2.

■ BOX 7.1 PROCESS OF STRUCTURING SERVICES IN AN ADMINISTRATIVE UNIT

1   Define the public issue.
2   Define the political issue.
3   Identify the legal bases.
4   Structure 'outputs' into groups of services and services.
5   Determine the tasks and process needed for a service to be delivered.
6   Identify service beneficiaries.
7   Set indicators (goals linked to a service).
8   Establish links needed for data capture.

■ BOX 7.2 STRUCTURING SERVICES LINKED TO THE PROTECTION OF CULTURAL GOODS

Buildings of historical significance, whether ancient (ruins, castles, churches, old farmhouses, etc.) or modern (e.g. houses or buildings designed by famous architects) are protected in many countries by laws obliging owners to respect rules of upkeep and renovation. Owners may receive help and financial support (subsidies).

Preliminary phase:

To facilitate structuring and establish a link with the time spent in data capture and analytical accountancy, the functional classification of public tasks is often used.[1]

0.   *General administration*
1.   *Public safety*
2.   *Teaching*
3.   *Culture, sport and leisure*

    3.1 Cultural heritage

        3.1.2   Preservation of historic monuments and protection of nature

Phase 1: Defining public issues
Cultural goods are fundamental elements of human culture and civilization. Any reduction of this centuries-old cultural heritage counts as a loss.

continued . . .

■ BOX 7.2 STRUCTURING SERVICES LINKED TO THE PROTECTION OF CULTURAL GOODS ... *continued*

Phase 2: Defining political issues

■ *Lawmakers wish to protect all cultural goods – whether moveable or immoveable, old or new – which are important to the community as evidence of spiritual activity, artistic creativity or social life.*

Phase 3: Identifying the legal bases

■ *Federal law on the protection of nature and landscapes*
■ *Federal law on the protection of cultural goods in case of armed conflicts, etc.*

Phase 4: Structuring 'outputs' into groups of services and services
Group of services for the 'protection of cultural goods':

■ *inventories*
■ *placing under protection*
■ *protection in event of conflicts or crises.*

Group of services for the 'preservation of cultural goods':

■ *advance permit applications*
■ *allocating subsidies*

Group of services for 'publications and awareness':

■ *publications*
■ *actions to promote awareness.*

Group of services for 'internal services':

■ *unit representation in commissions*
■ *unit direction and management.*

Phase 5: Determining the tasks and process needed to provide a service (e.g. for 'inventories' service)
Building inventories:

■ *on-site visits*
■ *photographs*
■ *archive research*
■ *data capture.*

Phase 6: Identifying service beneficiaries

■ *Administrative services*
■ *Tourist promotion services*
■ *Other public communities (e.g. communes)*

continued . . .

■ **BOX 7.2 STRUCTURING SERVICES LINKED TO THE PROTECTION OF CULTURAL GOODS** ... *continued*

Phase 7: Setting indicators
Having an exhaustive, up-to-date inventory of the cultural goods to be protected, or likely to need protection in future

Phase 8: Establishing the necessary links for data capture

Level	Number	Subject
Group of services	1000	Protection of cultural goods
Service	1100	Inventories
Tasks	1100–01	On-site visits
1100–02	Photographs	
1100–03	Archive research	
1100–04	Recording data	

Note:
1   The functional classification groups all public tasks into ten categories: 0 General administration; 1 Public safety; 2 Teaching and training; 3 Culture, sport and leisure; 4 Health; 5 Social contingency planning; 6 Traffic; 7 Environmental protection and territorial development; 8 Public economy; 9 Finance and tax.

Source: Adapted from Davet (2006).

The first phase involves defining the public issue. In a democratic system, the State is called on to act only if the reason for its intervention has already been collectively defined as a public issue. For instance, environmental protection was not considered a public issue 30–40 years ago, and State intervention in the field remained negligible (e.g. the water supply and water table were protected to guarantee people's health, not with a balanced eco-system in mind). It can take decades for a public issue to be recognized, and the approach can vary considerably from one State to the next. Then, for services to be clearly identified and structured, attention must be drawn to the public issue for which political institutions consider it necessary to provide services.

Once the public issue has been identified, political authorities need to decide to act (lawmakers' intentions) as regards public policies, goals and, above all, the types and methods of State intervention. (Should the State regulate private activity, mandate bodies to provide services, or provide the services itself?) It is especially important to obtain this information if political discussions linked to State intervention took place some time ago, and administrative units have greatly developed in the interim.

Identifying and obtaining the legal bases is the third stage. One should of course pay attention not just to the law but also to all the texts regulating and guiding the action of the administrative units – many tasks assigned to these units are stipulated by decrees, regulations, directives, etc., rather than the law itself.

The fourth and most important stage as regards the targeted objective involves structuring the activities of the administrative unit into groups of services and services. This means using criteria that appear in the definition of a service and in the service's characteristics. The next phase is to assign all the tasks performed by the unit to the various services defined.

The last stages are more technical. First, one needs to identify the service beneficiaries (internal or external to the administration), then set indicators for the service (what are its specific goals?). Finally, each task or unit activity needs to be given a functional classification number, so that the number of hours spent on an activity, and the costs involved (paying a mandated third party), can be assessed.

Quality of public services

Studies of the quality of public services are largely based on the principles of New Public Management – especially on the concept of the State as service provider; from a higher demand for efficiency; and on a 'client' orientation in supplying services. However, contrary to private bodies – for which analysing service quality has long been a major issue (Parasuraman et al., 1985; Zeithaml et al., 1990; plus other marketing sources) – public bodies cannot limit themselves to commercial criteria (reliability, relational qualities, etc.) and must also consider criteria linked to general interest and social justice (theories of fairness). In the context of public services, individual satisfaction (e.g. a building permit believed to have been fraudulently obtained) can be in contradiction with the general interest (nature preservation). So it is crucial that the process enabling the service to be carried out be perceived as fair (Rawls, 1971; Tyler, 1988, 2005). In democratic systems, the persons concerned are usually all the more tolerant about the services provided and their consequences (service quality) if they think the way they have been carried out is fair (equal treatment, fair-minded decision making, etc.).

By returning to the various types of relationship that can develop between the administration and service beneficiaries (see Chapter 3), the criteria for assessing the quality of the service can be identified (see Figure 7.4). The first set of criteria is linked principally to the traditional relationship between administration and citizens as to the decision-making process. These criteria include respect for rules, transparent procedures and equality of treatment. The more constrained people's relationship with a public body, the more these criteria are fundamental in assessing the service provided.

The second set of criteria concern the relationship between the administration and people as consumers. It is not so much the procedure itself which influences how the service is appreciated (ability to explain decisions, their transparency, etc.) as the decisions taken, and how they are communicated. The traditional assessment of a service within a commercial relationship involves the client's degree of satisfaction and the corresponding criteria (reliability, empathy, accessibility, etc.).

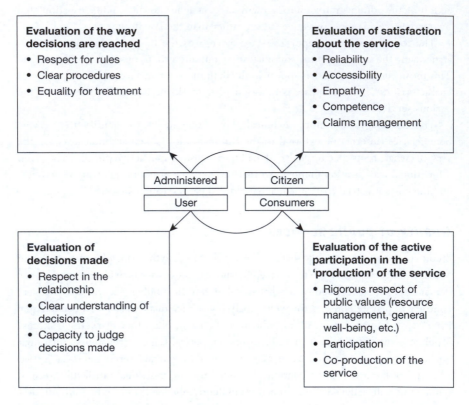

Figure 7.4 *Public service quality criteria*

The final set of criteria must allow for people taking an active part in providing the service. Within this 'citizen relationship,' respect for higher values (such as rigorous resource management), and direct involvement in producing the service, matter as much as (if not more than) the service itself.

It is important to specify that a public service is not just evaluated according to one set of criteria, but to all of them. Depending on the service, and to what extent it is commercial, certain criteria may have more or less importance. A practical example of the criteria adopted for defining the quality of a public service is given in Box 7.3.

PRICING OF PUBLIC SERVICES

In the private sector the price is the compensation paid by the client, with companies aiming to maximize profit. But prices in the public sector play a totally different role, in that many services are free for beneficiaries; prices charged for some services do not cover their cost; and there are even services which the State pays for beneficiaries to use (e.g. when the State woos companies by offering them land free of charge).

■ BOX 7.3 DECLARATION ON SERVICE QUALITY FROM THE CANADIAN GOVERNMENT

A Declaration of Quality Service

The Government of Canada and its employees are committed to delivering quality services within the resources Canada can afford. When you seek services, you will know what level of service to expect through the specific service standards each department and agency is publishing. We aim to ensure your satisfaction, abiding by the following principles:

Accessible, Dependable and Timely

We want to be easy to reach and to deal with. Our priority is dependable, prompt and accurate service delivered with your convenience in mind. Wherever practical, we aim to bring together all the services you need. We will serve you in the official language of your choice at the designated locations.

Clear and Open

We want you to understand what services are available and how much they cost you as a taxpayer. We will clearly explain the rules, regulations and decisions that apply to you. We will identify who is serving you and who is in charge.

Fair and Respectful

We will treat you fairly and courteously, recognizing your distinct needs, even when regulatory services impose conditions or sanctions on you. We will respect your legal rights, privacy and safety.

Good Value for your Tax Dollar

We will tell you how well we are doing in relation to published service standards. Affordability is one of our primary concerns and we are committed to delivering and demonstrating good value for money – quality services provided as efficiently and economically as possible, based on integrity and sound judgement.

Responsive and Committed to Improvement

We will regularly seek your views on what works well and what needs to be improved. If you wish to complain, it will be effective and easy to do. Where we have made a mistake, we will work to set things right. We welcome your suggestions and complaints – they represent our opportunity to improve.

Source: Treasury Board of Canada (1994).

Three aspects are considered in this section: the notions of free services, taxes and price; pricing and the strategies applicable; and monetary and non-monetary incentives.

Free services, taxes, licence fees and price

Given that the public sector inevitably supplies collective goods (public service), the notion of price differs considerably from that in the private sector. There are four specific concepts:

■ *Free services:* numerous public services (schooling, police, roads, etc.) are free, and financed by taxation.

■ *Tax:* a levy charged to use a public service, with two main features: the sum charged has no connection to the actual cost of the service; nor is it proportional to actual use of the service. The tax must be paid even if the service is not used. In Switzerland, for instance, the State taxes cars to use the highway network (obligatory voucher costing CHF40, to be displayed on the car windshield). This fee has no link with the actual cost of constructing and maintaining the network, and is due regardless of how often the car is used.

■ *Licence fee:* the amount is linked directly to how much the service is used, proportionate to the service provided. To take another Swiss example, heavy vehicles (trucks carrying goods) are fitted with a meter, and the vehicle owner must pay two to three cents per kilometre. Like the tax, the licence fee does not reflect the actual cost of the service.

■ *Price:* we speak of the price of a public service when the sum demanded takes the actual use of the service into account, and when it has to cover at least most of the costs engendered (link between price and costs).

Two criteria linked to the differentiation between a public and a private entity explain why public services are not charged to beneficiaries, and why the latter are only liable for some of the costs: non-competition and non-exclusion (Le Gall-Ely, 2003; Urbain and Le Gall-Ely, 2009).

Non-competition means that service beneficiaries are not in competition for the use of goods or services. Unless there are traffic jams, car drivers can use the road network without hindering other drivers. Similarly, any individual can breathe in air without preventing other people doing the same. Non-exclusion means individuals cannot be prevented from having access to a service or product. All members of the community benefit from services like security, control of epidemics, etc.; and it is virtually impossible to stop anyone swimming in a lake or walking up a mountain.

Table 7.1 provides an overview of the various combinations between criteria of competition and exclusion. Traditional market mechanisms (supply and demand) are inappropriate when public goods display characteristics of non-competition and non-exclusion. The service cannot be paying (free), and is financed by taxes (paid by

Table 7.1 *Public goods and types of price*

Exclusion	Competition	
	No	Yes
No	**Public goods** Free	**Common goods** (More unusual) rivalry for a limited renewable resource like water in certain countries
Yes	**Club goods** (No rivalry between users but a contribution to be paid) Some public services (water, garbage collection)	**Private goods** Possible intervention of the State that plays a tutelary role (school medicine)

beneficiaries and non-beneficiaries alike). Yet many services are of a non-competitive nature, while being able either to identify the beneficiaries, or exclude those which do not respect established rules (water treatment, using a road network, visiting a museum, etc.). It is then possible to ask beneficiaries to contribute towards the cost of the service (tax or fee).

Cases where it is not possible to exclude beneficiaries – while observing consumer competition – are less frequent. Among those most often cited are deep-sea fishing and the use of water in some countries. Price here is not usually an instrument for regulating consumption; other instruments, like the introduction of quotas, are needed. This evokes private goods (competition and exclusion possible) with the State playing a tutelary role in seeking to encourage consumption (the goods would be unaffordable for many people without the State's intervention). Education in general, along with more specialized services like medical training or providing bikes for cheap public hire in cities like Paris, Madrid or Montreal, are examples of the State exercising a tutelary function as regards what are essentially private goods (see Box 7.4 for the *Vélib'* system run by the City of Paris).

Pricing strategies for public services

If the price for a public service can be linked to its cost (taxes and licence fees being 'political' prices), it is important to study the function sought by the price (Greffe, 1999) and the possible strategies for fixing it (Urbain and Le Gall-Ely, 2009).

Prices can indicate the value of the product or service. As people are ready to pay to acquire a good, its price should correspond to the degree of satisfaction it gives them. Fixing the price is, however, tricky if users have no pricing reference, and no market mechanisms (competing proposals) exist.

■ BOX 7.4 BICYCLE HIRE IN PARIS

Vélib' (http://www.velib.paris.fr) is a bike-hire system in Paris, with nearly 20,000 bicycles available for hire at over 1,200 stations across the city. Users need to take out a subscription then pay according to use (first half-hour free). The service is provided by the City of Paris in collaboration with the advertising company Decaux.

Decaux's ten-year contract with the City of Paris (until 2017) obliges them to install and maintain the bicycles and stations, and pay the City of Paris an annual fee of €3.4 million. In return, Decaux have exclusive access to nearly 1,600 station billboards.

Price can also be a tool for rationing demand. If resources or capacities are limited, and to ensure excessive demand does not clog up the organization and prevent it from carrying out its mission, a price may be introduced for the service, providing principles of fairness are respected. One may also talk of 'de-marketing', or rationing demand. This was the case in a previous example (see Box 6.4), when a body offering students and adults career advice began to charge adults, so as to reduce demand and be able to continue its mission with students.

The price's main *raison d'être* may also be to gather the main resources needed for the organization to function – if, say, the organization faces a fall in subsidies – and has to seek new resources by commercializing services at the going rate. Since the early 1990s, various public meteorology services – faced with growing needs (new technologies, models of calculation, etc.) – have introduced a whole range of paying services in response to their public funding being scaled back.

Lastly, the price can be used to make public agents manage more responsibly. If they realize that some of the organization's revenue depends directly on the sale of services, it is in their interest to ensure the quality of those services is reflected in their price.

Fixing prices in the public sector can reflect various strategies. First, the price can be based on the marginal costs: users pay all the variable costs without having to contribute towards the fixed costs. Then, a price strategy may have no direct link to the actual cost – either because this is simpler, or to spread the cost among service users (the price of sending a letter, for instance, is fixed irrespective of distance). The final strategy, widespread in the private sector and increasingly so in the public sector, involves differentiating price according to a variety of factors:

- *Objective aspects of the service offered:* in the public transport or culture sectors, price differences based on the class or category chosen have long been common.
- *Time of day:* prices are based on when the service is used so as to modify people's behaviour if possible, and discourage use of the service at peak times; such a policy is practised by museums, for certain types of public transport, etc.

■ **138**

■ *Method of distribution:* to encourage people to book on the internet rather than at the ticket office, for instance, booking online can be free or cheaper.

■ *The person(s) concerned:* this is naturally a tricky subject in the public sector, but often used according to (a) zone of residence, with separate prices for residents (who already pay towards the service via taxes) and non-residents who are charged more (and tend to be less bothered about the price than residents); (b) demographic criteria, such as age (preferential prices for young people and senior citizens); and (c) social criteria, favouring people from under-privileged group (unemployed, on social benefit) or families (third child free, etc.).

■ *Specific differentiation (season tickets):* setting a fixed price for unlimited use fosters user loyalty and provides greater flexibility; for the organization, this type of differentiation offers the advantage of helping cash-flow and reducing sales structures.

Any price differentiation should, in theory, take account of equal treatment and a certain fairness in the criteria adopted. And some differentiations can lead to a loss of income – which the organization must compensate through a corresponding subsidy.

Monetary and non-monetary incentives

Prices in the public sector can be used to incite people to act in a desired way, or sanction them for unacceptable or undesirable behaviour. Prices here (whether monetary or non-monetary) are not linked to cost; and the administration, rather than providing a service as such, decides how people should behave. This is the main issue about incentives, which lend themselves to two types of study: monetary or non-monetary incentives; and positive or negative incentives.

Positive monetary incentives seek to reward people for behaving in a certain way. For instance, in some countries, to ensure children attend school and are not employed in economic activity, the government gives parents financial help if their children go to school. In the USA, anyone who agrees to join the army receives a bonus of up to several thousand dollars. Negative monetary incentives, in contrast, include fining individuals or bodies who break the law, and seek to sanction those responsible and dissuade them from behaving in the same way in future.

Positive and negative incentives may also be non-monetary, encouraging certain types of behaviour (e.g. granting official recognition to a firm that displays a responsible ecological approach) or discouraging others (e.g. banning single-passenger vehicles from dual carriageways).

ACCESS TO PUBLIC SERVICES (DISTRIBUTION)

Distribution is the marketing instrument whereby goods or services are delivered from producer to consumer. While the distribution system for physical goods like cars is familiar and well-structured (producer/importer/distributor/garage owner/consumer), the system used for services, specifically public services, is very different – for two reasons. On the one hand (and this concerns nearly all services), organizations distribute their services themselves, mainly because it is not possible to separate production from service consumption (banking services are provided mostly when clients visit their branch or log on to the bank's website). On the other hand, public services are generally distributed via territorial structures – which tend to have evolved historically, according to the State's administrative organization, rather than according to the nature of the service and the needs of beneficiaries.

Study of service distribution used to be neglected, but has now developed considerably given that access to services (proximity, opening times, waiting time, etc.) has become important in assessing their quality. An organization's best possible services are of limited impact if people need to take a day off work to be able to use them (distance, inadequate structures to absorb demand, etc.).

Distribution circuits and channels

A distribution circuit involves all those taking part in transferring goods from production to distribution. Put simply: we can distinguish between a direct circuit, with no intermediaries between producer and consumer; and an indirect circuit, where various intermediaries (wholesaler, retailer) take charge of the goods or service, along with other goods or services from other producers, and offer them to beneficiaries. A distribution channel is a delivery path for goods and services whose distribution structures (network of shops or sale methods) are of the same type.

At public-sector level, even if direct face-to-face relationships between public sector agents and beneficiaries have become more common, several distribution circuits and channels can be identified, as outlined in Figure 7.5.

As we can see above, the most frequent type of relationship in the context of fixed structures is a personal one (children going to school, filing a complaint with the police, etc.). Itinerant or personal structures are rarer but have developed, becoming very important in rural areas (or if a high number of beneficiaries are concerned). Examples include mobile libraries (a bus that travels from district to district at certain times), road safety in schools (police officers visiting schools to teach children basic safety rules) or fiscal administration (staff visiting small municipalities to help people fill in their tax forms). Whether as part of fixed or itinerant structures, a distinction can still be made between self-service and a face-to-face service. The former is cheaper but rarer, and usually limited to providing free access to available information (in modern libraries, users enjoy direct access to all the books, and are only checked as they leave; but in older libraries users must fill in a form and hand it in at the front desk, and only receive their book once a staff member has been to fetch it for them).

Even if direct contact is maintained, the relationship between the administration and beneficiaries may become impersonal. This is the case, for instance, with services ordered by telephone and sent by post. This form of service delivery has developed extensively with the arrival of internet and, more generally, electronic means and systems

Direct circuit			Indirect circuit
Personal relations		Impersonal relations	
Fixed	Mobile		
Traditional counter	Mobile structure	Telephone, internet	Collaboration with partners (private)

Figure 7.5 *Distribution of public services*

of communication (cyber-administration, call-centre, etc.). It enables a wide range of services to be offered at all times and reduced cost.

It is not so frequent for the administration to use indirect circuits, i.e. calling on intermediaries to deliver services. But this procedure has developed, with third parties being contracted to deliver services – either for economic reasons, or to ensure that decentralized regions also enjoy basic services. In many countries, including the Netherlands, Sweden, Germany and Switzerland, people must pay for household waste disposal (as per the polluter/payer principle), i.e. buy a voucher to affix to the garbage bags. Without the voucher the bags are not collected and the persons may be fined. People must be able to buy their vouchers easily, so they are sold in petrol stations, department stores and local shops (with shopkeepers keeping a percentage for the service provided). This distribution circuit is thus organized with partners who are external to the administration.

Physical aspects of distribution

For historical reasons linked to the nature of the core public services (schools, hospitals, justice, police, etc.), distribution of these services has mainly been organized on the basis of institutional and political territorial structures, with each country having a distinct political and administrative structuring of its territory. Reorganizing the distribution of these services is often essential, for several reasons. First, the spread of electronic communication helps people avoid having to move around (tax offices have set up call centres to answer taxpayers' questions, avoiding the need for them to make unnecessary trips). Then, distribution structures are not always adapted to the mobility of the population or its density in certain regions (more and more post offices are being opened in shopping centres, to the detriment of traditional village post offices).

Another reason is linked to the need for some types of service to have a minimal basic infrastructure size to function satisfactorily. For example, a medical transplant service must carry out a minimum number of operations each year in order to maintain a high degree of competence. This means such services – along with the necessary investment – can only be offered in a very limited number of hospitals. Finally, the physical structures of service distribution are very costly and, for economic reasons, many public communities are forced to reduce or alter them.

Along with venues which often have great symbolic importance in the public sector (tribunals, schools, town halls, etc.), the material aspects and the service's physical accessibility also need to be considered. A first, major factor is opening times. When services are open from 8:30–11:30am and 2:00pm–4:30pm, users are virtually obliged to take time off work to carry out an administrative formality or obtain a service. So, to bring the service closer to citizens, some public agencies are now open non-stop during the day (8am–5pm), or stay open one evening a week (e.g. Thursdays until 8pm), making it easier for working people to have access to the service.

Another aspect concerns the internal architecture of the buildings concerned. Many administrative offices were not designed to encourage a relationship between exchange partners, and great efforts must still be made to improve the material conditions for such an exchange. In Switzerland, a service in charge of personal bankruptcies was formerly housed in an old building with one long counter topped by frosted glass windows. There was invariably tension when personal files were submitted; everyone could hear what was being discussed; there was no room set aside for depositing personal files (which often fell on the floor); nor were there any chairs for people having to wait, let alone a cafeteria, etc. When the service moved, the management – dismayed at the material conditions of the relationship between their organization and citizens filing for personal bankruptcy – insisted their new premises be designed to reduce such tension to a minimum ('open-space' premises with partition walls to help preserve confidentiality; a new, comfortable waiting-room well away from the interview 'desks'; the possibility of sitting during the interview and depositing personal files, and one's coat, without a problem, etc). These changes to how the public were received greatly reduced tension and potential causes of conflict. So it is important, for the comfort of beneficiaries, that close attention is paid to the material conditions of public service accessibility.

CYBER-ADMINISTRATION

Cyber-administration, also known as e-administration or e-government, means using all available information and communication technology to offer services on behalf of the administration, and render public information accessible. The number of public administration portals continues to grow, as do the number of services provided via such technology. This field is currently the subject of extensive research due notably to the internet's vast potential, but remains under-used, and the attitude of the public varies considerably.

There are many advantages, both for the administration and beneficiaries, in using these new tools. One of the main ones is undoubtedly that all services are available round the clock, irrespective of where they are ordered (you can fill in a form at any time of day or night wherever you are, even abroad). Next, the cost is usually less – both for the beneficiary, who does not need to travel; and for the organization, which can deal with subjects according to its resources and possibilities, without relying on the physical presence of the persons concerned. Finally, providing the service lends itself to this, the offer is not limited, and all public services can be accessed via the same portal.

These undeniable advantages should not obviate the limits of internet use in the relationship between the administration and beneficiaries. We first need to bear in mind that many people do not have internet access, or know how to use the available services properly (filling in a tax return online, using an electronic signature, etc.). Then, although some services can be carried out on the internet, it may still be necessary to visit the administration to complete certain formalities – to obtain a biometric passport, for instance, a person must fill in a form, book an appointment, make advance payment online and apply to receive their passport by post . . . but they still have to come in person to have their fingerprints taken. And, finally, the internet cannot assume the task of maintaining and reinforcing social links between people. So cyber-administration may be regarded as an additional distribution channel for improving the quality of the services provided, rather than as a substitute for traditional channels.

CHOOSING A PUBLIC SERVICE DISTRIBUTION SYSTEM – DECISION-MAKING CRITERIA

As indicated above, public service distribution is largely dependent on territorial structures, the legal bases linked to introducing the service and political imperatives (e.g. political pressure to maintain services in certain places). A series of other criteria may also be noted as part of a more technical analysis of a public service distribution system:

- *Existing infrastructure:* as the infrastructure in use is often costly and impossible to move (hospitals, schools, etc.), it cannot be ignored when discussing service distribution. But transforming such buildings or assigning them new roles (e.g. turning a hospital into a medico-social establishment) often needs to be contemplated.
- *Equal access to services:* it is naturally impossible for each inhabitant to live the same distance from all public services. But it is important – above all for essential public

143 ■

services – to ensure that distance does not hinder accessibility, especially for people with reduced mobility, senior citizens, etc. If a maximum distance cannot be formed (various criteria must be considered, such as frequency or degree of importance to the beneficiary), large distances can lead to people renouncing their rights, and to confidence in the administrative system being undermined. (If individuals have to attend in person in order to contest, say, a parking fine, and the administration's offices are situated over an hour's drive away, it is highly probable that most people, even with right on their side, will prefer to pay the fine rather than waste a day in travelling and waiting.)

- *Service quality:* this does not necessarily depend on proximity, insofar as certain services require infrastructures and skills which it is not possible to develop in many places. In certain cases (hospitals, police, etc.), physical proximity with inadequate resources may even reduce the level of service quality quite considerably. Also, when it comes to service quality, the possibility of hiring personnel able to offer advice and deal with users' needs has an impact on the distribution structure.

- *Free services:* paying services can generate different expectations from free ones.

- *Versatility:* this is important, with many administrative services introducing the concept of a 'one-stop' centre where most procedures linked to a particular issue can be dealt with, preferably by one and the same employee (e.g. a company service to process all the formalities required to create a new company). The development of 'one-stop' centres tends to mean beneficiaries face greater travelling, as a large number of multi-skilled staff must be concentrated in one place.

- *Personal involvement of beneficiaries:* if this is extensive (launching a business, undergoing a major operation, visiting a leading museum, etc.), people will be more prepared to travel large distances. On the other hand, for services where personal involvement is less important or non-existent, they will be loath to make a special effort. In this case greater proximity is needed, with services available more simply and readily.

- *Public transport:* a structure may be geographically close at hand, yet considered far away if it is not readily accessible by conveniently organized public transport (times, connections, etc.).

- *Economic aspects:* these can be decisive, given the high cost of administrative structures or economic structures dependent on public bodies.

CONCLUSION

The marketing mix will be putting all these elements (product, price, promotion, place, people, process and physical facilities) into a coherent and well-adapted concept. There are not one size-fits-all solutions, but rather mixes that are more or less adapted to the service being marketed by a specific type of organization.

EXERCISE 7.1

Analyse two of your organization's services on the basis of the four Ps approach and compare the results with colleagues in other organizations. Is the weight of each element the same? What makes the mix of these elements different? Is it the nature of the service, the type of organization, etc.?

DISCUSSION QUESTIONS

1   Is the definition of the price of a public service really a marketing decision? Isn't it a public policy decision? How would you differentiate the two?
2   Aside from the four Ps and the three additional elements presented (people, process and physical facilities) do you believe your organization's specificities would require an additional category?

NOTE

1   The phrase 'public service' is mentioned just once in the EC Treaty, Article 73, which states: 'Aids shall be compatible with this Treaty if they meet the needs of co-ordination of transport of if they represent reimbursement for the discharge of certain obligations inherent in the concept of a public service.'

REFERENCES

Bitner, J. and Booms, B. (1981) Marketing Strategies and Organizational Structures for Service Firms, in Donnelly, J. and George, W. (eds) *Marketing of Services*, Chicago, American Marketing Association.

Borden, N. H. (1965) The Concept of the Marketing Mix, in Schnertz, G. *Science in Marketing*, Chichester, John Wiley & Sons.

Commission of the European Communities (2003) Green Paper on Services of General Interest, Brussels, Commission of the European Communities.

Davet, P. (2006) Gestion par Prestation au Niveau Cantonal: Développement d'un Concept pour la Définition des Prestations dans une Logique de Pilotage Politique et Opérationnel, Lausanne, Institut de Hautes Études en Administration Publique.

Greffe, X. (1999) *Gestion Publique*, Paris, Dalloz.

Kotler, P. K. (2009) *Marketing Management*, New York, Prentice Hall.

Kühn, R., Reimer, A. and Fasnacht, R. (2006) *Marketing: System, Strategie und Instrumente*, Bern, Haupt Verlag Ag.

Le Gall-Ely, M. (2003) Le Marketing Public, E-theque (www.numilog.com).

McCarthy, E. J. (1960) *Basic Marketing: A Managerial Approach*, Illinois, Irwin.

Parasuraman, A., Zeithaml, V. A. and Berry, L. L. (1985) A Conceptual Model of Service Quality and Its Implications for Future Research, *Journal of Marketing*, 49, 41–50.

Rawls, J. (1971) *Theory of Justice*, Cambridge, Belknap Press of Harvard University Press.

Treasury Board of Canada (1994) Quality and Affordable Service for Canadians: Establishing Service Standards in the Federal Government – an Overview, Ottawa, Government of Canada.

Tyler, T. R. (1988) What Is Procedural Justice? Criteria Used by Citizens to Assess the Fairness of Legal Procedures, *Law & Society Review*, 22, 103–35.

—— (2005) *Readings in Procedural Justice*, Burlington, Ashgate.

Urbain, C. and Le Gall-Ely, M. (2009) *Prix et Stratégie Marketing*, Paris, Dunod.

Zeithaml, V., Parasuraman, A. and Berry, L. L. (1990) *Delivering Quality Service: Balancing Customer Perceptions and Expectations*, New York, Free Press.

Part III

Chapter 8

Public communications
– an introduction

LEARNING OBJECTIVES

By the end of this chapter you should be able to:

- Identify the underpinnings of modern communications in the public sector.
- Distinguish between the various levels of communications, from government communications to crisis communications.
- Understand the issues and challenges involved in government transparency.

KEY POINTS OF THIS CHAPTER

- Public communications is taking an increasingly important place in advanced democratic societies, serving a number of functions: to inform, to influence, to promote value, and to be accountable.
- Public communications has developed in response to changes in society, changes in the roles of public-sector organizations, and changes in the media sector.
- There are a number of differences between public and private communications, among them the importance of the organization's legal bases and the obligation of neutrality.
- There are various levels of public communications, each with its own specific attributes. The emphasis – or lack thereof – on the political aspects is one of the most significant factors in determining the level of a communication.
- Transparency, implemented among other things through access-to-information legislation, is now an essential element in a modern democratic state, linked to the increased need for information from citizens and the goals of increased accountability, greater participation, and better relations with citizens.
- Despite the legal obligation imposed by access-to-information legislation, organizations have developed numerous strategies to counter the move towards transparency.

KEY TERMS

Public communications – communications used in a public-sector setting that take into account the ensuing specificities, notably the importance of neutrality and specific legal framework.

Active communications – voluntary, planned communications strategy by a public organization.

Passive communications – information provided by an organization in response to requests from various parties.

Access to information – the legal right of citizens to have access to information held by their government.

INTRODUCTION

Communication is a fundamental component of our society, the basis of social relationships between people. The field of communications assumes enormous importance in complex, democratic societies: it takes very varied forms (written, oral, visible, virtual, etc.) and is carried by varied media used in combination with each other. A particular feature of democratic societies is that the common good is debated in the public sphere in view of, and with the involvement of, citizens. Public communications cannot therefore be dissociated from democratic societies: it must make information available to those participating in the debate and must take into account the growing complexity of relations between the individuals and organizations that make up society.

There are many possible fields for the analysis of communications, but this chapter and the following deal solely with communications by public organizations. By this is meant the transmission of information or elements of meaning for the purpose of influencing the knowledge, attitudes, opinions, expectations or behaviour of the recipients. Consequently, nonverbal communications and personal communication are not dealt with in this book.

FUNCTIONS, DEVELOPMENT AND PRINCIPLES OF PUBLIC COMMUNICATIONS

One of the main characteristics of public communications is its diversity: diversity in the senders and receivers, their interactions and the roles they play, the possible forms and objectives of communication, etc. Box 8.1 gives a few examples of public communications to illustrate this diversity.

A closer look at this diversity reveals the main communications elements presented in Figure 8.1.

> **■ BOX 8.1 EXAMPLES OF FORMS OF PUBLIC COMMUNICATIONS**
>
> ■ Participation by managers of public organizations in public debates
> ■ Press conferences to present and explain decisions
> ■ Communicating information through press releases
> ■ Responses to questions and criticisms from the media and other actors in public life (political parties, civil-society organizations, citizens, etc.)
> ■ Distribution of information brochures to parents
> ■ Paid advertisements in the press or other media for prevention campaigns
> ■ Mailing of letters and e-mail messages as part of normal public-sector activity
> ■ Management and hosting of websites
> ■ Participation in shows and fairs
> ■ Open days
> ■ Publication of periodicals and books

The first element to consider is the originators of acts of communication (the 'senders'). Here, a distinctions must be drawn between the State, the civil service and all administrative and public bodies, which have a degree of autonomy that they often use to develop communications activities of their own. At the other end of the communications chain we find the receivers, where a distinction must be drawn between individuals with the various roles they may play (citizens, subjects, customers), and groups of individuals (including political parties and associations, businesses, institutions and public communities, and government bodies). Communication between senders and receivers can be intentional or unintentional, declared or undeclared, personal or impersonal, etc. To this must be added types of communications and their functions and objectives. The last two points are covered in the following sections.

The functions of public communications

Even though the functions of private organizations go beyond simply buying and selling, the functions of public organizations are much more varied and complex. The first function is to inform. The government must not only inform the public of all decisions taken by political authorities and government departments, but must also explain these decisions and why they were taken. With the expansion of public services, this function has become especially important because everyone concerned by the government's decisions and services must be kept informed, or at least must be able to have easy access to clear, accurate information. A lack of information about a public action can have serious consequences. For example, on 27 April 2009 a Boeing 747 belonging to the American Presidency, escorted by a fighter plane, flew over

151 ■

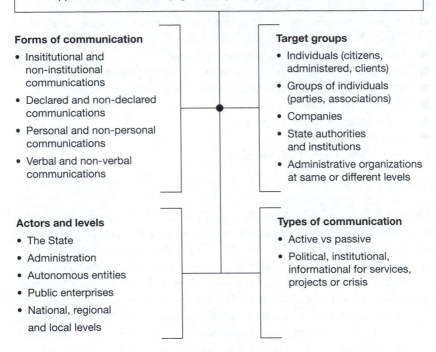

Functions and objectives of communication
- Inform (e.g. decisions, information useful to daily life)
- Influence (e.g. prevention)
- Confirm, prove (e.g. give an account of activities)
- Position (e.g. give a profile to the organization)
- Support values, motivate (e.g. citizen participation in political life)

Forms of communication
- Insititutional and non-institutional communications
- Declared and non-declared communications
- Personal and non-personal communications
- Verbal and non-verbal communications

Target groups
- Individuals (citizens, administered, clients)
- Groups of individuals (parties, associations)
- Companies
- State authorities and institutions
- Administrative organizations at same or different levels

Actors and levels
- The State
- Administration
- Autonomous entities
- Public enterprises
- National, regional and local levels

Types of communication
- Active vs passive
- Political, institutional, informational for services, projects or crisis

Figure 8.1 Elements of public communications

Manhattan at low altitude to take photographs. Fearing a new terrorist attack, thousands of people panicked and came out of their offices. Regardless of the wisdom of flying over the city of New York at low altitudes with such a plane, information distributed widely in advance to the entire population could have prevented inhabitants from reliving a moment of horror (Sulzberger and Matthew, 2009).

Influencing or attempting to change the behaviour of people is another function of communications – one in which large sums of money are invested! Through many communications campaigns and activities, the government or organizations mandated by it endeavour to warn against behaviours that pose a risk to individuals and to society in general. Such prevention measures are becoming more and more widespread, aimed in particular at reducing drinking and smoking, driving behaviour, protection during sexual acts in order to prevent the spread of AIDS and other STDs, the fight against illegal drugs and other addictions, and the promotion of healthy diet.

Another function of public communications is to explain, confirm and attest to tasks and initiatives that have been carried out. Public organizations must be accountable, which means that they must report on their actions, attest to the fact that they are well founded, and reply to enquiries about them. Communications activities such as these will take up an increasing share of the time of managers of public organizations.

Because certain public bodies have been made autonomous or have been given specific, clearly delimited tasks, they have developed communications activities aimed at giving them a profile and an image distinct from those of the government as a whole (their own visual identity, their own set of values, their own communications agenda). The National Aeronautics and Space Agency (NASA) in the United States provides a good example. The aim is to allow the agency to position itself relative to all the organizations that issue communications.

Lastly, public organizations are also charged with promoting the main values of the political system in which they operate. In a democratic environment, public organizations must – through their actions and behaviour, and actively in their communications – stand for and promote values such as equity, integrity, transparency and the respect for law.

Reasons for the development of communications in public organizations

A number of reasons explain the growing importance of communications for public organizations. These reasons fall into three groups: those having to do with changes in society and its expectations of the political–administrative system; those having to do with the roles and functioning of administrations; and those having to do with the evolution of the media.

In our society, information has become a vitally important public resource. Without information, citizens, political parties, associations and journalists cannot participate in the political debate and contribute to the workings of democracy. The government has a great deal of information at its disposal and an increasing disparity is being observed between the quantity of information it collects and the quantity it disseminates. Consequently, political authorities are seeking to enshrine in laws a broad obligation to provide information to citizens and to individuals or organizations concerned by decisions and other important information. This opening up of the government, its activities, its decisions and its functioning to citizens strengthens their confidence in a system that gathers a great deal of data. Communications thus become a public task which government departments must perform actively.

Other reasons are to be found in the place and the role of government departments in the political system. Until relatively recently, the civil service was a closed Weberian system accountable only to political authorities (parliamentary control, monitoring of finances and management) and legal authorities (legal redress, complaints, etc.); see

Chapter 1. Outside these clearly defined and quite constraining avenues, government departments had little need to open up and expose themselves to the scrutiny of other actors in civil society. With the advent of New Public Management principles, and particularly the development of a more customer-oriented relationship with the beneficiaries of public action, with administrative bodies being granted partial autonomy, and with demands for results, public bodies have very actively developed measures to communicate with beneficiaries, persuade them of the merits of services (either proposed or imposed) and more generally work towards increasing their satisfaction. This management autonomy has also led public organizations to develop their own visual identity and specific communications style to set them apart from the rest of the government. As criticism began to be levelled at New Public Management, and as new principles of democratic governance (accountability, transparency, citizens' involvement) were introduced, organizations did not cut back on their communications activities but instead shifted them to adapt to these new requirements. This means that regardless of the reference model for administrative conduct, organization-specific communications tasks have increased. There are other reasons, again with reference to the conception of the administrative system, why public organizations extend their communications activities: to respond to pressure on their budgets and to ensure that the public policies for which they are responsible remain on the political agenda.

Lastly, the evolution of the media is another factor underlying the trend for organizations to communicate more. As the number of media has increased, and with their liberalization and the role they play in society in general – and more specifically in enlivening political debate – public organizations are solicited by the media because the areas for which they are responsible are of general interest and of interest to the public (education, police, social protection, unemployment, etc.). Added to this is the fact that the multiplication and diversification of communications media reduce the effectiveness of every communications activity taken in isolation. As a result, to attain the same communications objective, communications activities must be stepped up appreciably in comparison with the past. This trend seems set to continue into the future.

Basic principles of public communications

Unlike private organizations, which have great freedom in communications, public bodies must abide by a number of principles in their communications, which must be:

- based on provisions of the law
- nonpartisan and independent of political circumstances
- transparent with regard to the issuing body and its funding
- carried out in timely fashion and usually continuously
- as objective and complete as possible
- adapted to the needs of target groups and the media
- proportionate to the objectives and the target groups.

Public communications must be developed and implemented on the basis of legal provisions. In most political systems there are laws or rules that authorize or even oblige the administration to develop and implement communications activities. These rules may be either general and valid for all administrative units (see Box 8.2) or specific, and connected with tasks such as promoting prevention campaigns, defence of values, etc.

A more difficult requirement, but one that is vitally important for gaining credibility over time, is the necessity for public communications to be nonpartisan and as far as possible to avoid playing a political game. Reality frequently reminds us that the communications activities of government departments are taken over by ministers as elections loom or in particular political circumstances. Although this kind of takeover is very difficult to avoid, government departments must ensure that as far as possible their communications remain independent of partisan considerations. Communications that succeed in doing so are bound to enjoy increased credibility with target audiences.

■ BOX 8.2 LEGAL FOUNDATIONS OF COMMUNICATIONS ACTIVITIES

In Switzerland, government communications are governed by a specific article of the constitution (art. 180 Cst) which stipulates that the Federal Council (the executive) must inform the public about its activities in a timely and detailed manner provided that there is no objection from any preponderant public or private interest.

In France, government communications are based on decree no. 2000–1027 dated 18 October 2000 in respect of the government information department (SIG).[1]

In Belgium, the legal basis for public communications is the *Loi du 11 avril 1994 relative à la publicité de l'administration* and the *Arrêté royal du 19 juillet 2001* implementing article 2, paragraph 1 of this law.

In Germany, government communications are based on the general principles of the constitution (articles 5 and 20 setting out the right to freedom of opinion, freedom of the press and the foundations of democratic order) and especially a decision of the constitutional court of 2 March 1977 stressing the importance of the state's information work (Sellier, 2006).

Note:
1 Zémor (1999, p.115) describes the development of this department. At its inception in 1963, the *Service de liaison interministériel pour l'information* was placed under the authority of the Ministre de l'information. From 1976 onwards, the department, initially dubbed SID for Service d'information et de diffusion in 1976 and then SIG for Service d'information du gouvernement in 1996, was placed under the authority of the prime minister.

The publisher and the funding of any political communication must be clear and unambiguous. A message's origin is as important as its content, and must be obvious to its receiver. The same goes for funding, because hiding behind an organization that finances communications activities are often clear intentions and objectives with respect to target groups. If public communications are financed directly or indirectly other than with public funds, this must be clearly indicated so that the receiver can interpret the message in the light of the relationship between the publisher and whoever is paying for the message.

The value of information depends on the use that can be made of it at different times. The dissemination of information must therefore take into account times when the probability of its being received by target groups is highest. Outside these times, there is a significant risk of its going unnoticed. In addition, information must, generally speaking, be repeated and continuously available. If a message is to be noticed and understood, it cannot be communicated only once. Messages must be repeated and made accessible whenever those concerned need them. In this respect, the internet allows complete information to be made available continuously.

Total objectivity may be impossible, but public information must strive towards objectivity and must also be as complete as is necessary for the message to be noticed and understood. This principle illustrates a clear distinction between private and public communications, because private organizations deliver only the information that they wish to disclose – information, moreover, that is rarely objective. The objectivity of a communication will be perceived, naturally, through the message itself, but also on the basis of the media chosen to convey the message and on the frequency of dissemination. With regard to completeness, a communication must contain sufficient information for the message to be understood; but loading the communication with too much additional information could hinder understanding of the message.

Public organizations must take particular care to adapt messages to target groups and to the media. This is because public information must be comprehensible to all recipients of the message, regardless of their intellectual, linguistic and social abilities. For example, letters sent by public bodies may sometimes contain many expressions or technical terms that make them difficult to understand. In addition – and this subject has given rise to lively debate in many countries – messages should also be understandable to people with insufficient language skills (naturally, this concerns foreigners who are not fluent in the national language(s), but also those who are illiterate or have poor reading skills). The use of foreign languages or other forms of language (sign language, specific visual aids, etc.) must be considered where necessary to ensure that the message reaches those at whom it is aimed. With regard to the media, apart from the need to use a vocabulary that is understandable or expressly documented (glossary, lexicon, etc.), their cycles, deadlines and needs (photographs, data for computer graphics, interviews, additional information, etc.) must be taken into account.

Lastly, public communications must be proportionate to target groups and objectives. Too often, communications in the public sector are deployed with insufficient intensity and over too short a period for them to be able to produce appreciable effects. The goal of achieving sufficiently intense communications can be achieved, for example, by using several distinct media in order to reach the target groups in different ways. Conversely, although this is relatively rare, public communications must not incur disproportionate costs that may subsequently be criticized by financial auditors, or even directly by citizens. Generally speaking, largely due to the increase in the number of organizations that are communicating and the diversity of communications media, public organizations are obliged to increase and diversify their communications activities in order to attain their objectives.

TYPES AND LEVELS OF PUBLIC COMMUNICATIONS

Types of public communications

A distinction must be drawn between two main types of public communications: active communications and passive communications. Active communications covers all information provided spontaneously and generally in an organized manner by the authorities and by government departments to the public or to defined target groups. Most communications activities by public organizations are active, since they are planned, organized and financed by the organizations themselves (see Box 8.3).

Passive communications, on the other hand, refers to information transmitted by public bodies in response to requests based on access-to-information legislation that exists in most countries. Generally, the sole obligations of public bodies are to make available registers of documents available so that citizens can identify and request those that interest them, and to deal diligently with requests received.

The following paragraphs are essentially devoted to active communications, but a presentation of the bases and implications of passive communications is set out in the next section of this chapter.

Levels of communication

Table 8.1 contains an overview of types of public communications along with a few examples. Although it is important to distinguish between political communications and public communications, the latter necessarily contains information of a political nature.

Although it is difficult to generalize about the strength of the political component of a type of communication, information that favourably presents government activity is considered to have the strongest political nature. The same is true of crisis communications, in that virtually any crisis or conflict in the public sector leads to intervention by all political and public actors and very frequently generates political debate. Communications related to citizens' rights and obligations and communications as an instrument of public policy are not free of political considerations but are less

■ BOX 8.3 THE GOTTHARD TUNNEL

As part of its transport policy, Switzerland decided to build two new tunnels under the Alps: the Lötschberg tunnel (which came into service in 2007) and the Gotthard base tunnel (due to come into service in 2017). When breakthrough in the Gotthard tunnel was achieved in October 2010, marking the construction of the world's longest tunnel at 57 kilometres, a major communications operation was organized:

- The piercing of the last few metres was broadcast live on public television.
- European transport ministers, meeting in Luxembourg, watched the proceedings live; the Swiss delegation presented each minister with a gift of a fragment of Gotthard rock on which was mounted a watch.
- Special programmes were broadcast during the days leading up to and following the breakthrough.
- Invitations were sent to journalists all over the world.
- Numerous activities were organized surrounding the event.

strongly connected to immediate political issues. Lastly, other types of communications, such as those dealing with government services and internal communications, are almost completely free of political considerations.

Government communications

In democratic countries, to ensure that institutions function properly, governments are required by the constitution, by laws passed by the parliament or by common law to inform the public, encourage dialogue and account for their activities. This means that they must communicate, and in many countries the departments set up to perform this task have substantial human and financial resources at their disposal. Generally speaking, government communications perform four tasks, although the importance of these tasks may vary considerably from one country to another:

- *Providing information on the government's actions:* Governments must provide all necessary information to elected representatives, the media and the general public on their intentions, decisions and actions. The way this obligation is understood gives rise to very different practices. In some countries, the government departments concerned focus on transmitting important information about government decisions and activities through press releases and press conferences and by making this information available on internet sites or in official documents (newspapers, magazines, etc.). They are also responsible for official portals of the

Table 8.1 Levels of public communications

Types	Examples	Political nature of public information
		Low High
Government communications	Information and explanations of government decisions and actions	
Communications related to citizens' rights and obligations	Making available information on laws; promotion of civic rights; making available information on political issues (e.g. on official statistics)	
Communications as an instrument of public policy	Prevention and awareness campaigns	
Institutional communications	Publications aimed at promoting the organization	
Communications related to public services	Information brochures, detailed explanations, etc.	
Communications regarding projects	Communications on major projects (bridges, tunnels, metro systems, etc.)	
Internal communications	Communications for staff	
Crisis communications	Any communications activity in a crisis situation	

government and the country. In other countries, these departments also have the responsibility for conducting communications campaigns that include events, paid advertising and a wide range of communications tools.

■ *Being responsive to the public:* The second task that falls to government information departments is to inform the government about the needs, expectations and concerns of the population and about the opinion of various groups that may influence policy, such as foreign media. Governments are making increasing use of such tools as press reviews of the country's media and major foreign media, opinion polls and, sometimes, quantitative surveys.

■ *Coordinating communications activities:* These departments are also charged with coordinating the communications activities of the entire administrative apparatus – a task made necessary by the constant growth in the amount of information being issued by all administrative entities. Coordination can be of three types. First, thematic coordination. For reasons of its political agenda, or depending on its activities, a government may wish the themes addressed to be actively coordinated so as to guarantee consistency in communications. Next, temporal coordination is designed to prevent damaging short-term overlapping of the communications activities of different administrative entities. When several government departments wish to communicate on various subjects at the same time, it is important that one of them should arrange the timing of messages so that, in particular, accredited journalists are able to cover all press conferences without putting departments or administrative bodies into competition with each other. Third, financial coordination of the communications budgets of the various departments allows prices to be negotiated, particularly the purchasing of advertising space from communications agencies and the media. For example, in Australia, all government departments and agencies are required to work with a specific agency for campaign advertising and for non-campaign advertising (recruitment advertisements, for example) (Australian Government, n.d.).

■ *Advising government departments:* Less frequently, and depending on their skills and resources, government communications departments may provide advice to all departments of the administration, as communications agencies might do. In the United Kingdom, the Central Office of Information is a true agency, offering its services to government bodies, including strategic consulting, production of campaigns, the hiring and training of communications specialists, etc.[1]

Government information departments are characterized by three elements. First, they are directly subject to the authority of the head of the government or the government as a whole: in France, the SIG is subject to the prime minister and in Germany the chancellor; in Switzerland, the vice-chancellor responsible for information attends sessions of the government. Second, the source of information is clearly identifiable as being institutional, being credited in writing and by the corresponding logos. Third, the communications of these departments are not concentrated on a single field of public policy such as health or safety, but on all the government's activities or on their promotion.

Communications in connection with citizens' rights and obligations

This is one of the foundations of public communications and covers, on the one hand, the obligation to make information available to the media and to the public (principle of openness) and, on the other hand, reminding citizens of their rights and duties and inviting them to participate in political life (civic information). In some countries, these tasks are carried out by the government's own information department and in others by specialized departments.

As we have seen, democratic life is particularly dependent on citizens' capacity to have access to information that they need to exercise their rights. Although this obligation on the government was for a long time limited to legislative and legal decisions and on the opening of debates to the public, the principle of openness now applies more broadly to all information held by the government, except in cases where there are preponderant public or private interests. States must ensure, on the one hand, that information is indexed and archived in such a way that citizens can find the information they want, and on the other hand that they deliver information proactively ('proactive disclosure') in order to enable political debate.

A second tier of activities involves disseminating civic information. This is information that reminds citizens of their rights and duties, as well as the fundamental values of the democratic state; explains how institutions work in order to increase their accessibility and legitimacy; and encourages participation in political life, particularly in elections and votes at all levels of government. These tasks are becoming increasingly important since 'incivility' is increasing, criticisms of the legitimacy of institutions are more frequent, and voter participation in elections often falls below 50 per cent.[2]

Communications as an instrument of public policy

While communications accompany almost all the government's decisions and actions as a tool, it has also become a fully-fledged instrument of public policy, being used in the same way as incentive, disincentive or regulatory measures. The aims may include discouraging certain behaviours (e.g. not driving under the influence of alcohol), raising awareness of various attitudes (sorting household waste for recycling) and inviting people to take concrete action (getting vaccinated). For these purposes websites are created, newsletters are distributed to households and to businesses, publicity campaigns are disseminated via the main media such as television and billboards, competitions are organized, personalized letters are sent, etc. The government therefore uses communications tools to attain objectives that form part of public policy. Communications campaigns in some fields, such as health and economic promotion, date back a long time, while others such as the environment, education and safety have appeared only more recently.

Institutional communications

An increasing share of communications activities is devoted to promoting public institutions and organizations. This is not a matter of highlighting the work of these bodies so much as the organizations themselves. Three main reasons explain this trend. First, new entities such as the *Cour des comptes* in the Canton of Geneva (created

161 ■

in 2005 following a referendum) and HALDE[3] in France are being created and need to make themselves known to the public in order to fulfil their missions properly. Next, to facilitate access to their services or reinforce their legitimacy, public organizations are developing a range of measures, from open days and the production of brochures to invitations to journalists to produce special reports. Lastly, organizations need to position themselves and build a positive image that will facilitate attainment of their objectives, for example when recruiting staff, marketing their services, or attracting businesses, residents or tourists.

This type of communications also encompasses all information concerning the life of the organization, such as appointments, organizational changes and, particularly, reports on activities. In spite of the fact that, in the classical view of bureaucracy, the civil service has no legal personality and must limit itself to implementing rules and procedures set out in legislation, clearly it is becoming increasingly important for public organizations to be known to the general public, enjoy a high level of trust and account regularly for their activities.

Communications regarding services

Communications regarding services is not a public policy measure but is aimed at providing information on services offered by the government. Clear information on services and eligibility for these services, on procedures to follow, on documents required, on the time it will take to obtain a reply or a decision, on possible recourse, on prices and methods of payment, on opening hours, etc. greatly facilitates the lives of citizens. These aspects are all the more important because in the public sector the perceived quality of a service is judged not so much on the service itself but on peripheral elements. Information and the attitude of personnel are vital elements in this perception of quality.

Project communications

The public sector undertakes projects that require specific communications activities for a number of reasons. Major projects such as the Millau Viaduct, the Confederation Bridge in Canada, Boston's 'Big Dig' tunnel project and the new Gotthard tunnel in Switzerland involve numerous public and private actors all needing to be kept informed of progress on the project, and of the technical and financial difficulties encountered.

Projects have a defined temporal framework, with a beginning and an end, and important stages that are traditionally highlighted (laying of the first stone, tunnel breakthrough, etc.) and serve as milestones for communications purposes. Lastly, projects such as these also constitute the achievements of a generation, national or territorial symbols that are valuable not only because they bring a community together but also because they serve as flagships for the outside world (see Box 8.3).

Today, no major project goes without a communications concept and a substantial budget for communications built into the costs of the project.

162

Internal communications

In addition to communications aimed at external actors, consideration must be given to communications aimed at staff. While this may appear obvious, there is an unfortunate tendency to overlook the fact that staff are the civil service's main resource and that they are frequently the first vectors of an organization's communications. If they receive information at the same time or even after the general public or certain specific actors, they will be unable to act as facilitators in the transmission of messages. For example, in the case of one crisis affecting a public-sector organization many staff members openly complained that they had no information with which to respond to the remarks and criticisms made by their families, friends, neighbours and acquaintances (Pasquier and Fivat, 2009).

Internal communications activities have also increased considerably with intranet sites, internal newspapers, newsletters, the organization of events, etc.

Crisis communications

The final type of communications that governments need to consider is crisis communications. What is unusual about crisis communications is that it can affect any field of government activity: a problem involving relations with political institutions, a crisis of confidence at the organizational level, a serious problem in a major project, a defective service or an internal crisis. In addition, a crisis will concern an entire organization because the general public are generally not able to draw a clear distinction between the service provided by an organization and its global image. Crisis communications will also go beyond government agencies to involve political authorities and parties since, depending on the type of crisis, it is highly probable that these actors will contribute to communications through their questions and the positions they adopt. For this reason, conflict and crises affecting the public sector frequently take on a political dimension, either through the intervention of political actors or through a political discussion of the problems that are the origins of the crisis.

PASSIVE COMMUNICATION, ACCESS TO INFORMATION OR THE CONCEPT OF TRANSPARENCY

The concept of transparency has taken root over the past few decades as a necessity to counter both organizational and individual lapses (corruption, fraud, financial scandals) and to improve the governance of organizations in both the public and private sectors (Transparency International, 2004). Laws on free access to information held by government departments and agencies, and laws concerning the opening of all proceedings of parliament, commissions and agencies, are essentially designed to increase the transparency of government activities. And yet, although organizations are obliged to demonstrate transparency, it is clear that they are very often reluctant to disclose information spontaneously and willingly.

Definition and origin

In spite of numerous references to transparency in both official discourse and scientific literature, it is difficult to find a set definition. Literally, transparency is what allows us to see through something (Blomgren and Sahlin, 2007), or to see what is happening inside something (Naurin, 2006). This definition cannot be directly transposed to government transparency, since no organization allows the public to have direct access to its premises, to consult its files freely or to attend its various meetings.

In this context, transparency means the opening up of an organization's processes and internal decisions to third parties, regardless of whether they are involved in the organization (Florini, 1998), and, as defined by Hood (2001, p.701), the making available by government of information about its actions and decisions: 'government according to fixed and published rules, on the basis of information and procedures that are accessible to the public and (in some usages) within clearly demarcated fields of activity'.

The origins of the concept of transparency and its application to public organizations can be found in philosophical, epistemological, economic and political reflections (Popper, 1949; Mill, 1961; Habermas, 2003). As early as 1859, John Stuart Mill considered that putting arguments into the public sphere was an unconditional benefit, making it possible to discriminate between good and bad arguments. Globally, transparency is directly linked to the construction of modern democratic states (Stiglitz, 1999) and to challenges to traditional bureaucratic models in which the relationship between the administration and citizens was one of one-sided dependency (Chevallier, 1988; Hood, 1991; Cottier, 2001). Table 8.2 presents the dates of the establishment of an access to information regime in various countries.

Reasons underlying the development of transparency

Four main reasons explain the development of the concept of transparency and related practices.

First, transparency must be understood as an exchange of information. In our societies, in order to accomplish its various tasks, the State requests ever more information from citizens (surveys, forms, etc.). At the same time, the value of information is growing. In the context of the so-called information society and with the revolution in means of communication, information is being transformed. From being a resource essential to the sound administration of citizens, it has become an indispensable public resource (Juillet and Paquet, 2001). This being said, a strong imbalance can be observed between information held by governments (growing in both quantity and value) and that in the hands of citizens (Sanchez, 2002). Giving citizens the ability to have free access to information that concerns them (in Switzerland, *Loi sur la protection des données LPD*, 19 June 1992) and information held by government agencies (in Switzerland, *Loi sur la transparence LTrans*, 17 December 2004) is aimed at achieving a better balance of information between citizens and governments.

Table 8.2 *The legal bases of access-to-information rights*

Country	Year	Law
Australia	1982	Freedom of Information Act
Canada	1983	Access to Information Act
China	2008	Open Government Information Regulations (*Zhengfu xinxi gongkai tiaoli*)
European Union	2001	FOI Regulation
France	1978	Law on freedom of access to administrative documents (*Loi de la liberté d'accès aux documents administratifs*)
Germany	2006	Federal act governing access to information (*Informationfreiheitsgesetz*)
India	2005	RTI: Right to Information Act
Sweden	1766	Freedom of the press act (*Tryckfrihetsförordningen*)
Switzerland	2006	Federal law on the principle of administrative transparency (*Loi sur la transparence/Öffentlichkeitsgesetz*)
United Kingdom	2005	Freedom of Information Act
United States	1966	Freedom of Information Act

Second, the goal of transparency is to improve relations between governing bodies and citizens. In a context marked by the thorny problem of public deficits, loss of confidence in administrations, demands for greater accountability of elected officials, and the fight against corruption, access to information makes it possible to reverse some of these trends and re-establish a relationship of trust between government and citizens. The aim is, therefore, to improve the management of government departments and agencies through an external pressure mechanism and the making public of internal operations (Juillet and Paquet, 2001; Reid, 2004).

Transparency is also a tool that fosters the involvement of citizens in the development and implementation of public policies. A growing propensity of citizens to participate in decision making and the political processes of the State is being observed (Lunde, 1996; Rowe and Shepherd, 2002; Juillet and Paquet, 2001; Open government, 2004; OECD, 2005). More active participation of citizens in the governance of the State requires greater quantities of information, and the information must be of higher quality. In this context, transparency of the State's activities becomes a prerequisite for good governance and active involvement of citizens in political processes.

165

Lastly, transparency must be understood as a method of management that improves organizations' efficiency and effectiveness (Caron and Hunt, 2006). While bureaucratic culture is characterized by secrecy (Reid, 2004), transparency forces public organizations to provide information about themselves (for example, expense accounts or internal guidelines) and, together with greater accountability of public actors, to explain and justify actions taken (Roberts, 2004; Sanchez, 2002). In this way it compels organizations to manage the resources made available more efficiently.

Different forms of transparency

When applied to public organizations, transparency can take a number of forms (Pasquier and Villeneuve, 2005; Audria, 2004) that can be referred to collectively as a 'transparency framework' (Caron and Hunt, 2006):

- *Documentary transparency:* this is access to information held by or collated by the administration, either in connection with an individual, or more generally. Active information, spontaneously made available to the public, via the internet for example, must be distinct from passive information delivered in response to a request from a citizen. Although laws on transparency and access to information sometimes contain clauses on proactive release of information, they are largely aimed at regulating passive information. This is the most widespread and most highly codified form of transparency in administration.
- *Organizational transparency:* this means knowledge of the organization and its functioning (processes, rules and decisional criteria). The goal is to show not only what is produced but above all how it is produced. This type of transparency also applies to electoral processes managed by the government and the opening to public observation of the proceedings of various commissions internal to the government. In the United States, for example, the 'Sunshine Act' applies to government agencies headed by a collegial body (several departments working together) and which have regulatory functions. They are required, for example, to open their sessions to the public.
- *Accounting and budgetary transparency:* here the purpose is to link the origin of funds with their use in public action, either administratively, through the production and official reporting of financial information to the political authorities, or through external auditing mechanisms.
- *Transparency of action and administrative responsibilities:* here the onus is on the government to make known and explain the meaning of its decisions and actions and to ensure that civil servants and the civil service as a whole comply with their obligations.

Although these forms of transparency are applied – albeit in very diverse ways – in processes of parliamentary control and are very broadly documented, free access to all information held by the government (documentary transparency) is more recent.

It developed in response to the multiplication of access-to-information laws during the 1980s (Banisar, 2004).

Historically, the Swedes, with the introduction of their Freedom of the Press Act in 1766, laid the foundations of the principle of access to government information. In recent history, Finland was the first country, in 1951, to build citizens' access-to-information rights into its laws. Since then, many countries have framed laws of this kind, including the United States in 1966, France in 1978 and Canada in 1983. More recently, similar laws came into force in the United Kingdom (2005), Germany and Switzerland (2006). To date, about 70 countries have adopted laws facilitating citizens' access to government information (Banisar, 2006).

Although access-to-information laws essentially concern national governments, it is worth mentioning that international institutions and organizations such as the United Nations and the European Union have made some advances in the field of access to information. For example, in 2001 the European Parliament and the Council of Europe adopted regulation 1049/2001 concerning access to documents of the European Parliament, the Council of Europe and the European Commission (Maiani *et al.*, 2010).

Analytical framework for transparency laws

The principles underlying the various laws on transparency are fairly similar from one country to another; they vary principally in their scope and application. For the purposes of comparative analysis, two levels of study are possible. First, the text of the law can be examined in order to identify the ways in which information can be accessed and from there the extent of the prescribed field of transparency. Second, we must look at the manner in which the law is applied in practice by the organization concerned and how it is used by citizens.

The first level consists in analysing the law's characteristics, and is principally based on the content of various legislative documents (laws, orders, implementing regulations and other guidelines). In particular, the following elements require study (Frankel, 2001; Banisar, 2003; Office of the Information Commissioner of Canada, 2003, 2004):

- *Accessible information:* the basis of any access-to-information law lies in the opportunity given to the citizen to request information, or a document containing the desired information, without having to justify the request. The document in question may take very varied forms: reports, notes, minutes of meetings, letters, e-mail messages and even unwritten documents such as telephone conversations. Access-to-information laws must therefore explicitly specify what information is accessible and what is not.
- *Exceptions:* generally, such laws apply to all governmental and administrative entities. However, provision will be made for exceptions related to the defence of the national interest (international relations, security services) or the higher interests of citizens (courts, privacy).

- *Assistance provided by the State in the search for information:* given the complexity of government operations, it is unreasonable to expect citizens to be aware of all the documents that are prepared and therefore accessible to them. Depending on the country or institution, instruments or information counters are set up to inform citizens of the type of documents produced by the government.
- *Time required for delivery of information:* laws or regulations generally specify a period of time during which the government or entity concerned must respond to the access-to-information request. The government cannot therefore make citizens wait unduly. This is vital because information often loses its value over time (subject no longer topical, an important vote has been held, etc.).
- *Research costs and charges:* the costs of a request are set out in the law. If research costs, which are frequently quite high (photocopies, research time, etc.), exceed a certain threshold, the possibility of invoicing for them is provided. However, the amounts must remain reasonable, since otherwise some citizens will be deprived of their rights.
- *Appeals procedures:* a distinction is made between procedures for appeal within the government and the possibility of asserting access-to-information rights in the courts in response to refusal by the administration, failure to respond within the allowed time period, or overcharging.

These parameters may vary from one law to another, thereby affecting the scope of the transparency model. In Canada, for example, access rights are limited to Canadian citizens and permanent residents, whereas in most other countries having a similar law, access is open to anybody and requests may remain anonymous. Practically all transparency laws provide exemption for certain organizations, and in some countries the list of exempt organizations is extensive. In Canada, many autonomous legal entities that perform public tasks are excluded from the field of application of the Access to Information Act (Secrétariat du Conseil du Trésor du Canada, 2005). The type of information accessible may also take very varied forms: reports, notes, minutes of meetings, mail (Sweden), e-mail (United States, Canada, Great Britain) and even unread documents such as telephone conversations (Denmark). Exceptions provided for in the law and the margin of interpretation allowed to government bodies in applying the law also vary from one law to another. Finally, the time allowed for an organization to respond to a request, rules for the charging of fees, and possibilities for redress provided for in the law must also be taken into account in determining the degree of openness of a law.

The second level of analysis concerns the concrete application of the law and its effects. These certainly depend on the infrastructure and resources made available, but may also vary considerably depending on the administration's behaviour regarding making information available and the use that citizens make of the law.

Resistance to transparency

While documentary transparency is firmly established in the legal framework, resistance to this transparency and the development of avoidance strategies by organizations can be seen, obstructing the right of inspection legally granted to civil society (Pasquier and Villeneuve, 2004, 2005, 2007):

- *Non-transparency* is characterized by the fact that an organization or part of its activities are legally exempt from the obligation to disclose information.
- *Averted transparency* refers to the behaviour of an organization that is subject to the law but which actively and illegally prevents access to information.
- *Obstructed transparency* means the use of all legal means to limit access to information (redaction, mis-classification of documents, restrictions in the transparency of the request handling process, etc.).
- *Strained transparency* designates behaviours of the administration which, consciously or unconsciously, limit access to information, either through the absence of resources to deal with requests, ignorance about documents, etc.
- *Maximized transparency* might appear to be a panacea, because it refers to the behaviour of an organization which makes available all the information it holds. Citizens then no longer need to make requests. However, it can also provide a hindrance since, if people do not have indexes, a system of filing of records, etc., they may not be able to access the information that interest them or they may have great difficulty locating it. In other words, too much transparency may kill transparency. These various dynamics are classified according to their optional or mandatory nature and their legal natures in Table 8.3.

Table 8.3 Types of obstacles to transparency

	Optional		Mandatory		
Situation	Legal	Illegal	Legal	Legal	Legal
Type of obstacle	Non-transparency	Averted transparency	Obstructed transparency	Strained transparency	Maximized transparency
Description	The concept of transparency does not apply; transparency is purely voluntary	Organizations directly contravene the law (refuse to participate)	Obstacles to transparency through the use of the provisions of the law	Inability to comply with the transparency requirements due to a lack of resources or ignorance of information	Behaviour designed to anticipate requests by making all available information available
Justification	'It's not necessary'	'The file doesn't exist'	'It would be irresponsible'	'We don't have the necessary resources'	'It is simpler and cheaper'

Communication, whether active or passive, is now a mandatory activity for public organizations. The following chapters detail the specificities of communicating in a public-sector environment.

DISCUSSION QUESTIONS

1   In times of economic crisis, are public communications an unaffordable luxury for the State?
2   Can/should governments be transparent? Is access to information a force for good or simply an administrative fad?

NOTES

1   The wording of the Central Office of Information website is unambiguous: 'The Client Account Team (CAT) helps to ensure that COI always puts the client's needs first. The team's remit is to build strategic partnerships with clients and develop the best possible understanding of their business so that COI can offer effective advice and delivery across all marketing and communications specialisms' (Zémor, 1999, p.115).
2   In Switzerland, voter participation in votation (elections and referendums) in the past decade has stood at between 40 per cent and 50 per cent. In France, voter turnout at the 2009 European elections was 40.6 per cent and in the second round of the 2010 regional elections, 51.2 per cent.
3   Created in 2004 by the Haute Autorité de Lutte Contre les Discriminations et Pour L'égalité (30 December).

REFERENCES

Audria, R. (2004) *New Public Management et Transparence: Essai de Déconstruction d'un Mythe Actuel,* Geneva, doctoral thesis, University of Geneva.

Australian Government (n.d.) Central Advertising System. Online at http://www.finance.gov.au/advertising/cas.html (accessed 24 July 2011).

Banisar, D. (2003) The www.freedominfo.org Global Survey: Freedom of Information and Access to Government Record Laws around the World, Privacy International.

—— (2004) The freedominfo.org Global Survey: Freedom of Information and Access to Government Record Laws around the World, Privacy International.

—— (2006) Freedom of Information around the World 2006: A Global Survey of Access to Government Information Laws, Privacy International.

Blomgren, M. and Sahlin, K. (2007) Quests for Transparency: Signs of a New Institutional Era in the Health Care Field, *Transcending New Public Management: The Transformation of Public Sector Reform,* Aldershot, Ashgate.

Caron, D. J. and Hunt, T. D. (2006) Accountability and Disclosure: The Proper Use of Transparency Instruments and their Implications for Canadian Public Administration, in Sciences, I. I. O. A. (ed.) Third Regional International Conference: Transparency for Better Governance, Monterrey.

Chevallier, J. (1988) Le Mythe de la Transparence Administrative, in Curapp (ed.) *Information et Transparence Administrative*, Paris, Presses Universitaire de France.

Cottier, B. (2001) De l'administration Secrète à l'administration Transparente ou les Enjeux d'un Prochain Renversement de Paradigme, Lugano, Commissione ticinese per la formazione permanente dei giuristi.

Florini, A. (1998) The End of Secrecy, *Foreign Policy,* 111, 50–63.

Frankel, M. (2001) Freedom of Information and Corruption, *Global Forum on Fighting Corruption and Safeguarding Integrity*, London.

Habermas, J. (2003) *The Structural Transformation of the Public Sphere*, Cambridge, Polity Press.

Hood, C. (1991) A Public Management for All Seasons, *Public Administration*, 69, 3–19.

—— (2001) Transparency, in Clarke, P. B. and Foweraker, J. (eds) *Encyclopaedia of Democratic Thought*, London, Routledge.

Juillet, L. and Paquet, G. (2001) Politique D'information et Gouvernance, Ottawa, Gouvernement du Canada.

Lunde, T. (1996) Client Consultation and Participation: Consumers and Public Services, in OECD (ed.) *Responsive Government: Service Quality Initiatives*, Paris, OECD.

Maiani, F., Villeneuve, J.P., Pasquier, M. (2010) Less is More? The Commission Proposal on Access to EU Documents and the Proper Limits of Transparency, Lausanne, Institut de hautes études en administration publique.

Mill, J. S. (1961) On Liberty, in Cohen, M. (ed.) *The Philosophy of John Stuart Mill*, New York, Modern Library.

Naurin, D. (2006) Transparency, Publicity, Accountability – The Missing Links, *Schweizerische Zeitschrift für Politkwissenschaften,* 12, 90–8.

Office of the Information Commissioner Of Canada (2003) Rapport Annuel du Commissaire à l'information 2002–3, Ottawa, Commissariat à l'information du Canada.

—— (2004) Rapport Annuel du Commissaire à l'information 2003–4, Ottawa, Commissariat à l'information du Canada.

Open Government (2004) Freedom of Information Coalition, Freedom of Information Coalition.

Organisation for Economic Co-operation and Development (OECD) (2005) Engaging Citizens in Policymaking, Paris, OECD.

Pasquier, M. and Fivat, E. (2009) Crise à l'Université de Genève: Une Étude de Cas, *Cahier de l'IDHEAP,* 2009.

Pasquier, M. and Villeneuve, J.-P. (2004) Les Entraves Politiques et Administratives à la Transparence Gouvernementale, *Revue économique et sociale*, December.

—— (2005) Typologie des Comportements Organisationnels des Administrations Publiques Visant à Limiter l'accès à l'information, Working Paper, IDHEAP.

—— (2007) Organizational Barriers to Transparency: A Typology and Analysis of Organizational Behaviour Tending to Prevent or Restrict Access to Information, *International Review of Administrative Sciences,* 73, 147–62.

Popper, K. (1949) *The Open Society and Its Enemies*, London, Routledge & Sons.

Reid, J. M. (2004) Discours Sur l'Accès à l'information, Toronto, Groupe Ginger.

Roberts, A. (2004) Orcon Creep: Information Sharing and the Threat to Government Accountability, *Government Information Quarterly,* 21, 249–67.

Rowe, R. and Shepherd, M. (2002) Public Participation in the New NHS: No Closer to Citizen Control? *Social Policy & Administration,* 36, 275–90.

Sanchez, A. C. (2002) The Right of Access to Information and Public Scrutiny: Transparency as a Democratic Control Instrument, in OECD (ed.) *Public Sector Transparency and Accountability: Making It Happen,* Paris, OECD.

Secrétariat du Conseil du Trésor du Canada (2005) Examen du Cadre de Gouvernance des Sociétés d'État du Canada – Répondre aux Attentes des Canadiennes et des Canadiens, Ottawa, Secrétariat du Conseil du Trésor du Canada.

Sellier, D. (2006) *La Communication Gouvernementale en Europe,* Paris, L'Harmattan.

Stiglitz, J. E. (1999) On Liberty, the Right to Know, and Public Discourse: The Role of Transparency in Public Life, Oxford Amnesty Lecture, Oxford.

Sulzberger, A. G. and Matthew, L. (2009) White House Apologizes for Air Force Flyover, *New York Times,* 27 April, New York.

Transparency International (2004) *Global Corruption Report,* Berlin, Transparency International.

Zémor, P. (1999) *La communication publique,* Paris, Presses Universitaires de France.

Chapter 9

Communications models and strategies

LEARNING OBJECTIVES

By the end of this chapter you should be able to:

- Clearly identify the various elements that make up a communications model.
- Construct and analyse a communications campaign.
- Define a coherent, integrated communications strategy.
- Identify the objectives of a communications initiative.

KEY POINTS OF THIS CHAPTER

- Communication is a process that can be simple or complex, intentional or unintentional.
- A communications model includes a sender, a message and a receiver, all linked together in a relationship framed by a common code and occurring in a given context.
- A communications strategy has four main steps: (1) defining the general framework, (2) identifying the target audience, (3) designing the message and identifying the medium to be used and (4) finally launching the communications campaign.
- A modern communications strategy must, as far as possible, be integrated, achieving consistency of form, content and timing.

KEY TERMS

Communications model – schematic construct of the various elements allowing the establishment of communication.

continued . . .

KEY TERMS ... *continued*

Communications strategy – an iterative process involving a series of key decisions on the consistency between objectives and the concrete measures to be developed.

Integrated communications – logical, self-reinforcing coordination of the various elements of a communications campaign.

INTRODUCTION

Constructing a communication is a complex task that requires, on the one hand, an understanding of how communication is established and, on the other hand, following the steps involved in conceiving a message and conveying it. The first part of this chapter presents the main components of the communications model, while the second part describes the steps involved in developing a communications strategy. The third, shorter, part presents the concept of integrated communications, which stresses the need to ensure that communications activities are consistent in form, content and timing.

COMMUNICATIONS MODEL

Communication is a process of transmitting elements of information to someone. While this extremely simple definition does not convey all conceptions of communication, it at least highlights the main characteristics.

The process of communication can be intentional or unintentional, simple or complex. A newspaper advertisement is of course an intentional form of communication, while style of dress, body language, remarks made in a corridor or in the cafeteria may all be elements of unintentional, or at least unplanned, communication. Communication can be relatively simple (asking for information about a museum's opening hours) or highly complex – as study of the entire set of interpersonal relationships in a group of individuals will reveal. Communication establishes a relationship with another person in order to transmit information, generally with the intention of producing an effect on the intended recipient(s) (an increase in their knowledge, a change in their attitude or their behaviour, etc.). Many methods and techniques – from very simple to very sophisticated – can be used for this purpose (work session, newsletter, website, systematic blogging, etc.).

The communication process has been modelled in various ways depending on the reference discipline: Weaver and Shannon (1963) took a technical, mathematical approach, Lasswell (1927; 1948) formulated a persuasive political conception, Jakobson (1963) used linguistics as a reference, while Gerbner (1955) adopted a sociological approach.

The basic elements of a communications model are shown in Figure 9.1.

174

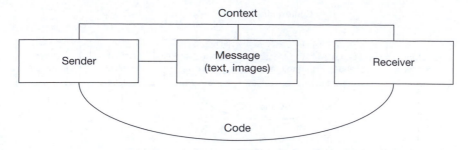

Figure 9.1 *Schematic model of communication*

Communication requires a sender (who emits the communication) and one or more receivers (the recipients, or those who receive the communication). The message is a set of information (text, images, sounds, etc.) conveyed by a medium (spoken word, newspaper, document, advertising spot, etc.). Communication occurs in a context, that is, at a given moment, in a given place and in relation to a given situation. This context is not part of the communication but accompanies it and can be the source of interference or, to use a specialized term, 'noise' that may influence the desired effect in one direction or another. For example, if police announce that members of an organized gang have been arrested, the news may not produce the same effect in a region where crime rates are low as in a locality that has recently witnessed a series of violent attacks. Lastly, communication requires a code allowing the sender and receiver to understand one another (common understanding of signs and their usage). Numerous classic examples of the absence of a common code can be observed in intercultural relations. For example, a Japanese invited to a friend's home in Switzerland for a meal offers a chrysanthemum, considered to be one of the most beautiful flowers in Japan. Because for the Swiss this flower symbolizes bereavement, the gift may not have the desired effect. Another example of differentiated code can be found in road signs (see Figure 9.2).

Figure 9.2 *Road signs indicating a level crossing*

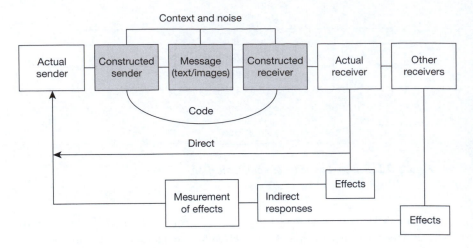

Figure 9.3 *Integrated communications model*

Although the simplified schematic diagram in Figure 9.1 shows the main elements in a communications process, it is inadequate to describe the increasing complexity of communication. Figure 9.3 shows an integrated communications model.

The first distinction to be made is in the nature of the sender and receiver (actual versus constructed sender/receiver). It is not so much an organization that issues a communication as the organization's representation of itself and the perception that receivers have of it. Depending on the message it wants to convey, and also on the image it has of itself or that it produces in others, it will make choices regarding the coding of the message (choice of text, image, sounds, etc.). The message will be conveyed through a medium whose neutrality can vary considerably (a message in a serious newspaper regarded as reliable would most certainly not be perceived in the same manner if it was placed in a popular tabloid). With regard to reception, we must also distinguish between receivers' ability to decode the message (reconstruction of the message on the basis of what they see and hear) and the potential effects on these same persons given their knowledge, experience and environment. In addition, we must also take into account other receivers who were not originally targeted but who may be reached by the communication relayed by a receiver (discussions in the family or among friends, word of mouth, etc.). The last major element to take into account is feedback, which is the message sent back to the sender by the receiver. Feedback can be direct (confirmation that the message has been received, a request for additional information, etc.) or indirect, when response to the communication is measured (someone stops smoking further to prevention messages). After taking these responses into consideration, the sender will develop, refine or suspend the communication: this is known as a feedback loop.

The communications model highlights all the major elements that make up a communication and allows us to analyse it:

- Who is the sender?
- What is the message?
- What is the instrument (means of communication) or medium?
- To whom is the message addressed?
- What are the planned and actual effects?

Boxes 9.1 and 9.2 illustrate the analyses that can be performed on the elements of communication.

■ BOX 9.1 THE EUROPEAN UNION 50TH ANNIVERSARY LOGO

To mark its 50th anniversary in 2007, the European Union launched a contest for the design of an anniversary logo, which was won by the Polish graphic designer Szymon Skrzypczak (from among over 1,700 entries) – see Plate 9.1. At the ceremony, the EU vice president, Margot Wallström, stated: 'the winning logo represents the diversity and vigour of Europe and at the same time it underlines the desired unity and solidarity of our continent' (European Union, 2006).

■ **Plate 9.1** *The European Union 50th anniversary logo*
Source: European Union.

A brief study of this logo reveals that identifying the sender is difficult since it does not carry the European Union's 'signature'. Although the coding of the message (unity in diversity) is made relatively clear through the use of characters from several different typefaces for the word 'together', it is reasonable to wonder whether those who see the logo are able to decode it and successfully identify the original message. Use of the ® symbol for the letter R came in for criticism, since in American law this would indicate that a trademark has been registered. With regard to the logo's effect, it would be interesting to study the extent to which it assisted recognition of the events that formed part of the festivities and stimulated a stronger adherence to the corresponding values.

◼ BOX 9.2 CAMPAIGN TO PROMOTE BORROWING BY THE FRENCH GOVERNMENT

◼ *Plate 9.2* *Campaign to promote borrowing*
Source: Government of France.

The advertising campaign shown in Plate 9.2 cost approximately €1 million (spent on advertising space in the press and on the web) and was sponsored by the French government to promote a €35 billion governmental loan for investment aimed at increasing France's competitiveness.

continued . . .

◼ **178**

■ **BOX 9.2 CAMPAIGN TO PROMOTE
BORROWING BY THE FRENCH
GOVERNMENT ...** *continued*

The sender (the French government) is easily identifiable thanks to the logo
and the information it contains. The message is very clear, despite its coding being
somewhat unusual for communication with the public. Allegory, a rhetorical device,
is used to reinforce the message contained in the text (the figure of Marianne
representing France and the symbol of maternity representing the future). It is
highly probable that those at whom the message was aimed – the French public
– were easily able to decode the message. Because private individuals could not
benefit from the loan, we can assume that the campaign's main aim was to inform
citizens about the decision to borrow and foster their support for this decision
and the policy that lay behind it.

COMMUNICATIONS STRATEGY

Communications strategy is an iterative process that consists of taking a series of decisions
aimed at achieving consistency between objectives and concrete measures. Very often
measures taken are not in line with objectives, either because the latter are too
ambitious in relation to available resources or because the means of communication
chosen are not suited to the messages that are intended to be conveyed. This is why
it is necessary to take a series of steps, systematically checking that each is consistent
with the others.

Figure 9.4 gives a schematic presentation of the main steps in a communications
strategy.

The eight steps of this process can be grouped into four major parts or decision
groups. The first of these contains the first step only and consists of drawing up a list
of framework conditions to restrict the decision-making margin when formulating the
strategy. The second group of decisions concerns the target groups and the objectives
to attain with these groups (steps 2 & 3). This is, naturally, the heart of the process
because the decisions taken will have an impact on all subsequent steps. The third part
includes the conception of the message and the choice of means, or instruments, of
communication (steps 4 & 5). These two elements must be considered at the same
time because they are closely linked (the choice of instrument depends on the message
to be conveyed and vice versa). The fourth and last group of steps, more operational
in nature, includes checking the communications plan and its concrete execution
and gauging its effectiveness (steps 6, 7 & 8). The following paragraphs describe the
various stages of this process in detail.

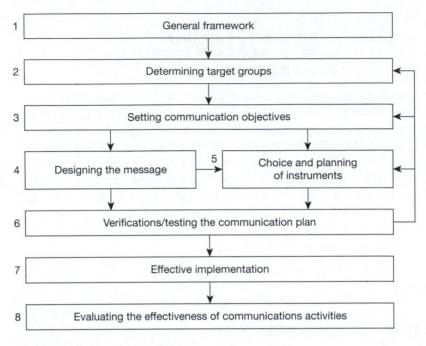

Figure 9.4 *Steps in a communications strategy*

The general framework

Before developing a new communications campaign or new measures information must be gathered so that the framework within which the communications activities will be carried out can be established. Three types of items need to be taken into account.

The first concerns the environment and the general context of the communication (including the political and social environment). Consideration must be given to other organizations that are currently communicating on the same subject or may do so later, together with their objectives and their concrete measures. Although in principle public organizations have no direct competitors that could interfere in their communications, they must check whether communications activities are being planned by other organizations at a different level of government (regional as opposed to national, for example), other organizations at the same level (another government department working on closely related subjects) or nongovernmental organizations (NGOs) whether mandated by the government or not. Different messages from different organizations risk creating confusion in the minds of recipients rather than mutual reinforcement and synergy. The State, and frequently the public sector in its entirety, are seen by some as a single interlocutor, with no distinction made between the various organizations and missions.

The second element that will influence the development of communications activities is items of information specific to the organization. First among these are the organization's policy and its past and present communications activities. These must be taken into account in order to avoid contradictions in the message and to ensure a degree of continuity. The organization's public profile and its credibility in the minds of the main recipients must be analysed. Many organizations tend to overestimate their own profile and hence their ability to persuade the public with a communications message. Lastly, formal elements of the communication must be identified and respected (visual elements such as logos and other elements of the graphic charter, organizational elements such as coordination rules and predefined or contractual elements such as the choice of certain media or certain instruments, etc.).

The last element that frames the development of communications activities is the budget. In principle, the budget should result from decisions taken at the various stages. However, because the costs of communications are high and greatly dependent on the instruments chosen it is recommended that a budget framework be set to serve as a reference for the decisions made during the process. Obviously, this budget framework should not be so restrictive as to hobble creativity during development of the message and the choice of instruments. Although optimization models for defining the budget framework exist, very often it is based on the objectives that have been set, and more often still on the experience of previous years or on the means available in the budget determined by political authorities.

Determining target groups

In the public sector, determining specific target groups can be difficult where the communication concerns all citizens and residents of the territory in question (general information for the public in a municipality, information on a vaccination campaign for H1N1 influenza, etc.). However, in many situations, aiming at a very large population group is the best way to reach nobody. Moreover, communications activities are increasingly aimed at defined target groups (professional groups such as doctors or teachers, parents of schoolchildren, residents of a district, the elderly, etc.).

In many cases, describing the people to whom the organization wishes to send a message presents no great obstacle: the real difficulty lies in the choice of media or instruments to reach them. Since all these people will not necessarily have homogeneous behaviour regarding the media they consult, target groups need to be defined on the basis of their characteristics but also on the basis of their attitudes and behaviour regarding all communications instruments and media. Let us take as an example a municipality wishing to provide regular information on the city's services and activities. Describing the target audience is easy enough (all residents), but what they read, where they go and so on need to be taken into account. The municipality could use public noticeboards or poster pillars or, in more modern fashion, electronic panels in various places, but there is no guarantee that the movements of parts of the population will take them past the displays or that they will be disposed to stop and look (see Box 9.3). On the

■ BOX 9.3 GENERAL INFORMATION FOR THE PUBLIC

During the summer of 2004, in response to high summer temperatures and ozone air pollution, a prefectoral decision was taken in the Provence Côte d'Azur region (south of France) to reduce the speed limits on roads and highways.

A number of municipalities in the region chose to inform the public of this decision by posting a copy of the prefectoral decree on the door of the town hall. While the municipality cannot be accused of having failed to communicate the decision, it is a safe bet that almost nobody took the time to stop in front of the town hall and read the entire text. Luckily, the media relayed the decision to some extent and people passing through the region were informed by electronic signs on the highways.

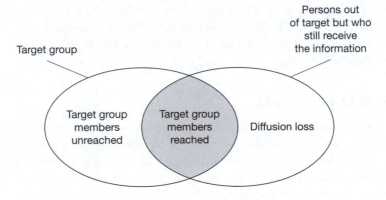

■ *Figure 9.5* Target group reached and dispersion loss

other hand, people outside the municipality may regularly see this information that is of no relevance to them.

This means it is important to define target groups in such a way that they can be reached by communications activities while minimizing diffusion loss – that is, the number of people reached who do not belong to the target group. Figure 9.5 illustrates the problem.

Setting communications objectives

Once communications targets have been defined, the next step is to set communications objectives. These are derived from the model developed by Elias St-Elmo Lewis in

1898 (Barry, 1987) and summed up by the formula AIDA (Attention – Interest – Desire – Action). In other words, a communication must first attract attention (be visible), then elicit interest in its content before provoking desire. Finally, action, or the behavioural aspect, is the ultimate objective. Many other models for achieving communications effectiveness have been developed, including the DAGMAR model (Defining Advertising Goals for Measured Advertising Results, Colley, 1961).

Although the basis of these models is valid for the public sector, it needs to be adapted for two main reasons. First, the ultimate objective is not to induce a person to make a purchase, which is the main goal of business communications. Second, these models have been designed as a series of steps to be taken, whereas public communications may be perfectly content with 'only' attaining the first level (simply transmitting information without any further objective). Table 9.1 sets out the various types of objectives of public communications together with the main levels to be considered.

Knowledge, or basic information, is the first type of objective to consider. Organizations need to provide basic information on activities, events or actions (appointment of a new manager, report on activities, etc.). With regard to services, the same type of objective will be aimed at providing information on the content of the service, its accessibility and so on. Very often, public organizations can restrict themselves to conveying very basic information so that recipients have the required information when needed. But it is vitally important for an organization to provide at least this minimum amount of information in order to give it and its services a degree of visibility and to simplify matters for beneficiaries.

The second type of objective goes further than simple dissemination of information and is aimed at legitimizing public action. This might involve explaining and justifying the reasons for a decision, setting out the pros and cons of a project (temporary inconvenience for nearby residents) or presenting the main characteristics of a new service (explaining to foreign investors the fiscal benefits of setting up in business in the region). In many countries, the introduction of biometric passports has stirred up a lively civil-society debate. Political and administrative authorities have been obliged to explain in the media and in a variety of documents exactly what data are gathered, why it is no longer possible in many cases to supply one's own photographs, what the State intends to do with the information gathered, who is entitled to consult this information and so on. It is clear that in cases like this the organization must go beyond simply making information available and instead educate the public and be responsive (frequent repetition of easily understood messages).

The third type of communications objective is more complex because it is aimed at helping to create or modify attitudes towards an organization or a project, or at creating a climate of trust. Suppose that asbestos is discovered in a school building. Even though the risks to children may be nil, the public organization cannot limit itself to providing information and explaining the situation. It must in addition ensure that a climate of trust is created in order to ensure that the attitude of students, parents and organizations concerned remains constructive. For example, every week it could inform the public of readings taken by a recognized company even if specialists consider

183 ▪

Table 9.1 Objectives of public communications

	Objectives levels	Basic information	Further knowledge and understanding	Attitude/opinion	Preference/behaviour
External communication	Organization	Knowledge of the life of the organization (project) outside the organization	Knowledge and legitimization of the organization (project) in socio-economic-political life	Attitude/opinion (confidence)	Adherence to the interests and values promoted by the organization
	Projects			Attitude/opinion (guarantee, security, proximity)	Adherence to the project
	Services	Knowledge of the service and its content, benefits and accessibility	Recognition of a service and its main attributes	Attitude towards the service or brand (brand image)	Preferences, trials, purchases, repeat purchases
Internal communication	Collaborators	Knowledge of the life of the organization and its actions and commitments	Identification with the life of the organization (involvement)	Pride, sense of belonging	Loyalty, active advocacy of the organization, particularly outside the organization

this measure to be completely unnecessary. In the same way, it could provide regular updates on progress in the renovation project (public information sessions, press briefings, newsletter sent to parents, etc.) even if very little new concrete information is available. All these communications measures will be mainly designed to reassure people and to prevent them from developing an overly critical attitude towards the organization. As far as collaborators are concerned, these communications objectives will consist in creating a sense of belonging, developing their pride in working for the organization and thus adopting values specific to the culture of the organization. The case of the soccer World Cup in Germany provides an interesting example. The country seized the opportunity of hosting a large-scale sporting event to act on its brand image through the image that the Germans have of themselves. An internal campaign involving numerous government, economic and social institutions succeeded in substantially improving the straight-laced, serious image, tinged with the shame of past nationalist violence, that was generally associated with the country. The enthusiasm, openness and tolerance shown by the Germans combined with flawless organization of the event to project a more positive and more up-to-date image of the country (Dinnie, 2008).

The final type of objective that can be aimed for in communications terms is a change in behaviour or, at least, the establishment of stated preferences. This is, obviously, the main goal of marketing businesses. For public organizations, this objective comes into play particularly in prevention campaigns aimed at changing people's behaviour (wearing seat belts, stopping smoking, using condoms to prevent transmission of the AIDS virus, urging people to get out and vote, and so on), but also in cases where an active behaviour is sought from the target audience (for parents: providing better support for their children's schooling; for all residents: watching out for elderly neighbours or friends during heatwaves). The issue here is for the public to adhere to the values and attitudes put forward by the organization, to actively support a project or, with regard to services, to try them and to use them appropriately. As for the organization's collaborators, the main aim is to make them into advocates of the organization and its values and activities. Because of the large number of active collaborators in the public sector (teachers, police officers, other civil servants), it is important that they should contribute freely to explaining the organization's activities and changes that have been made, thus becoming, in a sense, promoters of the organization. Of course, they need to be correctly informed in advance and convinced of the worth of the organization's activities and the values.

Although each communications objective can be considered on its own, it must not be forgotten that, in order to attain emotional and behavioural objectives, a good basic knowledge of the organization or its services is vital. Box 9.4 provides a clear illustration of this.

Designing the message

Designing a communications message often demands creativity and precision, particularly if the message is complex and must be conveyed through advertising media

■ BOX 9.4 SCHOOL MEALS GUIDELINES

Childhood obesity in Western countries is generally seen as a public health problem. In France, one child in five is considered to be overweight.

To remedy this problem, in 2001 the French government ministers concerned (national education, health, agriculture) drafted an official memo (*circulaire*) 'on the composition of meals served in school cafeterias and on food safety'. Five years later a survey of 784 schools revealed that more than 40 per cent of these establishments had never, or only vaguely, heard of the memo. Source: *Le Canard Enchaîné,* 28.03.2007

Very often, sending an item of information only once is not sufficient to convey the desired message and produce a change in behaviour. The message must be repeated frequently and disseminated on a variety of media. Checks must also be carried out to see that it has been received properly so that, where necessary, the measures taken can be corrected.

(newspaper advertisements, posters in the street, etc.). Without downplaying their importance, the creative aspects can be accompanied and guided by considering the objectives of the message and its content in relation to the motivation of the target groups.

Three main questions must be asked about the message:

■ What will recipients get from the communication? In other words, what benefits will derived from absorbing the message?

■ What will make recipients change their perception, opinion or behaviour in one way or another?

■ What is the tone or general impression conveyed by the communication? Is it highly official, austere in its choice of words and visuals, or is it more playful, with drawings, pictograms and a message that is easy and enjoyable to read?

Let us take as an example a municipality that has adopted a new policy for waste collection and management (all household waste must be sorted into categories each having a specific collection system, residents to be charged by weight for waste that cannot be recycled but must be incinerated, etc.). The municipality will certainly have to develop a communications campaign to inform the public of its new policy and, above all, of all the consequences for residents (information in the media, public information sessions, detailed brochure for residents, flyers giving an overview of the most important information, posters at collection sites, etc.). Depending on the region, some of these communications measures may have to be translated into other languages to make sure that the people concerned are correctly informed (Spanish in certain American states, English in some districts of highly cosmopolitan cities, etc.).

The recipients of the messages should understand the municipality's main reasons for adopting this policy (the benefits for all residents) and especially should have all the information they need to minimize the inconvenience that sorting will bring. Those who take in the various messages must then take on board the elements encouraging them or obliging them to change their behaviour. As regards the form, the organization will have to decide whether to opt for a mainly technical presentation of information with all the necessary details, or use a more playful form, possibly with cartoons or pictograms allowing everybody to understand the new principles for sorting and collection of waste. For example, a regional taxation authority in Switzerland includes cartoons in its documentation that explains to individuals how to fill in their tax returns.

Other elements will help in the design of the message and shape the attitude of its recipients. Two criteria should be taken into consideration (Rossiter and Percy, 1987): people's interest in the subject (involvement) and their motivation with regard to the organization or its services.

If the degree of involvement or interest is low, communication must be very simple, get straight to the point and avoid any kind of rhetorical language removed from the needs of people. On the other hand, if the degree of involvement is high and people are ready for and interested in the information, the organization can develop it further, providing all the necessary information even where this is quite technical.

The second criterion is motivation which, simply put, can be either negative or positive. Negative motivation involves a situation in which a person is interested in information or a service in order to resolve a problem or because they have no choice (buying cleaning products, taking out car insurance) while positive motivation arises in situations where people freely buy a service to satisfy a pleasurable desire (e.g. going on vacation). In the public sector, situations are most frequently linked with negative motivation (requesting authorization, paying taxes, calling an emergency service, etc.), although situations involving more positive motivation do arise (children's education, developing the tourism sector or setting up businesses, etc.). In negative situations, the recommended approach is to communicate in a rational manner while also highlighting the benefits (for example, explaining the purpose of taxation). Where the motivation is positive, a more emotive style of communication making use of figures of speech can be envisaged (see the example in Box 9.2).

Choice and planning of instruments

The choice of instruments is closely bound up with the message. A highly complex message will normally require the use of instruments involving prolonged contact with the recipient (information session, a brochure that can be read several times, etc.) while basic messages can be conveyed on media where the contact time is shorter (posters, flyers, letters to the household, etc.).

Whether one or several communications instruments and media are chosen depends on a number of criteria, the most important of which are set out here:

187 ■

■ *Audience, or capacity to reach target groups:* this is the percentage of people in the target group having at least one chance of contact with the medium in a defined period. For example, if an organization has the names and addresses of all those it wishes to reach, it is relatively simple to send a brochure to those people and secure an audience of close to 100 per cent. On the other hand, obtaining the addresses of all young people to whom an organization might wish to send an AIDS prevention message is impossible. This means that other instruments and media must be chosen and attempts must be made to minimize the risk of dispersion loss.

■ *Frequency:* this means the average number of contacts that a person will have with a medium during a defined period. Some messages are very easy to understand and a single reading or viewing will suffice. A message that is – like most – more complex needs to be repeated frequently in order to be understood and assimilated.

■ *Period and duration:* the timing of the message and continuity in its dissemination are also important. During the weeks that followed the attacks of 11 September 2001, many messages from public organizations went unnoticed because people were mainly focused on discussions about security policies and the human and geopolitical consequences of these attacks. Lighter subjects – such as maintenance of forest and natural spaces – and special initiatives should try to benefit from periods of the year when current affairs take up less space in the media (school holidays and summer holidays) in order to gain more notice.

■ *Credibility of the medium:* in communications, the medium or channel of transmission is often as important as the meaning or content of the message itself (see McLuhan, 1964's assertion that 'the medium is the message'). The importance of the medium and its credibility in the eyes of target groups can therefore determine whether the message is received. For example, a report on environmental protection broadcast on a television channel recognized as being serious may have greater effect than flyers deposited in residents' letterboxes.

■ *Control over content:* organizations can choose between developing and hence paying for their own medium, purchasing space in a medium (paid advertising) or organizing communications in such a way that the medium itself relays the information in its editorial sections. In the last case, the organization can control the information made available to the media, but not the media's treatment of it. In the other two situations mentioned, the organization retains complete control over form and content.

The main instruments are presented in Chapter 11.

Testing the communications plan and evaluating the effectiveness of communications activities

A clear distinction must be drawn between two steps: testing the communications plan and gauging the effectiveness of the communication.

When any communications plan is developed – even when it is limited to presenting a public policy measure in a press conference or a press release – a check of the concept and a test of this communication with recipients are recommended. Testing the concept consists mainly of ensuring consistency in all the decisions taken in the previous steps. Is the message well-suited to the communications objective? Does the choice of instruments comply with internal rules regarding communications? Will the available budget and the choice of instruments allow the desired continuity in the dissemination of the message? These and other questions are designed to prevent gross errors being made and effectiveness been compromised by lack of consistency. It is also essential to test the message on target groups before going into production with the campaign's documents and materials. Certainly, for budgetary and/or time reasons, it is often impossible to arrange a pre-test involving a representative sample of the target audience. However, it is always possible to have a press release read by two or three people who are unfamiliar with the topic discussed or to organize a focus group to make comparison judgements between various draft advertisements or circulars. Although this type of summary check will not reveal every possible problematic detail, it will very often prevent errors with more serious consequences (incompatible message, too much importance attached to secondary information, message too complex or too abstract, etc.). If the budget set aside for the communication is large or if means are available then carrying out a professional pre-test of communications measures is strongly recommended.

Effectiveness testing is very often given very little credit in the whole communications process. One reason that is often advanced to explain the lack of resources devoted to this task is the difficulty of assessing the effectiveness of communications activities. Yet it is surprising to note the ease with which millions may be paid to secure spots on television or radio or to take part in a major event (country pavilions at universal exhibitions, for example) and the difficulty with which small budgets are granted to assess a few basic effects of communication (number of people reached, comprehension of the message, suitability of the medium for the message, etc.). The small amounts invested in gauging the effectiveness of a communication are most often explained by a lack of interest in a past event ('look towards the future'), the fear of being faced with unsatisfactory results, the need to interpret these results and thus devote time to doing so and the need to accept criticism. And yet measures that may be quite simple, when carried out regularly, will produce very useful lessons and make it possible to continually improve the communications measures taken by public organizations (see Chapter 12).

INTEGRATED COMMUNICATIONS

Mainly as the result of the increasing numbers of communications media and the growing difficulty and cost of reaching target audiences, the concept of integrated communications (from Integrated Marketing Communications, IMC) is increasingly being applied systematically by private companies and gradually being adopted by public organizations. The aim is to achieve consistency in all communications activities for the purpose of improving their effectiveness (Belch and Belch, 2006; Schultz, 1996; Bruhn, 2006).

More and more organizations are communicating on the same subject at the same time (prevention initiatives, for example), using increasingly varied media. To guarantee highly effective use of the means at their disposal, organizations must, in developing a communications strategy, ensure consistency and coherence in all communications activities (Bruhn, 2006):

- *Consistency of form:* this is often the most basic type of consistency, achieved through the integrated use of all formal elements of a communication (logos, typeface and font size, colours, images used, etc.) independently of the medium used. The principal objective is quick, clear identification of the issuer of the message and easy reading of the content.
- *Consistency of content:* this involves making the various messages consistent by coordinating the objectives, using similar logical arguments and repeating the same message for the duration so that it is understood. Typically, for communications aimed at prevention or at modifying people's behaviour (encouraging cyclists to wear helmets, and drivers to take regular breaks on long journeys, etc.), the same message with clear arguments must be stated consistently and in a coordinated fashion by organizations devoted to prevention, companies that manage highway infrastructures (electronic signs on autoroutes, for example) and the police.
- *Consistency of timing:* if several media and instruments are used in the same period, close coordination is very important in order to allow mutual reinforcement of communications activities. Unfortunately, examples of bad timing abound, with campaigns failing not as a result of the objectives or the message but of poor coordination (an item in the media sends people to a website to order a brochure or service, but the site is not yet ready or the link is broken; an advertising campaign designed to reinforce the message of television spots with a simplified repetition of the basic message is inserted a month after the spots have ended, etc.).

The integration of communications activities must form part of the whole communications process, from defining the general framework (setting formal rules) through to checking the effectiveness of measures taken (analysis of mutual reinforcement of measures, for example).

EXERCISE 9.1

Take three recent communications initiatives made by a single public organization. For each, try to evaluate the various communications objectives based on the elements presented in Table 9.1. Having selected one specific issue, look at the variation across campaigns in the other aspects presented in Figure 9.1 – the message, the receiver, the code and the context. Do these elements vary according to the objectives identified?

DISCUSSION QUESTIONS

1   Consider a public communications campaign you are familiar with. Can you identify: a) the sender; b) the message; c) the intended audience; and d) the expected effects?
2   A communications strategy implies a degree of coordination of communications efforts across government agencies. What might be some of the difficulties in developing such an approach?

REFERENCES

Barry, T. (1987) The Development of the Hierarchy of Effects: An Historical Perspective, *Current Issues & Research in Advertising*, 10, 251–295.

Belch, G. E. and Belch, M. A. (2006) *Advertising and Promotion: An Integrated Marketing Communications Perspective*, Boston, McGraw-Hill.

Bruhn, M. (2006) *Integrierte Unternehmens-und Markenkommunikation*, Schäffer-Poeschel.

Colley, R. H. (1961) *Defining Advertising Goals for Measured Advertising Results*, New York, Association of National Advertisers.

Dinnie, K. (2008) *Nation Branding: Concepts, Issues, Practice*, Burlington, Butterworth Heinemann.

European Union (2006) EU 50th Birthday Logo Selected. Online at http://europa.eu/rapid/pressReleasesAction.do?reference=IP/06/1415 (accessed 26 July 2011).

Gerbner, G. (1955) *Toward a Theory of Communication*, Los Angeles, University of Southern California.

Jakobson, R. (1963) *Essais de Linguistique Générale*, Paris, Editions de Minuit.

Lasswell, H. D. (1927) *Propaganda Techniques in the World War*, Cambridge, Massachussets, MIT Press.

—— (1948) *Power and Personality*, New York, W.W. Norton.

McLuhan, M. (1964) *Understanding Media: The Extensions of Man*, New York, McGraw-Hill.

Rossiter, J. R. and Percy, L. (1987) *Advertising and Promotion Management*, New York, McGraw-Hill.

Schultz, D. E. (1996) *The New Marketing Paradigm: Integrated Marketing Communications*, New York, McGraw-Hill.

Weaver, W. and Shannon, C. E. (1963) *The Mathematical Theory of Communication*, Illinois, University of Illinois Press.

Chapter 10

Communications instruments

LEARNING OBJECTIVES

By the end of this chapter you should be able to:

- Understand the characteristics and uses of various communications instruments.
- Evaluate communications instruments according to their nature (direct or mediated) and target audience (internal, prescribers, general public).
- Identify the key points of media relations for public-sector organizations.
- Classify the internet-based communications instruments of your organization.

KEY POINTS OF THIS CHAPTER

- Organizations use different communications instruments, both direct and mediated, depending on the target audience (internal, prescribers, general public) and the resources available (financial, human resources, etc.).
- Advertising has long been used by governments. Careful coordination of the actors involved, due consideration for budgetary matters and proper integration of the various media are essential.
- Media relations are essential for organizations aiming at reaching a large and diverse audience. They can be developed using various tools, including press releases, press conferences and press briefings.
- E-government initiatives need to be well planned and coordinated to achieve their full potential. Considerations specific to public-sector organizations mean that internet-based communications can only supplement, and not replace, other communications instruments.

KEY TERMS

Classical advertising – the traditional tool of communications using one or more media such as radio, print, television or the internet to convey a message. This approach allows direct targeting of the general public or a subgroup of citizens.

Media relations – the goal of media relations is to ensure that the media relay information on behalf of an organization. This involves targeting the media as key interlocutors.

E-government – the use of information technology by governments to enhance the quality and accessibility of their services. E-government splits into several categories, chiefly e-administration and e-democracy.

INTRODUCTION

Communications activities involve the use of various instruments. As in marketing, the instruments used are well known, but their choice, the way they are combined, the timing and the intensity of their use, and the degree of professionalism employed differ from one organization to another.

Because such a wide range of instruments is available, we begin this chapter by presenting an overview before exploring a smaller number of instruments in greater detail: classical advertising, media relations and internet communications.

AN OVERVIEW OF PUBLIC-COMMUNICATIONS INSTRUMENTS

A number of ways of classifying communications instruments have been proposed, using various criteria (Zikmund and D'Amico, 1993; Rossiter and Percy, 1987; Hartley and Pickton, 1999; Pickton and Broderick, 2005; Bruhn, 2009). The most widely used criterion is the distinction between direct, or personal, communications instruments and indirect, or mediated, instruments – those that require a medium. Direct communications instruments are those where information is transmitted directly through personal contact (bilateral or group discussions, lectures, seminars, presentations, etc.) with or without the use of a medium (paper document, electronic medium, etc.). Indirect communications, on the other hand, use a medium to convey information (newspaper, press release, website, etc.) – hence the descriptor 'mediated'. In this case there is no direct personal contact between the emitter of the message and the receiver. The second classification criterion is target audience(s). In public communications, three target groups are differentiated: members of the organization (internal communications), deciders and prescribers (persons and organizations that have a direct impact on the public policy at issue) and, lastly, the general public.

Other criteria have also been proposed in the literature. For example, a distinction can be made between individualized communications (where the content and even the form is adapted to each recipient) and mass communications (where a single message per medium is addressed globally to all recipients). A further distinction can be made between unilateral communications – with no possibility of observing a direct reaction from the receivers – and bilateral or multilateral communications where the issuer can, through the questions or reactions of those present, respond to and interact with them.

Table 10.1 combines the two main criteria to classify the main communications instruments relevant to the public sector. Personal communications addressed to members of the organization essentially consist of individual or group interviews, work sessions and conferences. These classical tools allow every organization to convey accurate, detailed, interactive information. Under the pressure of time, managers frequently fail to construct messages properly, to coordinate the timing of messages intended for staff and external messages (ideally, messages to staff should be released earlier) and to repeat essential information. Sometimes, when particular items of information are highly complex and difficult to communicate, seminars conducted by people from outside and/or inside the institution can be organized. This may be done when a major change for the organization is envisaged, for example when the status of the organization is modified (an administrative body is transformed into a more independent agency).

Communications for staff is completed by other instruments based on written or electronic media. Chief among these are letters and e-mails, memos, in-house journals, noticeboards and the intranet. Added to these instruments may be documents intended for, for example, new members of staff (brochure on the organization, summary of current rules, etc.).

Communications aimed at deciders and important partners of the organization are one of the peculiar features of the public sector. The taking and implementation of decisions in the public sector are governed by rules that are very different from those of the private sector (length of the decision-making process, need to achieve consensus, legal procedures, number and diversity of partners, trade-off between policy rationale and economic rationale, etc.). As a result, public organizations must identify partners who are important for their actions and ensure that many of their communications activities are targeted. For example, a department in charge of regional policy on forests must take regional factors into consideration (in mountainous areas, forests serve a protective function and a high forest density will contribute to fulfilling this purpose, whereas in drier, fire-prone regions scrub must be cleared to prevent the spread of fires and protect dwellings). This department will thus have to work closely with owners of forests (both private owners and local communities) and municipalities in order to raise the awareness of political deciders so that resources are assigned to these tasks. For this purpose, regular discussions, presentations and sessions to inform partners are important, as is maintaining personal contacts in formal and informal settings (in the case of a difficult or complex situation, relationships of trust with main partners can facilitate the implementation of a policy). But because personal contacts take up the time of many resources, indirect instruments are also widely used because they allow

Table 10.1 *The main public communications instruments*

	Direct, personal communications	Indirect or mediated communications
Staff or members of the organization	Speeches, oral messages	Letters and e-mails
	Personal interviews	Memos
	Work sessions	Bulletin boards
	Training seminars	In-house journal
		Intranet
		Documents about the organization
Deciders/prescribers and important partners	Personal interview	Letters and e-mails
	Testimony before a commission	Presentation kit
	Personal relations	Annual report, historical works
		Information letter and technical notes
General public	Trade fairs and shows	Advertisements
	Events (open days, anniversaries, etc.)	Information letters, corporate journals, historical works
		Sponsoring
		Media relations (press release, press conference, press briefings, interviews, participation in debates)
		Internet communications
		Documents on the organization, multimedia presentations
		Promotions
		Social networks

large quantities of more technical information to be provided in a permanent, structured manner. In addition to the instruments mentioned earlier, newsletters in paper or electronic form can be highly useful, giving effective back-up over time, provided that they bring true added value information and are published regularly.

Lastly, the general public. As the activities and tasks handed over to the public sector have grown, along with demands from all citizens and accountability requirements, public-sector organizations are devoting increasing amounts of resources to communications activities aimed at the entire population. Because of the numbers of people targeted in these activities and their cost, indirect communications instruments using external media are greatly preferred. Among these, media relations, advertisements and the internet constitute the virtually indispensable foundations of public communications. And yet, particularly because the media are free to choose what topics they wish to cover and how, and because these instruments do not allow direct contact with the target audience, there has been a revival of interest in personal communications instruments. Among these, participation in trade fairs and shows and the holding of open days are widely used by public-sector organizations (see Box 10.1).

■ BOX 10.1 OPEN DAY FOR JUSTICE

As part of the European Day of Civil Justice in 2004, the civil justice department of the Canton of Fribourg, Switzerland, organized an open day. For the organizers, the main aim of the day was to help the public realize that justice is a service available to citizens for settling private disputes and asserting their rights.

For an entire Saturday, all courts were open to the public and the following activities were organized:

- guided tour of premises
- fictitious trial using actors
- presentation of civil justice
- talks by judges
- free legal consultations
- opportunity to interact with judges and lawyers.

In addition to these activities for the public, on the previous day pupils from about 20 school classes attended a moot trial organized for the purpose.

Source: Swiss Canton of Fribourg (2004).

CLASSICAL ADVERTISING

Advertising is a nonpersonal form of communication using media generally designed for conveying news in order to disseminate messages that are declared to be advertisements. The use of these media requires payment and the advertiser retains control over the content disseminated.

Advertising in the modern sense of the term appeared in 1836 when Émile de Girardin first inserted into his newspaper commercial announcements in order to bring down the price and extend his readership (Thérenty and Vaillant, 2001). Billboards in the early twentieth century, followed by radio, cinema and television, subsequently generalized the use of information media for conveying advertising. More recently, advertising has strongly marked the development of new electronic media such as the internet. Today, virtually all media derive a substantial portion of their income from advertising. In France, a ban on advertising on public-service channels between 8pm and 6am was introduced in 2009. The revenue shortfall of about €450 million was largely offset by an increase in the amount of the government subsidy.

Until relatively recently, governments limited the use of advertising for both budgetary and political reasons, since advertising was deemed to be manipulative. But in recent decades advertising has been increasingly used by governments, particularly for prevention and awareness activities (see Box 10.2) but also for very diverse purposes such as informing citizens of their rights and duties, promoting certain behaviours (energy saving, integration of immigrants), the promotion of government services or reputation development (see examples in Box 10.3).

■ BOX 10.2 GOVERNMENT ADVERTISING IN SINGAPORE

The government of Singapore is the country's biggest advertiser, with close to 50 per cent of the market, and develops communications campaigns with a strong advertising component for subjects as diverse as:

- speaking more Mandarin
- speaking better English (http://www.goodenglish.org.sg/)
- being more polite
- not gambling
- being punctual.

One of the newest communications campaigns of the Ministry of Community Development, Youth and Sports will be aimed at boosting the rates of marriage and birth in the country. This follows the finding that many young women and men aged between 20 and 35 are not looking for lasting relationships in a highly competitive professional world. This initiative, which will begin with a series of television commercials, follows other campaigns entitled 'Romancing Singapore' to celebrate love and 'Superbly Imperfect' to spread the message that searching for an absolutely perfect partner is illusory.

Source: Singapore Ministry of Community Development, Youth and Sport (n.d.).

■ BOX 10.3 COMMUNICATIONS CAMPAIGNS IN CANADA

The federal government of Canada announced its Economic Action Plan through a media blitz worth CAD49.5 million. The initiative was aimed at communicating a plan that 'Provides $62 billion over two years to help protect and create jobs and invest in future prosperity'. The communication instruments used included a website (http://www.actionplan.gc.ca), television ads, a series of press conferences and briefings, radio ads and numerous project announcements.

For the same year the mass vaccination campaign against the H1N1 virus came in at CAD24.1 million. In this case, the same approach was taken with a specific focus on prescriber groups (doctors and nurses) and a more important reliance on new media (Facebook, Twitter, etc.)

Source: Public Health Agency of Canada (n.d.).

There are several facts to be aware of before conducting a classical advertising campaign. First, advertising involves a number of actors whose interactions should be controlled. These will include, at the least, a communications agency tasked with designing the campaign and producing advertisements (ads, film clips, posters, banners, etc.) and the advertising media used to disseminate the ads (newspapers, television, radio, websites, etc.). Depending on the size of the budget and the complexity of the campaign, other actors will also intervene, such as a media agency, specialized agencies, communications consultants and so on. Coordinating all these actors, as called for by the objectives of integrated communications, is imperative.

A second important element is the cost of campaigns. For the 2009–10 period the Australian government spent some AUD114 million through its central Advertising System; for 2009 the Canadian government spent some CAD130 million (Australian Government, 2011; Leblanc, 2010). Unless advertisements are limited to a small number of regional media with a very restricted number of broadcasts, classical advertising campaigns often cost several million euros. For example, in 2010 a full-page ad in *Le Monde* cost €126,000, and in *The New York Times* USD107,000. This means that campaigns must be managed professionally in order to achieve their objectives. Unfortunately, all too often insufficient preparation (e.g. overly general briefing, failure to take into account previous campaigns and their results) or a failure of coordination regarding dissemination on various media leads to disappointing results. In addition, since large sums of money are at issue, public organizations must comply with the rules for the awarding of public contracts.

There are complex choices to be made regarding media exposure. The number of possibilities for placing an advertisement, a commercial or a poster is extremely high, and all media actively seek to acquire business. At the same time, not all media can reach certain target groups or attain certain specific communications objectives.

Table 10.2 compares the main advertising media in terms of criteria such as availability, ability to reach specific target groups and cost. Because the media context varies greatly from one country to another, the importance of individual media for placing advertising can vary considerably. For example, the costs of advertising on classical media for 2008 totalled close to €60 billion in Italy and €33 billion in Germany. In Germany, spending on television advertising represents 40 per cent of total advertising expenditure on traditional media, as against only 28 per cent in France (Goldbach, 2009). In addition, with the continuing development of the internet and mobile media, the distribution of advertising budgets between various media is bound to continue changing in the coming years. The Global Entertainment and Media Outlook: 2010–14 survey showed that in 2009 the electronic advertising (e-advertising) market in the United States was already equivalent to the press advertising market (about $24 billion). It predicted that by 2014 e-advertising will have risen to $34 billion, with press advertising falling to about $22 billion (PriceWaterhouseCoopers, 2009).

Generally, a combination of media is chosen, with one main medium and one or two complementary media. For example, depending on the advertising objectives, television can be chosen to convey a basic message (with an investment representing 60–70 per cent of the budget) and billboards and internet as complementary media acting as simple reminders and repetitions of the message in the following weeks (about 10–15 per cent of the budget for each medium).

MEDIA RELATIONS

While advertising uses the media by purchasing part of their space in order to place an advertisement or a commercial, the purpose of media relations is to inform the media so that they convey all or part of a message as part of their normal business.

Economically, politically and socially, the media play a crucial role in our societies. Naturally they carry considerable economic weight and competition between them is increasingly intense. They constitute what de Tocqueville as early as 1835 called the 'fourth estate' (de Tocqueville, 1992 [1835]) in our democracies, alongside the legislative, executive and judiciary powers, referring to their capacity to exert control over political and public activities and influence opinion by virtue of the fact that they are the public's main source of information (the vast majority of the information at our disposal has been conveyed by the media and does not come from direct contact with the persons or organizations concerned).

With the liberalization of the media and the partial or complete privatization of radio and television, in most countries the media are completely independent of public institutions, and work independently. Consequently, it is important to know the rules governing media relations before making use of the main tools available – press releases, press conferences and press briefings.

Table 10.2 Comparative criteria of advertising media

Criteria	Press	Television	Cinema	Radio	Billboards	Internet
Availability	High	Often limited by law	Limited	Often limited by law	Limited surface area	Limited availability
Possibilities for targeting specific groups	Possible for large groups	Very limited	Limited	Very limited	Not possible	Possible for large target groups
Absolute costs (including production)	Moderate	High	Moderate	Low to moderate	Low	Low
Costs per person reached	Moderate to high	Moderate	High	Low	Low	Low to moderate
Environmental conditions	Editorial and advertising content mixed	Separate commercial breaks	Commercial period before the film	Separate commercial breaks	Purely advertising	Web and advertising content mixed

Note: The rating of these criteria may differ from one country to another depending on each medium's importance and the number of representatives, and on historical and legal situations peculiar to each country.

Source: Based on Steffenhagen (2000) and Bruhn (1997).

Rules for communication with the media

The media are businesses, mostly private, whose goal is to provide information and entertainment services to generally quite broad audiences. The costs of media production and broadcasting are so high that they must address a wide audience in order to be profitable or to fulfil the public-service mission assigned to them.

One of the first elements to take into consideration is that the media have their own business model (objectives, priorities, specific target groups, etc.), their own method of producing news and technical considerations that place large constraints on the treatment of information: in the written media, journalists will be given a maximum number of lines in which to cover the chosen article; on television, it is rare for stories in the TV news broadcast to exceed two or three minutes; on radio, information bulletins during the day are no longer than a few minutes. These constraints therefore force journalists to select a limited number of subjects and to focus on the essential points of each.

As the number and diversity of the media have grown, with their globalization, and with new information technologies that for little over a decade have made it possible to communicate in real time from any point on the globe, competition between media has increased strongly, and finding exclusive information that enables organizations to set themselves apart from the competition has become increasingly difficult. At the same time, the number of organizations striving to communicate through the media is also growing constantly, and most organizations – whether private, public or non-profit – are seeking to gain media visibility to raise their profile and improve their reputation. As an example, Associated Press, the largest and oldest international press agency, which supplies news information to its customers (the media) for publishing or broadcasting, produces dispatches in several languages totalling more than 20 million words every day (Rüttimann, 2006). It is therefore hardly surprising that a very large number of press releases and press conferences organized by governments are not relayed by the media: it is simply impossible for them to deal with the entire mass of information made available to them every day.

Similarly, because they have to satisfy readers, listeners, viewers or internet users who are ever more demanding and have a wide choice of news outlets, the media look for new subjects, exclusive information, different angles and sometimes 'juicy' information on people or organizations for their front pages. The adage 'nobody writes about trains that run on time' is very relevant here, explaining why many people attempting to communicate on certain topics are disappointed to find that they are ignored in the media. During the disastrous flooding in Pakistan in August 2010, many media organizations devoted articles to the dangers of epidemics, of cholera in particular, threatening the population. At the same time, an epidemic of cholera affecting thousands of people in central Africa was completely ignored by the media.

These general characteristics mean that it is essential to be aware of a few principles or rules that govern media relations. First, the independence of the media has to be accepted. The media are free to choose what information they cover and how, and

201

this independence, although sometimes abused, is necessary both from a political and democratic viewpoint and from an economic viewpoint (media that are tied to a government struggle to survive).

It is also necessary to know and anticipate the needs of the media. Each medium has its own rhythm and its own structure. Peak times for audiovisual media are midday and evening, while newspapers are generally distributed in the morning. Therefore the time when a news item is released will dictate that certain media will cover it in depth while others will lose interest or will publish it as a brief item because it has already been covered elsewhere. In addition, the media frequently need complementary elements such as pictures, video footage, eyewitness accounts, interviews and so on, because raw news is insufficient to guarantee editorial coverage. The availability of such complementary elements often determines whether the message is followed up and obtains sufficient visibility in relation to other topics covered.

Organizations that seek to have a message conveyed by the media must be ready to face controversy and unpleasantness. Critical questions and scrutiny are to be expected. This kind of interaction may prove trying, but to reject it will almost certainly encourage the media to focus on problem areas – or to lose interest in the subject completely.

Information must be active and clear. In the world of politics and in the public sector it is very difficult to keep information confidential. Demands for accountability, the interest of the public and the media in public affairs, political machinations and influence mean that much information, when not released officially, comes to the notice of the media via leaks. As a result it is very often wise to arrange for proactive disclosure of information, since failing to do so lays one open to criticism for attempting to hide information or events. In addition, the information must be clearly understandable to nonspecialists. Technical data and jargon risk causing the media to deal with the subject in a highly limited fashion at best, and to provide misleading or very incomplete information at worst.

It is vital to maintain regular direct contacts with the media. Managers of public organizations may sometimes view media relations with great reluctance, agreeing to make contact only when necessary. But, without necessarily developing relationships of connivance, regular meetings with media representatives in informal settings can allow them to acquire basic knowledge of the organization and its activities. Covering a complex subject will be much easier if the basic elements are known and if some grounding in the subject has been given.

Lastly, keeping some distance from information conveyed by the media may be a wise course. Information is often transient, and most people who hear or read it have usually forgotten about it within a few days. As a result, it is better to avoid arguing detailed points of editorial coverage, and to concentrate instead on the heart of the message.

Public communications through the media – although difficult, given the above (nonexhaustive) list of rules – is indispensable for reasons of speed, cost and the fulfilment of governments' basic mission. Speed, because the media can process possibly complex information virtually instantaneously (both the internet and the radio can broadcast an important news item in moments). Cost, because it would frequently be impossible to communicate general information to the entire population using government media. Respect for the basic mission, lastly, because only the media are able to reach a very broad segment of the population in all regions and thereby keep them informed of public and legal affairs and fuel democratic debate.

Tools for media relations

We have seen that informal contacts are an integral part of media relations. But four main tools are used in more formal, systematic relations: press releases, press conferences, reports and briefings.

Press releases are a very widely used tool in public communications because they enable summary information on a specific subject (an official appointment, a decision of an authority, a particular event, etc.) to be provided rapidly. They normally consist of a short, easily accessible text sent to all the media organizations concerned (normally those having accredited journalists). Based on the press release, the media can then relay the information without special coverage and without going into the topic in greater depth (by searching for further information or questioning other actors concerned). Box 10.4 sets out some rules to follow in drafting a press release.

■ BOX 10.4 RULES FOR THE DRAFTING OF A PRESS RELEASE

- Provide a concise, informative headline and a byline summarizing the message and attracting readers' attention.
- Put the essential information in the first paragraph.
- Restrict the length to about 200 words.
- Attach a press kit containing commentary, information, references, photographs and other documents that may be useful for the media.
- Give first names, last names and titles.
- Avoid using abbreviations or acronyms that may be unfamiliar to some readers.
- Give names, titles and telephone numbers of people available to provide additional information.
- Put a date on the press release and, if necessary, embargo details (information not to be divulged until a particular time).
- Have the press release read by a third party to check for errors and to make sure the message is understandable.

Source: Rüttimann (2006).

Press conferences are events to which journalists are invited, generally consisting of a presentation and an opportunity for journalists to ask questions. They are useful for providing news on an important subject or where the information requires explanations that are difficult to put across in a press release (strong political impact, highly sensitive subject, complex data that need to be interpreted, etc.). Because many press releases are not taken up by the media, a trend that is being observed is organizations increasing the number of press conferences in a bid to guarantee a degree of visibility for the event or the news. An abundance of press conferences that attract only sparse attendances is tending to dampen media interest. Box 10.5 provides an overview of some important rules for organizing press conferences.

The idea behind organizing a feature report lies in the fact that some subjects need to be illustrated to be understandable and interesting, and may be insufficiently topical to be covered by the media in an ordinary way. Making the public aware of the functions of forests, giving them insight into the difficulties of various public-service vocations (such as police officers, firefighters or teachers in difficult areas) and explaining the issues involved in various public policies (e.g. environmental protection) are not

■ BOX 10.5 RULES FOR ORGANIZING A PRESS CONFERENCE

- *Time and place:* the timing must take into account the availability of the media and their publishing or broadcasting rhythm (a press conference given at the end of the day will often not give the media time to explore the subject). The place can also take on a symbolic importance that should not be neglected.
- *Invitation:* except in an emergency, invitations should be sent two to three days in advance to allow the media to organize themselves and be represented. The media may be very eager to cover the words and deeds of the main actors in the government, but the same does not apply for events and information concerning the civil service and its implementation of public policy.
- *Press kit:* this must contain the documents to be presented at the press conference (text of speeches, images, etc.).
- *Duration:* the presentation should not exceed 30 minutes and sufficient time should be allowed for questions.
- *Availability:* those giving the conference should allow time after the press conference to respond to specific requests from each media organization represented (interviews).

Source: Rüttimann (2006).

subjects – barring a particular event – of great interest to the media. One can therefore invite, say, one or a small number of newspapers or television channels to create a feature report, thereby giving them a degree of exclusiveness that may lead them to cover the subject from a different angle. The organization must therefore arouse the interest of an editor or a journalist, provide documentation to help them prepare the report and finally ensure that the people who need to be consulted during the report's creation are sufficiently available.

Lastly, press briefings. Press briefings are useful in major projects, when the implementation of a public policy is long and complex, or when the government or an organization deals with varied, sensitive files. They provide an opportunity, without expecting the media to relay any information, to report on progress in a project or a case, to give off-the-record explanations, to speak critically about the way certain subjects have been covered and so on. These meetings with journalists – by invitation, and sometimes around a dining table – must be infrequent and must make it possible, as their name suggests, to brief journalists about a situation and thereby facilitate media relations at the time of subsequent official communications.

INTERNET COMMUNICATIONS

Definitions, and advantages and limitations

The internet has revolutionized not only the way that people communicate but also the interaction between individuals and between political and public institutions and citizens. For the European Union[1] e-government means the use of information and communications technologies (ICT) by public-sector organizations in order to improve the quality and accessibility of public services. Online administration can reduce costs and facilitate transactions between governments and citizens. It also contributes to making the public sector more open and transparent. A number of fields of application fall under the overall concept of e-government (see Figure 10.1), particularly:

- *E-administration:* the application of e-government in the relations that public organizations may have with all persons and businesses (and even other governments) in a customer-oriented model (providing information, conducting online transactions, etc.).
- *E-democracy (e-voting, e-participation):* this is the component that develops a relationship with citizens in their political role (electronic voting, citizens' participation in political debates and in developing public policies, etc.).

Some authors, such as Saint-Amant (2005), also include e-society, meaning the development of information and communication technologies in society (as a matter of public policy).

Communications is involved in both e-administration and e-democracy. To serve people better and facilitate procedures for them, but also to increase government transparency, government departments and agencies use the internet to disseminate large quantities of information. With regard to e-democracy, the government can also provide citizens with information on electronic voting and, above all, can supply information enabling political actors (citizens, political parties, interest groups, etc.) to exchange views and take part in debates.

The advantages of the internet as an information medium are many. First – and this is a factor that has appreciably contributed to changing the relationship between the government and citizens – the internet allows a degree of individualization of that relationship. People can search for information based on their own needs, while the government can target information, either according to types of target groups (persons, businesses, public bodies, etc.) or according to types of use (schools, taxes, etc.). In accordance with the principles of New Public Management, without calling into question the criteria of equality and equity, the internet also facilitates relations between all actors concerned. Another advantage lies in the multimedia possibilities offered by the internet: text, sound, images and video can be combined. Provided that these various possibilities are used properly, people can be reached in a highly educational manner. The topical nature of information, when kept up to date, allows both the government to communicate in real time and beneficiaries to have access to information that is always current. Other distinct advantages of the internet are that all information is available immediately and continuously (24/7) and that some transactions can be conducted regardless of business hours (change-of-address notification, online completion and filing of tax returns). This reduces the 'distance' between the government and citizens. Another benefit is the improvement in the interaction between the government and beneficiaries (speed of information and transactions, facilitation of dialogue, etc.).

While the internet has revolutionized relationships between individuals and between individuals and organizations (forums, blogs, online purchases, etc.), other more problematical aspects that affect the public sector in particular must not be underestimated. First, many people assume, particularly in times of budgetary

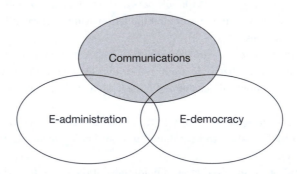

Figure 10.1 E-government and communications

restrictions, that the internet will make substantial savings possible (automating processes, reducing the business hours of service counters, etc.). While savings are indeed possible in some fields, the design and management of websites, together with the hardware and skills necessary, are primarily a cost factor and consume many resources. This aspect is all the more important because, unlike private organizations, government agencies cannot turn their backs on classical methods of communicating and of distributing services (service counters, telephone information, letters, etc.). A private business is entirely free to impose constraints on its customers (e.g. online ordering only). In order to guarantee access to services and information to everybody (including people having no internet access or lacking the necessary skills, and people with disabilities), governments are obliged to retain traditional tools, thereby limiting opportunities for savings. Despite the internet's undeniable advantages, it must not be forgotten that relations over this medium are largely dehumanized. As part of its function of creating and maintaining social bonds between people, the government cannot reduce its presence to electronic exchanges only and must ensure that it maintains a visible 'physical' presence. Last, the internet must be considered not as a medium that replaces all other media but as an additional medium that facilitates the transmission of information and the distribution of services.

E-GOVERNMENT SUCCESS FACTORS

Although certain general principles for using the internet are valid for both private and public organizations, particular features of the public sector mean that specific success factors must be taken into account (OECD, 2005).

First, it is widely recommended that a common portal be set up for all government services. This is what Switzerland has done with http://www.ch.ch, the United Kingdom with http://www.directgov.uk, France with http://www.service-public.fr and Canada with http://www.canada.gc.ca. Because of the diversity of public-service organizations and missions, the temptation is strong to develop a website for each, thereby giving the services or departments concerned better visibility and, sometimes, better individualization of relations with beneficiaries.

Three aspects need to be borne in mind, however. First, starting from the beneficiaries' point of view, it must be assumed that they do not have detailed knowledge of administrative structures and that they will not immediately be able to locate the organization or website where the information or service they are seeking is to be found. A common portal will assist most beneficiaries in their search for relevant web pages.

Second, a number of parallel sites generally means different designs, constructions and approaches. Legitimate public action requires clear identification of the issuing body, but this is not always the case with websites, where one is unsure whether the issuer is a public organization, a private organization to whom powers have been delegated or a completely private organization having no connection with the public sector.

Last, the financial aspect is by no means least important. A multiplicity of sites brings an increase in consistency problems, together with development and especially management costs. This last point is often forgotten: the benefits of the internet only become reality if management is continuous and professional.

For all these reasons, a common portal for the government as a whole is recommended. However, deviations from this policy can be allowed – as long as there are clear rules that are strictly applied – particularly for major projects or for government departments that have been made autonomous and whose activities go beyond the classical relations of a government department (e.g. an agency offering both public services and business services).

A second success factor that should be borne in mind is the need to identify the portal strongly and clearly and to promote it actively. Changing people's usage or consumption habits is difficult, and the mere existence of a portal will not suffice to modify them. If a government really wishes to benefit from the advantages of the internet, and to pass these benefits on to citizens, it must encourage use of the portal through active promotion.

The architecture and navigation model must be common to all departments and all online content. It is important that users can be directed to the desired department without difficulty or uncertainty. In every case it is recommended not to give portals a structure that reflects administrative structures, but one that reflects user groups (individuals, businesses, other governments) and needs, and also takes into account the way in which users define these needs (taxes, schools, identity documents, etc.).

Governments must make sure they protect the confidentiality of citizens' private data, ensuring that they cannot be intercepted or seen by an authorized third parties. Improper use of such data can not only have consequences for the people involved but can also lead to considerable loss of credibility for the organization in the performance of its tasks, completely denying the benefits of the internet. Another fact that must be taken into account is that most users are not ICT professionals (ergonomics of websites) and some have disabilities (respect for recognized international guidelines). The danger of turning the 'digital divide' into an administrative divide caused by limited access to government portals must be guarded against.

Last, and this is a factor that although obvious is often overlooked, comes the need to make available sufficient resources to meet objectives. Many governments get carried away by the multitude of possibilities offered by the internet and underestimate the resources needed to maintain websites and ensure very regular updates.

Website design

Many books and articles (Hallahan, 2001; Weinschenk, 2008) discuss principles and rules to follow in designing a website. Although some rules are valid for all communications tools, for example those calling for clear identification of user needs, others are specific to this new tool. An example is the 'three click' rule according to which a webpage or an item of information sought should not require more than three mouse clicks to display, since otherwise users may either lose patience or get sidetracked by other content.

Box 10.6 sets out important, specifically communications-related elements to bear in mind when creating a website. Although all the rules are important, updating information and links is vital. As a result, it is better to progressively develop a site that is relatively simple but always up to date rather than a site offering every possibility and all information but which quickly becomes obsolete because it is not kept up to date. The rate of updating depends of course on the site's organization and content, but in all cases a minimum of weekly checks and monthly updates is imperative.

■ BOX 10.6 IMPORTANT ELEMENTS IN WEBSITE CREATION

Content-related aspects:

- ■ Define the objectives of the website.
- ■ Provide useful content based on users' needs.
- ■ Take into account the various possible users (user categories, types of computer, types of connection, etc.).
- ■ Update content very regularly.
- ■ Ensure that the site is properly referenced.
- ■ Monitor and track usage (how many visitors, what pages, when, from what site, from what page users leave the site, etc.).
- ■ Ensure that practical information (addresses, business hours, telephone number, etc.) are easily and quickly accessible.

Formal and technical aspects:

- ■ Ensure that a clear domain name is used.
- ■ Coordinate graphic elements, harmonizing them with all communications tools (integrated communications).
- ■ Devise a navigation system to suit users' needs and skills.
- ■ Pay attention to ergonomics.
- ■ Organize information in a clear and logical manner.
- ■ Facilitate quick reading (short titles, sentences and paragraphs, etc.).
- ■ Minimize the number of clicks necessary to reach information.
- ■ Establish links between subject and information.

continued . . .

> ■ **BOX 10.6 IMPORTANT ELEMENTS IN WEBSITE CREATION** ... *continued*
>
> Financial and organizational aspects:
>
> ■ Determine content and structure before design.
> ■ Determine rules for making decisions and competences in adapting and updating content.
> ■ Organize resources for the development and especially for the updating of the site (trained staff).
> ■ Determine the budget.
>
> Sources: Research-based Web Design and usability Guidelines (http://www.usability.gov/ guidelines, consulted 20 November 2010); Glassey (2003).

Although the rules set out in Box 10.6 are valid for any website, public organizations need to take various elements into account in setting the content of webpages:

Quantity of information put online. Two extreme trends can be observed. At one end of the spectrum, some organizations are very parsimonious, placing a minimum of information online. Such organizations have to deal with many telephone or e-mail queries from people seeking information. At the other end, some organizations use websites to put a maximum amount of information (reports, opinions, files, etc.) online, with the danger, sometimes deliberate, of 'drowning' information that is important to citizens (the term 'infobesity' is sometimes used). It is not always easy for public organizations to take into account all types of needs for information or to comply with both the practical rules of website design and legal rules related to the principles of public communications and transparency (e-democracy).

Homogenization of rules for putting information online. Because the public sector is not homogeneous with regard either to the nature of tasks performed or to the type of organization performing these tasks, the degree of autonomy allowed to each administrative entity in the design and content of its own webpages should be determined.

Coordination of the internet tool with other communications tools. While this aspect is not limited to public organizations, it takes on a particular character in this sector. In order to achieve equality of treatment, people who cannot access or will have difficulties accessing information via the internet must not be given second-class treatment. This makes it very important to consider the complementarity between the various communications tools, and to do so in a very systematic manner. To save costs, some private organizations do not show a telephone number or address on their websites, thereby forcing users to navigate through the site and search for information by themselves. In principle, a public organization cannot proceed in this manner and must allow several access points, even if some may be limited (reduced opening hours for departments whose services are easy to access online).

E-democracy

E-democracy is a complement of e-government and refers to the use of ICT by institutions for the purpose of conducting their relations with citizens in the exercise of their democratic rights. There are three types of use:

■ *Making information available:* in order to facilitate citizens' participation in political debates and decisions, but also to strengthen their confidence in institutions, public-sector organizations put information online for citizens (information on civic rights, budgets and accounts, minutes of meetings, expert opinions, etc.).

■ *Moderation of the political debate and participation in interactive exchanges:* calls for ideas, surveys, forums, chat rooms, etc.

■ *Exercising voting rights over the internet:* this is a form of electronic voting that has been tried in recent years. It provides easy access to voting for certain groups (citizens living abroad, for example) and stimulates participation in elections for other groups such as young people.

Although the general rules for the design and maintenance of webpages are the same as for other pages on government sites, in e-democracy governments will strive to adopt the most objective position possible in order not to become a political actor (informational bias, tendentious comments, favoured target groups, etc.).

EXERCISE 10.1

Analyse a press release in the light of the criteria presented in Box 10.4. Analyse your organization's website in the light of the criteria presented in Box 10.6. Compare the results obtained for both the press release and the website. Are the evaluations similar, dissimilar?

DISCUSSION QUESTIONS

1   What should be the role of the internet in an organization's communications strategy? Do you see major problems in centring your approach on this new medium?

211 ■

2   The question of harmonization, across an entire government, of the various communications instruments is a challenge. Why do you believe it is so hard to get organizations onto a specific common platform? What does this say about the dynamics between organizations?

REFERENCES

Australian Government (2011) Campaign Advertising by the Australian Government, Full Year Financial Report, 2009–10, Canberra, Australian Government.

Bruhn, M. (1997) *Kommunikationspolitik*, München, Vahlen.

——— (2009) *Intergrierte Unternehmens-und Markenkommunikation*, Stuttgart, Schäffer-Poeschel-Verlag.

Glassey, D. (2003) Le Plus Petit Nombre de Clics, Working Paper of IDHEAP, M/2003.

Goldbach (2009) Goldbach Guide, Goldbach Media Publications. Online at http://issuu. com/goldbachmedia/docs/goldbachguide09_blaetterkatalog_f (accessed 9 August 2011).

Hallahan, K. (2001) Improving Public Relations Websites Through Usability Research, *Public Relations Review*, 223–39.

Hartley, b. and Pickton, D. (1999) Integrated Marketing Communications Requires a New Way of Thinking, *Journal of Marketing Communications*, 5, 97–106.

Leblanc, D. (2010) Conservatives Spent Record $130-Million on Advertising in 2009, *The Globe and Mail*, 20 September.

Organisation for Economic Co-operation and Development (OECD) (2005) E-government for Better Government, Paris, OECD.

Pickton, D. and Broderick, A. (2005) *Integrated Marketing Communications*, Essex, Pearson Education.

PriceWaterhouseCoopers (2009) Global Entertainment and Media Outlook 2009–13, PriceWaterhouseCoopers.

Public Health Agency of Canada (n.d.) Get the Facts on the H1N1 Flu Virus. Online at http://www.phac-aspc.gc.ca/alert-alerte/h1n1/index-eng.php (accessed 26 July 2011).

Rossiter, J. R. and Percy, L. (1987) *Advertising and Promotion Management*, New York, McGraw-Hill International.

Rüttimann, J. P. (2006) *Travailler Avec les Médias*, Fribourg, Département des sciences de la société de l'Université de Fribourg.

Saint-Amant, G. (2005) E-Gouvernement: Cadre d'évolution de l'administration Électronique, *Revue Système d'information et Management (SIM)*, 5.

Singapore Ministry of Community Development, Youth and Sport (n.d.). Website. Online at http://app1.mcys.gov.sg (accessed 1 April 2011).

Steffenhagen, H. (2000) *Wirkung der Werbung. Konzepte, Erklärung, Befunde*, Stuttgart, Wissenschaftsverlag Mainz.

Swiss Canton of Fribourg (2004) Open Days 2004. Online at http://admin.fr.ch/ pj/fr/pub/evenements/2004.htm (accessed 1 April 2011).

Thérenty, M. E. and Vaillant, A. (2001) *1836, L'an I de l'ère Médiatique. Analyse Littéraire et Historique de La Presse de Girardin*, Paris, Nouveau Monde Éditions.

Tocqueville, A. de (1992 [1835]) *De la Démocratie en Amérique I*, Paris, Gallimard.

Weinschenk, S. M. (2008) *Neuro Web Design*, Berkeley, New Riders.

Zikmund, W. G. and D'Amico, M. (1993) *Marketing*, New York, John Wiley & Sons.

Chapter 11

Communication control

LEARNING OBJECTIVES

By the end of this chapter you should be able to:

■ Identify the various control mechanisms for communication.
■ Select the approach best suited to a specific communication campaign.
■ Activate the evaluation of your communication initiatives.

KEY POINTS OF THIS CHAPTER

■ Communication activities are rarely evaluated – due both to cost and the difficulty in confronting failures and the desire to go forward. Result: an inability to improve communication initiatives.
■ Evaluating communication in the public sector is especially difficult, as many bodies and initiatives present the same message and try to reach the same policy objectives.
■ Three levels of evaluation can be made, measuring: output (e.g. number of contacts); outcome (modification of knowledge); and impact (changes in behaviour).

KEY TERMS

Communication control – monitoring of an organization's communication activities to gauge the validity of the concept as well as the outputs, outcomes and impacts.

continued . . .

> ## KEY TERMS ... *continued*
>
> **Effectiveness Analysis** – the most common form of assessment of a communica-
> tion campaign. It helps ascertain whether the objectives have been attained in
> terms of a specific target group to be reached.
>
> **Longitudinal Study** – evaluating a communication campaign over time.
>
> **Benchmark Study** – evaluating a communication campaign as compared to
> similar endeavours by other organizations.

INTRODUCTION

Controlling communication activities and, above all, assessing their effectiveness, are
tasks which are often neglected by both private and public bodies. Although these are
complex tasks, they are vital for ensuring that goals are attained and the measures taken
are re-assessed as necessary.

Along with a lack of desire to deal with these tasks and a reluctance to admit mistakes,
two factors make all this a complicated issue: first, it is very hard to isolate the effect
of one communication measure with regard to other measures in the same campaign;
second, in terms of communication, the effects on target groups do not just depend
on activities undertaken by an organization, but on all the activities and events of a
great many organizations. Many non-profit organizations, for instance, raised huge sums
through fund-raising campaigns after 9/11. The main reason was not that their
campaigns were more effective than those they had staged before, but because of the
heightened climate of insecurity caused by the attack. These explanatory factors can
be summed up in the famous words of Lord Leverhulme: 'I know half my advertising
is wasted. I just don't know which half!'

Communication control is even more complex in the public sector. Many organizations act on the same public policies through their own measures. Also, the public nature
of things means that the way in which the organization can direct and control its
communication (discussion in public and in the media) is restricted. What is more, the
details of these public policies are often left deliberately vague to ensure the greatest
possible support from political decision-makers in voting on the appropriate laws.

A good illustration of this situation can be found in measures taken to promote a
country's image. In the context of World Expos, like the one held in Shanghai in 2010,
countries spend large sums of money to be present with their own pavilion. This is
accompanied by various promotional measures, as outlined in Figure 11.1.

A country's presence at a World Expo results from a political mandate assigned to
an organization in charge of preparing and carrying out the project (such organizations
usually come under the Foreign Ministry). The flagship measure is a pavilion to host
exhibitions, welcome visitors and showcase various aspects of the country. It is usually

215 ▪

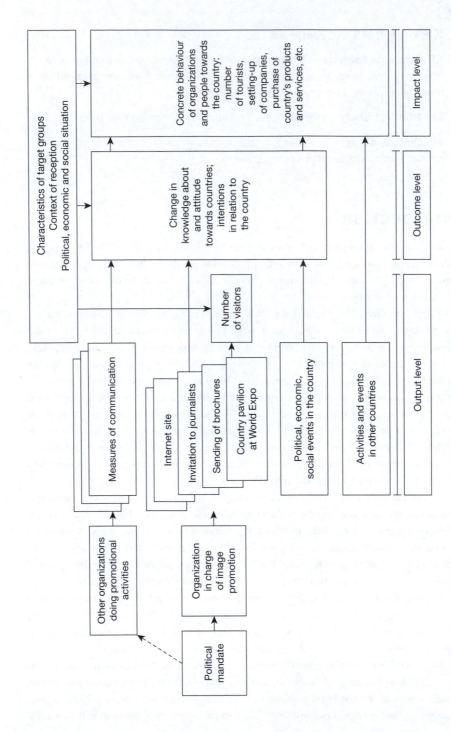

Figure 11.1 *Analytical overview of potential effects of a promotional measure*

accompanied by support measures such as a website, information documents, press conference, invitations to journalists to visit the country, etc.

Analysing the impact of these measures must take into account how they are received by their target groups. The socio-economic characteristics of the persons concerned (basic knowledge, level of education, etc.), and the situation in which they find themselves when in contact with these measures (economic situation, political context, logistical and technical aspects, etc.), will influence their ability to apprehend and understand the message. All these elements are moderating variables that amplify or reduce the potential impact of the organization's message.

There are three distinct levels of impact:

1) It is relatively easy to determine the number of visitors, evaluate the frequency or length of their visits and, after questioning them, how much they appreciated their visit (the pavilion's quality and appeal, what they learned, etc.).

2) An analysis of changes as to how a country is perceived – and any intentions as regards the goods and services produced or companies located in the country – can only be made bearing in mind all the measures taken by the other organizations involved in promoting the country (tourist offices, bodies in charge of attracting companies, embassies, etc.). Depending on the messages conveyed, and how well they are coordinated, these measures may strengthen or undermine the Pavilion's impact. It is, in any case, difficult to specify how a visitor's opinion of a country might be altered by visiting a national pavilion.

3) The impact sought by the political authorities within the framework of a given mandate – e.g. increasing the number of tourists, attracting more firms, helping companies with export activities, etc. – becomes even more difficult to assess, as one cannot ignore promotional events and activities staged by other countries.

After describing the types and conditions required to monitor communication activities, this chapter presents and explains the levels and basic variables to be considered when studying the effectiveness of communication measures.

TYPES AND CONDITIONS OF CONTROL

The act of monitoring communication activities can take four different, complementary forms:

The first is the 'monitoring the concept', also known as 'pre-test' control. As outlined in Chapter 9, it is vital to verify the concept before conceiving and carrying out communication measures. The following tasks can be identified:

■ *Assessing the concept's coherence:* particular attention must be paid to ensuring that the framework of conditions for communication activities is respected, and that the decisions taken during the process fit in with one another (e.g. as regards budget and goals, or budget and choice of means, etc.).

- *Ascertaining that the concept can be put into effect:* it is important to make sure that the required instruments are available (e.g. possibility of placing an advertisement in a newspaper or obtaining a stand at a fair) and, above all, coordinating the technical and time-related aspects (e.g. it may be necessary to cancel, postpone or bring forward communication activities according to events).
- *Controlling the message:* checking that the message for the target groups, goals and chosen support is understood, ideally by testing a representative sample. Both for reasons of time and means, such studies are hardly possible, but it is nonetheless recommended to carry out such tests using whatever samples are readily available (e.g. office colleagues, acquaintances and friends, etc.) and which, whether individually or within the framework of a group discussion, may yield critical comment: Is there enough time to read all the information? Do we have enough basic knowledge to understand the message? Does the principal message come across clearly? What effects does the message produce? etc.

The second, and often most important, type of monitoring is the 'control of goal-achievement', generally called 'effectiveness' control or 'post-test' control. This involves verifying whether the goals with regard to the defined target groups have been attained. The following section is devoted to this type of control. The two other types of monitoring – longitudinal (tracking) and comparative (benchmark) studies – are slightly less frequent, but often useful, especially in the public sector, and when it is hard to isolate the specific effect of individual measures.

Third, 'tracking' is used to evaluate the impact of a set of measures over time. One can obviously measure how the fame or reputation of an organization or country evolves,[1] but more subtle measures are also worth considering – especially when communication activities are carried out over time, on subjects for which extensive studies are not possible (see Box 11.1).

Fourth and last is the 'benchmark' study aimed at measuring the effectiveness of communication campaigns not in absolute terms, but relative to campaigns of other, similar organizations. When it comes to prevention, for instance, one can compare the budgets devoted to communication activities and the results obtained among target groups in different countries (providing, of course, such information is available). If a State agency sponsors a cycling team, for instance, it could (as well as analysing effectiveness compared to the goals fixed) compare how its own image has evolved compared to that of the sponsors of other teams.

Opportunities to monitor communication activities depend on various factors. The first, and most obvious, is the budget available. Professional and systematic monitoring of these activities can be costly and absorb extensive time resources; and it is clear that many public (and private) organizations struggle to devote the necessary means to this. A second condition is linked to the existence of goals with regard to target groups, and how clear they are. Such goals are often so vague ('improving the image of the law', 'encouraging cyclists to wear helmets') that measuring the effects serves little purpose. So, when the mandate is defined, the objectives with regard to precise target groups must be sufficiently explicit for the effect to be subsequently measured. Otherwise there will always be both positive and less positive effects, making any clear interpretation difficult.

Other factors to be considered are more technical, including the possibility of questioning target groups or obtaining reliable data. Take, for instance, communication measures to prevent obesity among children and teenagers. In many countries surveys of persons under 16 are not allowed, so it is not possible to obtain results among the target groups concerned. Only data obtained from indirect target groups (parents, doctors, teachers, etc.) can be envisaged.

Furthermore, data obtained from surveys of children, senior citizens or the under-privileged must be interpreted with caution, unless the product of measures which ensure a degree of data reliability (special qualifications of pollsters, control issues, limiting of possible third-party influence, etc.).

ANALYSING THE EFFECTIVENESS MODEL

Bases of the model

Analysing the effectiveness of communication campaigns and measures is the most frequent type of control, and usually the most important one for public bodies. It involves verifying whether the defined objectives among the target groups have been attained. Figure 11.2 presents a synthetic overview.

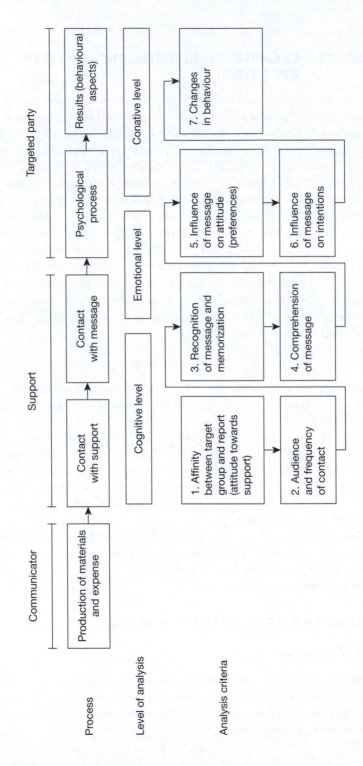

Figure 11.2 *Synthetic model for analysing effectiveness of communication measures and advertising campaigns*

The model concerns a basic communication approach and, among other things, differentiates between the party communicating, the support and the persons targeted. Such distinctions are important because, for communication to have an effect on the persons targeted, the latter need to be in contact with the support (i.e. read the newspaper or prospectus, consult the website, see the poster, etc.).

As regards the support, a distinction is usually made between the relationship with the support as such, and the relationship with the message. Take a press release whose basic contents are relayed by a newspaper article. A local inhabitant may subscribe to the newspaper and read it every day (contact with support), but may not see the article in question due to lack of time, interest or some other reason (no contact with message).

Impact on the parties targeted can be described in psychological terms, such as remembering a message or a change of attitude towards the organization or issue concerned. Then there are the behavioural aspects or end results which are usually aimed for (taking part in an activity, altered behaviour, paying for a service, etc.).

Theories of consumer behaviour are often split into cognitive, emotional and conative aspects, partly overlapping with the phases in the communications approach. The cognitive aspect corresponds to mental functions and the ability to perceive, read, hear, memorize and reason (understand and interpret). The emotional aspect covers motivations and the ability to establish preferences. The conative aspect concerns conscious actions (from intentions to actual behaviour) (Pasquier, 1997). In many situations, studying the impact of communication follows these three aspects in a linear fashion (becoming aware of information, forming an opinion and preferences, then actual behaviour). But research into consumer psychology has shown that often this order can be reversed.

In the event of behaviour which is spontaneous or motivated in a particular way (giving pleasure to someone else, satisfying some special wish), people may take decisions not in keeping with their knowledge or usual attitudes (e.g. someone who is environmentally conscious may choose to take the plane for a trip they would normally make by train). To minimize this apparent inconsistency, people may perceive, or even seek, information that rationalizes their decision. In this way, people's behaviour may affect how they view the service.

Analysis criteria

Based on the communication approach and the aspects outlined above, we can draw up a list of the criteria needed to assess communication's effectiveness.

The first criterion concerns 'physical' contact with the support and the frequency of such contact. For communication to be effective, it is first essential to ensure that the persons targeted have been in contact with the support, preferably more than once. Studies show that more frequent contact increases people's memory of an advertising campaign (Pasquier, 1997), and that the effectiveness of certain supports, like posters, depends above all on repeated contact.

The second criterion is connected to the affinity between the target group and the support. Attitudes towards the support (regular or occasional reading, time spent reading, etc.), its credibility and the value accorded to the information are all moderating variables that broaden or reduce communication's potential impact: the same information in different supports will not have the same effect, either because the quality of contact is not the same, or because the support does not have the same credibility.

Third, there is recognizing the message and remembering it. Some people may see a message several times, be able to describe it, yet remain incapable of identifying its principal theme, or the brand (or body) behind it. So we have recognition of the message – but mistaken attribution. Fourth, if we study the degree of understanding of the message, we can ascertain whether its main thrust and arguments have been correctly decoded.

Once the message has been seen and understood, the effects produced at an emotional and pre-behavioural level need to be assessed. Will there be a change in attitude towards the theme being dealt with among the people affected? Will they alter their choices? Are they prepared to change their behaviour? Criteria five and six try to answer such questions. In the field of prevention, in particular, a number of messages are seen and understood, but do not suffice to make people change their behaviour (sorting household waste, stop smoking, don't drink and drive, follow a balanced diet, take regular exercise, etc.). Reasons vary, and communication alone is often not enough to prompt the desired change.

The final criterion concerns the action taken by those affected. Both economic and non-economic effects can be evoked, especially in the public sector. Economic effects mean that the likely consequences of behavioural change can be measured in monetary terms (e.g. increasing fiscal receipts through a campaign inciting people to declare their earnings and fortune). Non-economic effects can be measured only through observing behaviour (stopping smoking, sorting household waste, etc.).

Although these criteria have been presented one after the other, according to the pre-defined levels, the actual choice depends on the defined goals. If the goal, say, is to encourage people to frequent their local library, the main criteria will be linked to a change in behaviour (number of new readers, number of people intending to go to the library, etc.). If the goals are not attained, the reasons must be identified. These could be down to the support (wrong choice, not enough readers, message not repeated often enough, etc.); the message (difficulty for certain foreign communities to understand it, for example, or too abstract and lacking precise information); the attitude of those targeted (no desire to change their habits, fear of trying something that seems too posh); or behavioural reasons (lack of time, unsuitable hours, difficult access, etc.). Investigating why goals have not been attained should take into account all the indicators or criteria ahead of the goal targeted.

Boxes 11.2 and 11.3 give examples of communication control.

■ BOX 11.2 BASIC CONTROL OF EFFECTIVENESS OF COMMUNICATION CAMPAIGN AGAINST 'UNDER THE TABLE' EMPLOYMENT

After introducing a new, much tougher law against illegal employment, the Swiss government adopted various measures, including a public communication campaign. One of the posters reads: *Cherche femme de ménage sachant tout faire sauf des accidents* (Seeks cleaning help. Must be able to do everything except accidents):

■ *Plate 11.1* Ad of a communication campaign against 'under the table' employment

A survey after the campaign (representative 15–44 age group sample in Lausanne and Bern) showed that:

- ■ Ninety-two per cent passed in front of a campaign poster.
- ■ Thirty-two per cent went past a campaign poster at least twelve times.
- ■ Fifty-four per cent recognized the subject of the posters.
- ■ Fifty-seven per cent were able to identify the organization behind the poster.

Source: Confédération Helvétique (2008).

■ BOX 11.3 VERIFYING THE IMPACT OF PUBLIC RELATIONS (PR)

PR aims to foster a good relationship with parties who are important to the organization. Two things are vital when assessing the impact of PR measures:

- ■ PR aims less to change the behaviour of those targeted than to spread information and build a positive attitude towards the organization.
- ■ Given the wide range of parties involved, potential types of relationship and large number of possible communication measures, it is hard for effectiveness to be gauged precisely.

The effectiveness of PR measures can be assessed at three main levels.

- ■ PR outputs – immediate results of an activity or programme:

Traditional Media	Internet	Events
– Which media relayed the information and when?	– Website traffic	– Number and type of participants
– What information was conveyed?	– References to website or article	– Amount of material or information provided
– Format and placing of articles	– Information relayed by other sites (number and nature)	– Number of personal contacts
– Context in which information conveyed		– Evaluation of information conveyed in media
– Overall impression or 'mood' of article		

- ■ PR out-takes – measures related to the message:

  - – attention paid to the message
  - – understanding of message as linked to goals
  - – memorizing message over short and medium term.

- ■ Measures at an emotional level (targeted party):

  - – analysis of people's attitudes and opinions
  - – analysis of potential impact on behaviour.

CONCLUSION

The evaluation of communication initiatives is essential to ascertain their effectiveness, and, if needed, to modify the approach taken. The difficulties in evaluating are numerous and stem from both practical considerations (budget), methodological considerations (difficulty of isolating one's campaign from other environmental factors) and political considerations (not wanting to underline failures). That said, the various analytical criteria available, and the wide range of evaluation option, make it possible, even if at an aggregated level, to get a sense of the pertinence and general impact of one's own initiatives.

EXERCISE 11.1

Using Figure 11.2 and, based on one of your organization's recent communication campaigns, try to identify the various analytical criteria that were used, and evaluate their pertinence in view of the level of analysis and the process.

DISCUSSION QUESTIONS

1   How far can public bodies justify the costly exercise of communication testing? Is this over-managing communication?
2   With reference to Figure 11.1, what are the potential difficulties about applying such an approach to a traditional public services like education or justice?

NOTE

1   The GfK Institute, in collaboration with Simon Anholt, publishes an annual study of countries' images worldwide (*Anholt-GfK Roper Nation Brands Index*); results can be compared year on year, and the evolution of a country's image tracked over time.

REFERENCES

Caron, D. J. and Hunt, T. D. (2006) Accountability and Disclosure: The Proper Use of Transparency Instruments and their Implications for Canadian Public Administration, in Sciences, I. I. O. A. (ed.) Third Regional International Conference: Transparency for Better Governance, Monterrey.

Confédération Helvétique (2008) *PPI Poster Performance Index 2008*, Berne, SECO and APG Affichage.

Pasquier, M. (1997) The Effectiveness of Outdoor Advertising: The European Research Experience, Federation of Outdoor Advertising.

Chapter 12

Crisis communication

LEARNING OBJECTIVES

By the end of this chapter you should be able to:

- Identify a crisis situation.
- Analyse the type of crisis being faced, and outline possible responses.
- Understand and avoid the main pitfalls in crisis communication.

KEY POINTS OF THIS CHAPTER

- A crisis is a change in all the parameters of an organization's human and physical environment, making all points of reference effectively disappear.
- There are two types of crises: 1) crises linked to accidents and emergencies, and 2) crises linked to information-management problems or problems internal to the organization. Each type will have different dynamics, sequences and solutions.
- One can identify key communication mistakes in a crisis. These include underestimating the risks entailed, refusing to communicate, denying or playing down facts, neglecting internal communication and attacking the media.
- Proper management of a crisis will involve steps taken before the crisis hits (risk analysis), during the crisis (activation of various measures) and after the crisis (officially declaring the end of the crisis and analysing the crisis).

KEY TERMS

Organizational crisis – situation in which all the parameters of an organization's human and physical environment change, making all points of reference effectively disappear.

continued . . .

KEY TERMS ... *continued*

Crisis communication – a specific sub-field of communication studies that deals with the dynamics involved in a crisis.

Communication strategy – approach used to counter, mitigate or limit the negative impacts of a crisis.

INTRODUCTION

For any organization, a crisis is a major event that may threaten the jobs of its executives and even jeopardize the organization's survival. Consequently, a crisis must be managed in a specific way distinct from the organization's normal processes. Although political crises (e.g. the Cuban missile crisis) and health crises (e.g. Spanish flu) have always occurred, those affecting organizations directly have assumed greater importance since World War II, particularly in the past few decades. A number of reasons account for this development, including a) the growing place of organizations in society; b) the importance given to impacts on persons and the subsequent judicial impacts of such events; c) the speed at which society is evolving; d) the evolution of the media; and e) technological developments.

First, organizations have taken on considerable importance in our societies, in terms of both their numbers and of their diversity; through their products and services they affect broad sections of the population. A major event in any organization is therefore highly likely to affect a large number of people directly or indirectly. They may suffer impacts on their health or their physical integrity (injuries, poisonings), be restricted in their movements (strikes, outages) or be outraged because of contempt shown for their values (corruption, lies, etc.). The growing importance placed on the human person and on individual rights has also helped strengthen the potential impact of crises. In the same way, the increasing role of the courts in determining liability and the growth of associations (which may have the time and resources to bring serious events into the public eye or prevent such events from being forgotten) mean that the dangers of crises for organizations are increasing, and that crises may be prolonged by the involvement of the courts and associations.

Next, systemic changes and changes within organizations have accelerated, increasing the risks of dysfunction, errors or opportunistic behaviour (e.g. people taking advantage of loopholes in the system). All this means that it is increasingly difficult for managers to have full knowledge of and control over their organization's processes and actions, since organizations have become highly complex and frequently operate internationally.

Another reason for the growth in crisis communication stems from the evolution of the mass media. The number and diversity of media mean that competition between them has become fiercer, particularly with regard to the search for original, exclusive information ('scoops'). They will strive to discover information and angles for which organizations are not prepared. Into the bargain, through the liberalization and partial privatization of broadcast media, political control over information in democratic countries has become much weaker, with the result that events that could have been covered up half a century ago are today laid out for all to see. A final aspect has to do with the technological upheavals occurring in the telecommunications sector in particular. With mobile phones and the internet, information can be broadcast immediately and continuously. As a result, news that formerly would have made the rounds several hours or even days after an event may be known to the media and broadcasted even before those in charge of the organization have learned of it. In many cases, organizations no longer have any margin of time for anticipating and managing a crisis.

CRISES AND CRISIS COMMUNICATION

Characteristics of a crisis

A crisis is defined by Crozier (1991) as 'a change in all the parameters of the physical and human environment with the result that reference points no longer exist and people do not know how to behave' and by Lerbringer (1997) as 'an unexpected event jeopardizing the organization's reputation and stability'. A crisis, therefore, marks a break with normal functioning and raises major uncertainties to which it is difficult to respond.

From a more analytical point of view, a crisis for organizations is characterized by the following elements (Coombs, 2007; Coombs and Holladay, 2010; Zaremba, 2010):

- A crisis affects an entire organization, not merely the sectors or departments responsible for the event that triggered the crisis.
- Crises disrupt normal operations. Processes and internal rules are abandoned, or cannot be applied, thus paralyzing the system.
- The causes of a crisis may be known but generally they are unforeseeable, and above all they take the organization by surprise. Generally, organizations do not have time to implement structures to respond to the crisis in the way they had expected.
- The consequences are unpredictable and are likely to jeopardize the organization's survival.
- Both inside and outside the organization, perceptions become more important than facts. Emotional reactions dominate and frequently it is impossible, at least initially, to discuss the causes and consequences of the crisis in a rational manner. The elements potentially leading to a crisis situation are outlined in Box 12.1.

■ **BOX 12.1 CRISIS FACTORS THAT BRING MAJOR RISKS**

- ■ Those affected are vulnerable (children, the elderly, pregnant women, etc.)
- ■ Recurrence of failures or technical or human errors (successive breakdowns, repeated financial scandals even when of lesser importance, etc.)
- ■ Sensitive subjects that have health impacts and are generally seized on by the media (nuclear, flu, dioxin, asbestos, foods, etc.)
- ■ Symbolic places or very well-known organizations are involved
- ■ Information that was denied is subsequently proven to be true
- ■ Absence of answers as to the causes, risks, duration and solutions
- ■ Situations in which the organization had ignored facts or risks of which it was aware
- ■ Institutional void (resignations, departure of personnel, etc.)
- ■ The event is geographically or culturally close
- ■ Persistent rumours

The importance of crisis communication

Although a crisis *per se* calls for professional management in order to find appropriate technical solutions (providing relief for victims, assisting people in difficulty, locating and resolving the breakdown, etc.) and to restore normal operations, communication about the crisis takes on enormous importance, going beyond the framework of the crisis itself in terms both of time and of the persons concerned. According to Libaert (2001a), there can be no good management of a crisis without good communication.

For Revéret and Moreau (1997) and Libaert (2001a), a number of elements explain the importance of effective communication in a crisis:

- ■ Because organizations can be imperilled by a crisis, it is vital that they demonstrate not only their ability to manage the crisis's technical aspects but also their capacity to show understanding, compassion, empathy, patience and pedagogy if necessary. Generally, the effects of a crisis can only be contained if the organization's main leaders become closely involved.
- ■ As mentioned previously, large numbers of people may feel involved because they or those close to them are directly affected, because they feel they could be in the shoes of those affected, or because values or basic rules have been flouted. These people feel entitled to be kept informed and to obtain answers. In a globalized world, with international social and cultural exchanges as well as world trade, and with the speed of communications today, the likelihood of large circles of people feeling affected by a crisis is increasingly high.

229 ■

■ Numerous actors intervene with their own reading of the facts and their own vision of solutions that should be applied. For professional or political reasons, many who would not normally express their views on the organization may seize the opportunity presented by the crisis to step into the media limelight (as experts, to defend their values and put forward general solutions, or to raise their own profile or that of their organization). Consequently, organizations themselves must communicate or risk losing all credibility by allowing others to take centre stage.

As a rule, requests for information and explanations come from outside the circle of those directly affected and the pressure exerted on the organization is important. Approaches may come from media or persons who are only remotely – if at all – familiar with the organization. The organization must therefore understand and deal with the intentions of actors that represent 'unknown quantities'. These requests will very quickly swamp the organization's normal communication capacity, especially if the crisis lasts for several days. Organizations must be able to implement communication strategies and structures to respond to the crisis (setting up a hotline, ensuring that spokespersons can respond to media requests including in the evenings and at weekends). Without such structures, the organization risks having to deal with a second crisis caused by its inability to react (criticism of the lack of information, or rumours spreading because the organization is struggling to respond to all requests).

A feature of crisis communication is that control of the crisis shifts outside the organization. Although technical management of the crisis normally follows procedures depending on the circumstances of the incident (providing relief to victims, restoring basic operations), what happens in the rest of the organization is dictated by external actors – the media, government authorities, and even employees and other concerned actors. For as long as the crisis lasts, the requests, revelations, questions raised and rumours will force the organization to react by explaining, informing and refuting. This means it will not be in control of the agenda and will constantly be obliged to adapt to a highly stressful pace (nights, weekends, vacation periods) dictated by others. A major stage in the crisis is reached when the media no longer covers the crisis spontaneously but only when the organization communicates on matters related to the crisis or other subjects.

CRISIS TYPES AND PHASES

Publications dealing with crisis problems frequently use examples such as the Cuban missile crisis (1962), oil tanker wrecks (the Amoco Cadiz in Brittany in 1978 and the Exxon Valdez in Alaska in 1989), or health crises such as BSE (Bovine Spongiform Encephalopathy, commonly known as 'mad cow disease') in the 1980s and SARS (Severe Acute Respiratory Syndrome) in the early 2000s. These familiar examples provide illustrations of statements about crises that everyone can relate to. But they are not very representative of the crises that public-sector organizations have to confront, with real and potential consequences that are closer to home and less far-reaching. Public organizations are often unprepared to manage crises such as pollution of the water table, embezzlement of public funds by an insider, discovery of sexual abuse of children by a teacher or youth leader – situations that the authorities and administration must deal with at the local level with few resources (particularly because such crises are fortunately infrequent).

Types of crisis

There are many crisis typologies (Coombs, 1999; Sartre, 2003a) based on criteria such as causes, the nature and degree of risk, internal or external nature, or consequences of crises. Because this chapter is confined to aspects of crisis communication by public-sector organizations, the distinctive features of their activities and the context of their operations need to be taken into account.

From this point of view, two main crisis types can be distinguished: (1) crises resulting from accidents, incidents and emergency situations, and (2) crises arising from problems of information management or internal operation (see Table 12.1). Two main criteria explain the differences between these two types of crisis:

- In the case of crises resulting from an accident or serious incident necessitating the deployment of emergency services or crews dispatched to bring the situation back to normal, management of the crisis itself can usually be separated from management of crisis communication: even if both are linked, they can be dealt with by separate teams and will very probably be conducted at different paces and dynamics. In the case of a power outage lasting several days, for example following violent storms or unusual weather conditions (such as the 1998 ice storm in Québec), the experience of the crisis will be very different for those whose job it is to restore the situation in the field and for those tasked with responding to requests from consumers, citizens and the media and with managing the problems arising from the intervention of multiple actors.

- The situation is different where the crisis is the result of problems of information management and internal operation in the organization (fraudulent use of public funds, for example). Very often, the same people will have both to manage the problem that has arisen (searching for information, solving internal problems, informing the political authority, initiating legal action, responding to the media, etc.) and to provide communication about the same elements. Although crises of this type generally have lesser human consequences, they are very problematic because of the issues of trust they may generate. The public nature of the organizations and the environment in which they operate (legal framework, obligation of diligence, etc.) makes this distinction important. While private concerns are not obliged to report on internal problems (for example, a bank will try to prevent embezzlement by an employee from coming to public notice), public organizations are less and less able to avoid doing so as a result of their legal framework and the current media environment.

231

■ **Table 12.1** Types of crisis

	Crises resulting from accidents, incidents and emergency situations (mainly exogenous causes)	Crises resulting from information-management or internal problems (mainly endogenous causes)
Origins	Accident, natural disaster, epidemic, sabotage, major outage, etc.	Shortcomings in the management of a programme or an organization, failures in the management of an emergency situation, errors of judgement, information cover-ups
Characteristics	Large numbers of people are harmed (death, injury, sickness) or hampered in their daily life (restricted mobility, restricted communications, home comforts, etc.), or major environmental damage is caused	People are affected because the organization or persons inside the organization failed to comply with rules, procedures or more generally, key values (human consequences usually much less extensive)
Main objective	Limit harm to persons, property and environment	Limit the loss of trust in institutions
Examples	Québec ice storm of 1998, major power outage in the USA and Canada of 2003, Exxon Valdez oil spill in Alaska in 1989 See also Box 12.2	*Association pour la recherche sur le cancer en France*: founder and president embezzled funds earmarked for cancer research (convicted in 2000). The revelation of his misdeeds led to a fall in donations not only to this but also to other organizations See also Box 12.3

Crises arising from an accident, a serious incident or an emergency situation such as an imminent major risk (e.g. a pandemic) have in common the fact that they affect people's physical integrity or cause them considerable inconvenience in their daily lives (breakdown of public transport, prolonged strike, power outage, etc.). An example is presented in Box 12.2. Although the exact causes may not be immediately identifiable, generally they are relatively easy to understand. The organization must activate structures that will bring relief to people, protect them from danger, and help them to cope with the problems arising out of obstacles to everyday life. If these tasks are neglected, a crisis of the second type may well arise because the organization's capacity to respond to and manage the crisis will be thrown into the spotlight. Management of the emergency situation can normally be separated from management of the accompanying communication. Normally, the crisis itself and crisis communication are managed by different people: this allows emergency personnel to concentrate on their job without having to shoulder the burden of responding to requests from outside. These requests can be dealt with by specialists who will as far as possible adapt to the pace of external actors such as political authorities, the media and associations. Obviously, excellent coordination between crisis management and communication management must be established in order to prevent any information problems and to allow appropriate, proactive communications.

Although communication is very important in a crisis, the priority must remain relief of victims and limitation of harm to people, property and environment. Communications can never be successful unless proportionate and appropriate relief and assistance are provided to people. Communications may even rely on the work of the emergency crews to highlight the organization's capacity to manage the crisis. Conversely, communications can never compensate for deficiencies in intervention (insufficient relief efforts, unsuitable equipment or delay in the implementation of response).

In crises arising out of information-management or internal-operation problems, the causes are both much more difficult to identify and more complex to explain and justify (see example in Box 12.3). For example, in the case of abuse of trust or allegations of harassment, only an administrative or judicial enquiry will be able to establish the facts and rule on the guilt of those concerned. Enquiries of this kind require considerable time and the various actors will not wait for the final results of the enquiry before bringing matters into the public sphere for debate. As a result, the organization is obliged to provide communication while the facts and causes still remain largely unclear. Moreover, communication is a delicate task when key values have been flouted by members of an organization, especially when all precautions required to prevent such occurrences had not been taken.

■ BOX 12.2 A CRISIS CAUSED BY A SERIOUS INCIDENT

Prestige: The shipwreck of an oil tanker

On 14 November 2002 the oil tanker *Prestige*, carrying 77,000 tonnes of heavy fuel, began to break up off the Galician coast and sank five days later. More than 50,000 tonnes of oil leaked from the wreck, polluting the northwest coast of Spain and parts of the French coast. It was one of Spain's worst ecological disasters. But on 26 November 2002, the Spanish government was still failing to acknowledge the presence of an oil slick, preferring to talk of isolated contaminated spots. Afterwards, the authorities refused to bring judicial proceedings against the principal actors of the disaster and the government failed to establish a fact-finding commission.

Sources: *Le Temps* newspaper 15 November 2002, 27 November 2002, 22 January 2003, 14 November 2003; Journal du Net (2005).

233 ■

■ BOX 12.3 A CRISIS CAUSED BY AN INFORMATION-MANAGEMENT PROBLEM

On 9 April 2006, a Sunday newspaper published an article entitled 'Scandale à l'Uni: des profs menaient la grande vie aux frais de l'Etat' (Professors are leading a posh lifestyle on the back of the State). The article revealed information based on an audit report from the University of Geneva. It underlined frauds on expense accounts that touch the whole institution. Of a total of CHF10 million, some 25 per cent of expense accounts did not meet the official requirements. Prior events from the same individuals had been known by the authorities of the institution.

Financial and accounting problems were revealed to be based on the recurring problems of management and governance of the University. These problems, and the absence of a clear communication strategy, generated interest from journalists and fuelled internal tensions. The rumours, as well as the errors and lacuna in the management of this crisis by the University, and also in part by the political authorities, greatly diminished the credibility of the institution.

This process was reinforced by a lack of confidence of citizens towards the institution following a series of similar scandals in the Canton of Geneva. After a number of inquiries, the sums presented at the height of the crisis were found to be inflated and had no common measure with reality.

At the organizational level, this crisis led to the resignation of the executive of the University (rectorat). At the institutional level, it pushed the political authorities to reform the University; a reform that was approved by popular vote in November 2008.

Source: Pasquier and Fivat (2009).

This type of crisis is therefore clearly distinct from the previous type, because management of the crisis and of crisis communication will be closely linked. Because no harm has been caused to persons, property, or the environment, and because the organization's credibility is at issue, the same people will often be called upon to resolve the problems that have come to light and to communicate about them. Although this facilitates coordination of crisis management and related communications, it places a heavy burden on the same people, who must not allow their different roles (investigator, party to a procedure, manager, communicator) to become confused.

The phases of a crisis

Because every crisis follows its own pattern and has its own duration, and in most cases both are impossible to predict, defining a generalized list of the phases of a crisis is difficult. Nevertheless, main phases based on the two types of crisis described above can be defined (Coombs and Holladay, 2010; Libaert, 2001a; Zaremba, 2010).

Crises resulting from an accident, an incident or an emergency situation generally fall into four phases (Lagadec, 1991):

■ The *preliminary phase* is when the first alert signals occur. It can begin with information suggesting the gravity of the event (information about the disappearance of an airplane or the wreck of a ship) or information that is difficult to interpret or apparently anodyne but that can lead to a crisis (allegations, rumours, etc.). Organizations must be able to pick up such information through strategic watch and weak-signal-detection devices.

■ The *acute phase* is when the effects of the events (announcement of the plane crash, arrival of oil slicks on the beaches) and harm caused to persons, property or the environment begin to emerge. For example, the wreck of the *Erika* on 12 December 1999 was perceived as a serious crisis only 14 days later when oil began to wash up over a 400-kilometre stretch of the Brittany coast (Libaert, 2001a, 2001b). See Figure 12.1 for a complete evaluation of this particular crisis.

■ The *chronic phase* ensues after a crisis has peaked. Media interest fades gradually either because there is no new information or because other topics have cropped up to garner media attention. Interest persists, however, and the organization continues to be approached. It might still not have control over the rhythm of communication.

■ The *healing phase* begins from the time the crisis is no longer topical and the media are no longer actively covering the situation. The only times at which the event is covered afresh are anniversary dates or when the organization communicates (questions asked at press conferences, for example).

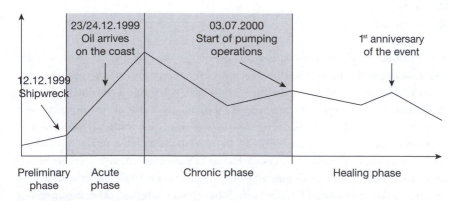

Figure 12.1 *Phases of a crisis resulting from a serious accident or incident*
Source: adapted from Libaert (2001).

The crisis surrounding the oil tanker Erika can be divided into four phases:

Preliminary phase: The tanker *Erika*, carrying 31,000 tonnes of heavy fuel oil, broke in two off the coast of Brittany during a storm on 12 December 1999. Despite leakage of between 2,000 and 8,000 litres of oil on the first day following the accident, the Centre for Documentation, Research and Experimentation on Accidental Water Pollution (Cedre) stated that there was no risk of oil slicks along the Breton coasts.

Acute phase: On 14 December 1999, the press reported that Cedre now believed that the oil would reach the coast. From then on, the press tracked the development of the oil slick along the Brittany and Vendée coasts every day. Other issues raised in the press were the silence of Total-Fina, the company that had chartered the *Erika*, and the question of its accountability. The crisis worsened on 23 and 24 December 1999, when the first slicks of heavy oil arrived on the coasts. In the subsequent days, the situation intensified along with the oil slick.

Chronic phase: Although new oil slicks were still arriving on the coast by February 1999, media interest in the crisis diminished. The press did not mention the fuel arriving on the coast however, and reported preparations for pumping procedures.

Healing phase: With the start of pumping procedures on 3 July 2000, the crisis entered into its last phase. The oil slick was no longer an item in the press, and only important events such as the ending of the pumping at the beginning of September 2000 or the anniversary of the shipwreck were still mentioned.

The structure of a crisis caused by information-management or internal-operation problems is often different for two reasons: (1) the onset of the crisis is much more difficult to identify, meaning that crossing from one place to another is not always perceptible and (2) the crisis often dissipates when the problem is resolved or at least recognized, and a commitment to implement solutions is made (see Box 12.4).

Three phases can be distinguished:

- development phase
- acute phase
- restoration phase.

The development phase involves, as in the other type of crisis, the disclosure of facts about the organization. At this stage, reactions from the various actors concerned and above all the reactions of the organization, combined with the general context in which the information is brought to the awareness of the public, are crucial. The organization's capacity to assess the risk following the disclosure of information, the answer it provides to questions asked, its credibility in its relations with the authorities and the media might allow it to succeed in not arousing increased attention from them or, on the contrary, may arouse lively interest. On top of this comes the context in which the information is communicated. If similar facts have come to light in other organizations or if the organization in question is known for somewhat lax management of problems, then the probability that the issue will turn into a controversy is very high (Box 12.5).

■ BOX 12.4 MPS' EXPENSE-ACCOUNT SCANDAL IN BRITAIN

The expense account scandal in the United Kingdom in 2009 is a good example of a crisis where communication is central. In May 2009, the *Daily Telegraph* newspaper started the publication of a series of articles on 'abusive' expenses claimed by Members of Parliament (MPs). Little by little, these allegations ended up involving some 600 members of the government, including the prime minister, Gordon Brown. The abuses ranged from reimbursement for a pool and a duck hut to lipsticks and matches.

The information given to the newspaper was, it appeared later, provided by someone employed in the processing of the expenses of MPs. That person was outraged at these expenses given the low level of equipment the British government provided to its soldiers in operation in Afghanistan.

Initially, the government went through the 'We are sorry' motions. It then promised the full reimbursement of all unjustifiable expenses. A reform of the system was even promised by the prime minister. Nevertheless, the scandal led to a large number of resignations, including that of some ministers. The prime minister saw his popularity plummet, and the *Daily Telegraph* its sales explode!

The acute phase is characterized by intense media coverage of the topic and is essentially determined by the capacity of the media to unearth information and that of the organization to supply clarification and proposals for solutions that will prevent similar occurrences in future. Escalation is frequently observed in proportion to proven fact. If the organization failed to show transparency from the outset and if trust is absent or has been lost, it is highly likely that the acute phase will last for as long as those seen as responsible for the incriminating facts remain in their jobs. Since pressure generally ramps up, organizations must often release all the information available and those in charge must step down.

If all the facts become known and those responsible are no longer in office, the crisis will rapidly move into a restoration phase. The media have no further reason to pursue their quest for information and other procedures that may be undertaken (administrative enquiry, prosecution, etc.) will not be covered until the reports are published. This means that the action in the crisis is no longer dictated by the media but solely by normal events further to the crisis such as the appointment of new managers, the publication of a report of enquiry, the introduction of new standards or new equipment, an anniversary date, etc.

As shown in Box 12.3, the crisis at the University of Geneva was essentially the result of internal dysfunction and an information-management problem. An analysis of the number of articles in the media reveals three main phases as shown in

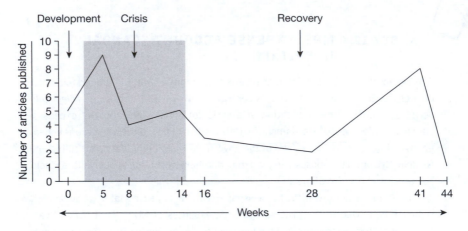

Figure 12.2 *Three main phases of the crisis at the University of Geneva*
Source: Pasquier and Fivat (2009).

Figure 12.2 (the vertical axis corresponds to the number of articles published in major Swiss newspapers):

■ *The development of the crisis:* the crisis began with the revelations in the press of financial irregularities inside the University. It gathered momentum when, following intervention from politicians, legal sanctions were sought.

■ *The acute crisis:* in subsequent weeks came successive revelations of new events, interpreted as increasingly serious. The University no longer had any control over the information. The press imposed its own agenda. This phase ended when the crisis peaked: practically all the elements that had created a scandal were unveiled, with the consequence that the University's executive (rectorat) resigned en bloc.

■ *The restoration phase:* media interest waned and the University controlled the communications agenda. The phase ended with the conclusions of the general investigation into the University which shed light on all the events. The affair was now closed.

ERRORS AND STRATEGIES IN CRISIS COMMUNICATION

Although in most cases a crisis cannot be prevented from emerging, it is possible to attempt to contain the crisis and above all to limit its negative effects on the organization in the long term (loss of trust, internal conflicts, etc.). This involves not making various unfortunately classic errors and developing a strategy in line with the organizational context and likely expectations of the actors concerned.

Classic errors

It cannot be over-emphasized that, since every crisis is different, a search for general characteristics, particularly with regard to errors, is difficult. However, analysis of numerous crises highlights common mistakes that exacerbate the crisis (Zaremba, 2010; Ulmer *et al.*, 2009; Fearn-Banks, 2007; Coombs, 2007; Anthonissen, 2008):

- underestimating the risks involved
- refusing to communicate or waiting too long before doing so
- making pronouncements about the causes and consequences without being aware of the details
- denying facts and attempting to cover up information
- minimizing the significance of facts
- entrusting communications to too many spokespersons
- giving responsibility for communications to someone with insufficient authority in the organization
- picking up on terms used by the media and giving free rein to exaggerated accounts
- attacking the media or other actors
- neglecting internal communication.

A very common error, particularly in crises related to the disclosure of fact, is to underestimate the risks involved. The causes of such behaviour vary: the heads of the organization may be absent (on vacation, travelling) when the facts are disclosed; the organization may be incapable of reacting or may lack experience of risk assessment; various people may attempt to hide information, etc. Risk assessment may be hazardous,

BOX 12.5 EXAMPLES OF ERRORS IN CRISIS COMMUNICATION

Making pronouncements without having gauged the nature and the causes of the crisis

The example of the fire in the Channel Tunnel on 18 November 1996 demonstrates the need to verify information and achieve consistency in communications. A statement released shortly after the accident boasted of the effectiveness of the security system and played down the consequences of the fire on traffic. Later, defects in the security system came to light and traffic took a long time to be restored. It was unnecessary to communicate so quickly and the company lost credibility, making it more difficult to convey the message subsequently (Gabay, 2001).

continued . . .

■ BOX 12.5 EXAMPLES OF ERRORS IN CRISIS COMMUNICATION ... *continued*

Communicating without knowing the facts

The disappearance of the Airbus from Río to Paris on 1 June 2009 was another case in which hypotheses were made and later disproved. For example, Air France's director of communications stated a few hours after the disaster that the most likely cause was that the aircraft was struck by lightning. Although no definitive conclusions have yet been drawn as to the causes of this accident, the lightning hypothesis was discarded in the days following the accident. Despite being invalidated, this alleged cause remains present in the world of information: in a Google search on 'Airbuses Río Paris', one of the first results is an article in *Le Parisien* with the headline 'Río-Paris Airbus hit by lightning' (*Le Parisien*, 2009).

Lying

The French authorities claimed that the cloud of radioactive particles produced by the Chernobyl nuclear accident (1986) had not crossed into France. Subsequent newspaper headlines read 'The radioactive lie' (*Liberation*), 'The day France was irradiated' (*VSD*), 'Nuclear disinformation' (*Le Monde*) and 'Radioactive contamination in France' (*Le Parisien*). The lie seriously compromised the credibility of the French authorities (Gabay, 2001).

Playing down facts that have come to light

The heat wave in the summer 2003 killed about 12,000 people in France; considerably more than in other countries. At first, the public authorities denied the problem of deaths due to the heat wave. They then started little by little to admit the problem: the general health directorate estimated between 1,600 and 3,000 deaths, then the health minister announced that 5,000 deaths could be possible and then, one day later, the general health director resigned. In spite of these developments, the government didn't take any responsibility for the failure of the sanitary mechanisms. And the French president gave only a speech after his summer holiday; a speech that didn't contain critical aspects regarding the problems in the sanitary systems. Aware that the government was acting too slowly on the heat wave crisis, the health minister announced after the heat wave that he would include measures in the new health law for avoiding similar crises (Gabay, 2001).

but underestimation means that, should the crisis eventually develop, considerable time has been lost when information could be gathered and communication prepared. Moreover, the underestimation of the dangers is likely to be picked up on by the media during their first contact with the organization (delayed responses, incomplete information, etc.) which could lead them to step up pressure on the organization.

The expression 'nature abhors a vacuum' is particularly relevant in a crisis and organizations must not fail to communicate or wait too long before doing so. Absence of communication or undue delays can have two consequences: other actors may step forward to speak, and confidence may be lost. In a crisis, silence from the main actor concerned is almost always compensated for by utterances from other actors or simply from the media. Assuming that the media will lose interest in the subject in the absence of explanation is a serious mistake because such an absence can encourage the development of assumptions and the spread of rumours tends to increase pressure on the media, which need to be supplied with information, and may be seen as a problem by citizens who expect a public organization to account for itself (the accountability principle).

While it is essential to communicate rapidly and continually in a crisis, special caution is called for: it is unwise to make pronouncements on the causes and possible consequences of the crisis while these remain unknown. It is very risky to begin formulating hypotheses, developing scenarios and so on until the facts have been established – especially because establishing the facts may take a great deal of time. The media and the general public will tend to accept such hypotheses as the true causes of the event, and persuading them to change their minds subsequently will prove very difficult because many people will not keep up with later news and traces of these 'causes' will linger especially on the internet.

Denying facts or deliberately hiding known, verified information is highly risky behaviour that can threaten the organization's survival, especially so in crises arising from information-management or internal problems. The temptation to deny the existence of facts or to cover up information in the hope that the media and other actors would lose interest in the problem is great. This is very unlikely to happen in democratic countries and others where the media play a significant role. The media are likely to step up the pressure, and seek out and publish contradictory information. The organization runs the risk of being caught lying and will lose all the ability in its future operations and communications.

Rather than denying the facts, some organizations will minimize them or play down their importance; this can prove counter-productive because this attitude may strengthen the feeling that the organization is far removed from the concerns and worries of citizens. Because the event is unusual and falls outside the organization's normal activities (such as an abusive interpretation of the rules regarding expense accounts), managers may attempt to play down the facts, claiming, for example, that their effect is minimal in comparison with the organization's operations or budget. And yet the media and the public will focus not on the rarity of the behaviour but on the fact of its existence and on the flouting of values.

Crises create uncertainty both inside the organization and in the minds of the actors concerned, and it is therefore important to provide credible reassurance to all those affected. For this reason, it is wise to avoid making frequent changes in spokespersons who appear before the media. The presence of a person who is known or will make themselves known by acting as spokesperson will have a reassuring effect. It conveys the idea of a degree of control over the crisis. It also prevents contradictory messages from being conveyed outside the organization, which would only fuel negative analyses. Similarly, the spokesperson must be kept completely and immediately informed of all events and information that come to the organization's knowledge. If the spokesperson is not involved in the process and does not have the authority required to be kept informed, he or she risks being confronted during a press conference or in an interview with a journalist with information that he or she is unaware of and for which he or she has been unable to prepare a credible response.

With regard to the media, and knowing that emotions tend to take precedence over rationality, organizations must avoid making use of the sometimes metaphorical terms used in the media. They must not be drawn into making the corresponding exaggerations and must above all reiterate the facts as established and show caution when speaking of causes and consequences. If such care is not taken, ownership of these metaphorical terms and exaggerations would transfer from the media to the organization and the media will legitimately be able to use them for the duration of the crisis. It is also essential not to criticize the media for their interest in the crisis or even for their assiduity in obtaining information by questionable means (late calls, repeated questions seen as of little relevance, etc.). First, it is not the place of the organization in crisis to judge the media, and second, such an attitude is likely to act as an incentive to the media to continue their search for information.

Lastly, since the organization may find a very significant proportion of its managerial capacities tied up by the crisis, it may forget its employees, who are dealing with requests from their family, friends and neighbours who all wish to be kept informed. Without necessarily making them spokespersons for the organization, they should be given clear information (What is known? What is the organization doing? What hypothesis can be refuted?) so that they can respond to questions and contribute to conveying a consistent message in their inner circles. This aspect is all the more important at the local or regional level where a high numbers of employees work and where fewer media are able to relay information.

Strategies and rules to follow

A number of communication strategies for crisis situations can be found in the literature (Sartre, 2003b):

- *Total acknowledgement strategies:* the organization acknowledges the facts and where applicable the corresponding responsibilities. In order to regain a degree of credibility quickly, the organization acknowledges the facts and the mistakes made and proposes solutions or rules to prevent their recurrence. In doing so it hopes to be pardoned by public opinion. Naturally, this strategy only works well if the organization voluntarily acknowledges errors, without being forced to do so.

- *Partial acknowledgement strategies:* these strategies, which carry a greater degree of risk, consist in acknowledging the main facts while absolving oneself of responsibility. This involves attempting to dissociate the organization's responsibilities and those of persons taken individually, linking the situation with other similar crises ('we are not the only ones') or accepting only a limited degree of liability ('we had no choice').

- *Avoidance strategies:* facts are neither acknowledged nor denied, and the organization attempts to create a diversion – for example, by attributing the problem to the absence of guidelines or confusing guidelines or by portraying itself as the victim of the crisis.

- *Denial strategies:* these strategies, which consist in systematically keeping silent or categorically denying the facts, are very risky. They can be considered when the facts or accusations have little credibility or when a very important or very serious offence occurs at the same time (terrorist attacks, a global event such as the football World Cup, etc.). The organization is counting on the fact that the attention of the main actors will be short-lived.

Although all the strategies may be considered by private companies or non-profit organizations, avoidance and refusal strategies should be rejected by public organizations. A public organization has a much greater obligation to provide information than a private company and non-judicial methods of uncovering the truth are many (parliamentary commissions, access to information rights, etc.), and the affairs of public organizations are frequently of greater interest to the media than matters in private companies. Generally speaking, a public organization must show the greatest transparency, at least as far as allegations are concerned, and actively contribute to determine responsibilities and put in place measures to prevent similar occurrences in the future. Any other strategy is very risky and should receive explicit prior approval from the political authority.

With this in mind, and also for the purpose of avoiding making crisis imitations errors, basic rules or principles should be followed (Coombs, 1999) (see Box 12.6).

Information must be provided actively and continuously. To prevent the organization from having to communicate in response to external pressure, a proactive attitude consisting in revealing facts as they become known and subsequently providing information regularly, repeating known facts and stating facts, together with information about the next steps, will provide a degree of control over crisis limitation. It is also important to check information conveyed and to reveal only established facts. Conveying erroneous or inaccurate information can have serious consequences and the organization will be criticized for it. For this reason, the organization and its managers must stick to the facts and avoid putting up theories or developing possible scenarios

243 ■

■ **BOX 12.6 RULES TO FOLLOW IN CRISIS LIMITATION**

- ■ Inform actively (don't wait for pressure from outside).
- ■ Inform continually.
- ■ Check information before releasing it and speak the truth.
- ■ Correct false information or unfounded rumours.
- ■ Avoid speculating.
- ■ Take emotional aspect into consideration.
- ■ Do not blame causes or persons unless you are absolutely certain.
- ■ Express yourself clearly and repeat information as needed.
- ■ Avoid inconsistencies between words and deeds.
- ■ Deal in the same way with all media and consider their priorities in terms of information.
- ■ Ensure that the content of information remains consistent.
- ■ Be open to dialogue and accept disagreement/allow yourself to be contradicted.
- ■ Pay attention to internal communication.

that will in many cases be disproved subsequently. Discussion of where responsibility lies can be undertaken in due course when all information is known, ideally after the crisis when debate can be dispassionate. While great attention must be paid to the emotional aspects of a crisis, showing empathy, a listening ear and, when people have been injured or killed, compassion, discussion of responsibilities and consequences must be rational and reasoned. Lessons will have to be drawn from the crisis; a process in which it is unwise to be hasty.

Since many people may be affected, most of whom are not specialists in the field concerned, managers of the organization must ensure they express themselves very clearly, if necessary repeating information in as helpful a manner as possible (avoiding technical jargon, reminding people of the order of events, etc.). For the same reason, managers must take care to show consistency between words and behaviour. For example, in a crisis involving misappropriation of funds or financial abuses, they must avoid attending a seminar in an expensive hotel with a festive programme, even though the event may have been planned long in advance. The credibility of their statements will be called into question by behaviour which, while it may be explainable, appears inappropriate in the context of the crisis.

Because of the important role played by the media, organizations must attempt as far as possible to treat them equally (they should all receive the same information) while taking into account their needs (photos, diagrams, interviews, etc.) and their priorities (broadcast time, time zone differences, editorial lead time, etc.). Ideally, the same person should always be in charge of relations with the media and other players outside the organization: this will make for consistency in information conveyed. If a number of people speak on behalf of the organization, close coordination will be required to avoid the risks of inconsistency. Because the media and the other players will ask questions that may be irritating or hostile, attempt to 'bully' the organization, pass off hypotheses as fact, make connections between unrelated facts, and so on, spokespersons must keep calm, be responsive to all requests, repeat the same answers several times if necessary, and accept disagreement. Fielding questions successfully is a vital part of establishing the organization's credibility.

Lastly, the organization must not forget its employees who will also have questions, be approached by outside players and sometimes give their opinion. Keeping them informed as quickly and completely as possible will enable them to correct misinformation, dispel rumours, set out the essential facts and thus contribute to increasing credibility. Most important of all, their confidence in the organization will be bolstered; a fact that will prove particularly important once the crisis is over.

The media and the crisis

The media will play a central role in any special event leading to the crisis because they serve as a 'resonating chamber' for the relaying of information. Sometimes the media are informed before the organization and may ask managers questions about an event they are unaware of. Without going into the function and operation of the media in our society, certain characteristics that affect the development of a crisis need to be understood. See Box 12.7 for further examples.

Information is a structured market. It is a market because it has become a consumer product. The media compete fiercely with each other to obtain original and exclusive information. It is not surprising, therefore, that when an incident occurs, the media will be hungry for information and will seek out information actively in order to be

■ BOX 12.7 SPEED AND INTRUSIVENESS OF MODERN MEDIA

The speed of the media: After the Concorde crash in Paris in July 2000, the media were already broadcasting eyewitness accounts of the accident and questioning former Concorde pilots before airport management, the airline or emergency services had a chance to express themselves.

The intrusiveness of the media: At the time of the avian flu crisis in 2006, poultry were contaminated in a French farm very probably by a television crew who had come from a contaminated site to the farm to film precautionary measures taken by the farmer.

quicker or different from the others. This market is structured because each medium has its own format and a specific relationship with its readers, listeners or viewers (radio in the morning, newspapers thereafter, television in the evening, internet throughout the day with a great deal of information and the analysis, etc.). The quantity of information and the form in which it is provided therefore varies considerably from one medium to another (headlines, pictures, etc.). This means it is very important to understand the specific needs of the various media and, to the extent possible, attempt to meet these needs.

The role of the media intensified still further with the advent and development of the internet. First, the internet has increased the competitive intensity between media and has changed the relationship between the media and their uses (all the classic media now also use the internet to convey information in addition to portals developed specifically for and on the internet).

Information transmitted over the internet is, at least for the moment, limited, reductionist, and often raw. It contains little analysis, heightening the importance of the accuracy of information for establishing the facts and making it vital to avoid spreading hypotheses or possible scenarios that could rapidly create rumours. As shown, traces linger long after the crisis and false information can circulate on the web years afterwards.

During and after the crisis, an analysis of reports will provide valuable information about the way the media evaluate facts, about correcting erroneous information, on aspects to be highlighted and others that should be left alone.

TOOLS TO MANAGE CRISES

Because organizations are taken by surprise and are unprepared for crises, it is useful to have checklists of tasks or elements to take into consideration. Although most of the points set out in Table 12.2 speak for themselves, some require additional explanation:

- before the crisis: risk analysis
- during the crisis: activation of the crisis communication cell
- after the crisis: declare the end of the crisis.

When a major event occurs, risk analysis is crucial. It will allow the organization to decide whether it should implement its crisis plans and set up the structures required, particularly the crisis cell. As there is no one criterion that can alone be used to decide the question, a number of factors must be used. They include all that emerges from a media watch:

- Innocent victims have been, or are in danger of being, killed or injured.
- The number of people affected or potentially affected is high.
- The subject will affect a wide section of the public and falls into a category that is given widespread media exposure (health, morals, sex, etc.).

■ **Table 12.2** *Crisis checklists*

Before the crisis	Risk analysis: probability of recurrence, level of risk incurred, extent to which the subject is understood
	Simulation of consequences: awareness of impacts, understanding of information
	Setting up a crisis cell: acknowledgement of the gravity of the situation
During the crisis	Analysis and assessment of the situation
	Implementation of operational and communications plans
	Take the initiative, provide information actively (do not wait for outside pressure to build up)
After the crisis	Declare the end of the crisis and resume normal activities
	Maintain communications with all partners and with the media
	Provide support to everyone who was involved and thank them
	Debriefing and post-mortem
	Produce a full report of experience and adapt operational and preparation plans (lessons learned)

Sources: Adapted from Gabay (2001) and Information Office of the Canton of Bern (2001).

■   The organization in question is well known.
■   The event is not isolated but is part of a series of similar events.
■   Rumours, doubts or contradictory information are circulating.

If one or more of these elements are present, the organization must, even if the managers are absent, analyse the situation in detail, decide whether or not to implement crisis plans or at least monitor the situation closely.

In the event of a crisis, the setting up of a crisis communication cell is very important for two main reasons. First, the organization will be bombarded with requests for several days or weeks, or even months, by outside agencies (media, authorities, etc.) and the organization's usual procedural and hierarchical rules will have to be modified very quickly (personnel assigned to a hotline, negations team mobilized, involvement of outside consultants, etc.). Only a cell dedicated to the crisis and equipped with personnel and material resources will be able to face up to this avalanche of varied, continual requests. Second, the message issued by the organization must absolutely be consistent and coordinated with the cell tasked with managing the crisis itself. In contrast with general rules for communication under which a number of spokespersons may be called upon to speak, it is wise to limit the number of people authorized to speak and to make sure there is excellent coordination with those

247 ■

managing the crisis. Only close coordination within a specific cell can guarantee that these basic rules will be observed.

At the end of the crisis, which is generally marked by the organization's retaking control after litigation and by a considerable reduction in pressure from the media, the organization must be able, internally at least, to declare the end of the crisis and embark on a process of returning to normal, while maintaining an active communication strategy. This is also a useful time to learn the lessons of the crisis (debriefing, post-mortem) and to thank those who were involved. All too often, the belief that the crisis is over leads organizations to want to forget a painful episode instead of preparing for a similar event; even though everyone hopes it will never happen again. It is only by drawing a complete picture of the crisis and by adapting planned measures that the organization can learn the lessons, and improve its maturity and its capacity to react in the face of the next crisis.

EXERCISE 12.1

Take the organization you currently for work for, and try to identify a crisis situation. One you have identified it, you should:

1 Determine of which type the crisis was.
2 Identify the various phases of the crisis.
3 Pinpoint the event that signalled the end of the crisis.
4 Identify the main mistakes that were made.

DISCUSSION QUESTIONS

1 What type of crisis do you find most dangerous for your organization and why? What criteria allow you to arrive at that answer?
2 What is the most easily avoidable communication mistake in a crisis situation? Does the answer vary according to the 'industry' the organization is involved in or is it a matter of the people in place?
3 How can an organization close prepare to best mitigate the consequences of an eventual crisis? Is the best approach to be well prepared or is this a waste of resources given that crises are by definition unpredictable?

REFERENCES

Anthonissen, P. F. (2008) *Crisis Communication: Practical PR Strategies for Reputation Management and Company Survival*, London, Kogan Page.

Coombs, T. W. (1999) *Ongoing Crisis Communication*, Thousand Oaks, Sage Publications.

—— (2007) *Ongoing Crisis Communication: Planning, Managing, and Responding*, Thousand Oaks, Sage Publications.

Coombs, T. W. and Holladay, S. J. (2010) *The Handbook of Crisis Communication*, Singapore, Blackwell Publishing Ltd.

Crozier, M. (1991) La Gestion de Crise, *Les Cahiers de la Sécurité Intérieure*, 6, 24.

Fearn-Banks, K. (2007) *Crisis Communication: A Casebook Approach*, Mahwah, New Jersey, Lawrence Erlbaum Associates.

Gabay, M. (2001) *La Nouvelle Communication de Crise: Concepts et Outils*, Issy-les-Moulineaux, Editions Stratégies.

Information Office of the Canton of Bern (2001) *Communiquer Correctement en Situation Difficile. Un Guide pour la Communication en cas de Crise et de Situation Extraordinaire à l'échelon de la Commune et du District*, Berne.

Journal du Net (2005) Communication de Crise: Vingt Crises qui ont Marqué les Esprits. Online at http://www.journaldunet.com/management/dossiers/050167crise/tablo.shtml (accessed 15 Febuary 2011).

Lagadec, P. (1991) *La Gestion des Crises: Outils de Réflexion à L'usage des Décideurs*, Paris, Ediscience International.

Le Parisien (2009) Vol Rio-Paris: Découverte de Nouveaux Debris, 1 June. Online at http://www.leparisien.fr/.../l-airbus-rio-paris-aurait-ete-foudroye-01-06-2009-533641.php (accessed 1 March 2011).

Lerbringer, L. O. (1997) *The Crisis Manager: Facing Risk and Responsibility*, Mahway, New Jersey, Erlbaum.

Libaert, T. (2001a) *La Communication de Crise*, Paris, Dunod.

—— (2001b) *La Communication de Proximité*, Paris, Rueil-Malmaison.

Pasquier, M. and Fivat, E. (2009) Crise à l'Université de Genève: une étude de cas, *Cahier de l'IDHEAP*, Lausanne, Swiss Graduate School of Public Administration.

Revéret, R. and Moreau, J.-N. (1997) *Les Médias et la Communication de Crise*, Paris, Economica.

Sartre, V. (2003a) *La Communication de Crise*, Paris, Les Éditions Demos.

—— (2003b) *La Communication de Crise: Anticiper et Communiquer en Situation de Crise*, Paris, Les Éditions Demos.

Ulmer, R. R., Sellnow, T. L. and Seeger, M. W. (2009) *Post Crisis Communication and Renewal: Understanding the Potential for Positive Outcomes in Crisis Communication*, New York, Routledge.

Zaremba, A. J. (2010) *Crisis Communication Theory and Practice*, New York, M. E. Sharpe.

A case study

OF MONEY, MARKETING AND COMMUNICATION

As is clear from the reading of the preceding chapters, marketing and communication cannot and should not be used indiscriminately in the public sector. The following case study is the application of some of the concepts presented in the previous chapters, in a sector that seems, at first, far removed from matters of marketing and communication: the printing and circulating of money.

Like other central public tasks such as justice or foreign affairs, money is at the core of the State's historical regalian functions. Nevertheless, the development, creation, circulation, regulation and general management of tangible money, in coin or paper format, are all aspects of the general delivery of a service and/or product to citizens: that of a convenient way of exchanging value.

But, can we truly talk about marketing and communication as to regards money? The following examples present various projects at marketing the introduction of new coins and new bills in the United States. They raise fundamental questions as to the use and limits of marketing and communication in the public sector.

In each case, some of the most salient features of the project are presented. A series of questions is then presented to further the discussion.

FROM PAPER TO METAL: THE INTRODUCTION OF THE SACAGAWEA

Paper bills of $1 are the norm in the USA. The American one dollar bill is one of the lowest value paper denominations in the developed world. Over the past decades, a number of attempts have been made at replacing some of them by coins. This desire to introduce coins to replace paper is based mostly on a financial calculation from the Government Accounting Office (GAO) estimating the potential savings at 500 million USD (GAO, 2002, p.1).

It is with that in mind that the United States 1$ Coin Act of 1997 mandated the US Federal Government to introduce a new $1 coin. It was named the Sacagawea in honour of the Shoshone guide and translator to the Lewis and Clark expedition that explored the western United States in the early nineteenth century.

Table A.1 Number of $1 coins produced

Coin design	Number produced as of November 2009	Production years
Susan B. Anthony	932 million	1979–82 and 1999–2000
Sacagawea	1,467 million	2000–8
Presidential series	1,722 million	2007–ongoing
Native American series	92 million	2009–ongoing
Total: 4,213 million		

Source: Adapted from GAO (2011).

This was part of a long list of attempts at convincing Americans to use a 1$ coin. Table A.1 presents the various coins, their production years and the number produced. There had been the early silver dollars (eighteenth century), but of more recent memory one can name the Eisenhower dollar (1970s) and the Suzanne B. Anthony (late 1970s and late 1990s), named in honour of a civil rights leader and a leader of the nineteenth-century women's right movement. None had much success in supplanting the dollar bill. Later attempts, the Presidential and Native American series did not succeed either.

In order to raise awareness for the Sacagawea, and to encourage American citizens to use it, the US Mint (charged with the manufacturing of coins in the United States) spent, from 1998 to 2001, some 67.1 million USD in marketing and communication. This programme came at the back of the relatively unsuccessful launch of the Suzanne B. Anthony coin in 1979. It had never caught on with the population. For the Sacagawea, a more active campaign was envisaged.

As part of the bill was the provision that the coin should be golden in colour and have various tactile elements clearly differentiating it from the quarter (25 cents) – a problem that arose with previous dollar coins. To ensure its widest possible use, it was to have the same size and electromagnetic signature as the Suzanne B. Anthony, thus ensuring it being accepted in all vending machines. The communication and marketing aspects were also directly enshrined in the act.

The Mint's programme had three different aspects: 1) research and identification of market opportunities; 2) national public awareness and education programme; and 3) a business marketing programme. The sums allocated were earmarked for elements such as: 'marketing and advertising program, public relations and publicity programmes; 23 partnerships with banking, entertainment, retail, grocery, and restaurant chains; and promotional events with transit agencies' (GAO, 2002, pp.2–3). The main campaign, using the reassuring image of George Washington, took 40.5 million USD of the total budget.

For the research aspect of the campaign, a private marketing research company was hired. The initial analysis focused on the Suzanne B. Anthony's use in various economic sectors. Analyses were made of the size of each sectors and the potential 'market' they represented for the new coin. Out of that analysis, a number of high-potential industries were identified (food and beverage, transit systems, postal machines, etc.). Several marketing efforts were made targeting these industries, including personal sale visits, discussions with industry leaders, participation in conferences and symposiums. Opinion polls were also conducted prior to the launch of the coin. The goal was to assess people's opinions and then to use these results to tailor the campaign accordingly. The primary target was 18- to 49-year-old adults in urban and suburban areas.

There followed 11 weeks of intensive advertising on various media (television, print, radio and internet). According to the GAO, 'The television ads reached an estimated 92 percent of the target audience an average of 15 times' (GAO, 2002, p.11). For a number of legal and political reasons, in these ads the Mint decided not to point out the benefits of using the coin and thus showing the down sides of using dollar bills.

Many popular venues were used to market the new coin. A Macy's Thanksgiving Day parade float was commissioned, coin-operated machines were installed in supermarkets, a branding agreement was made with Cheerios cereal from General Mills and the coin was featured on the popular television show *The Wheel of Fortune*. A specific partnership was struck with Wal-Mart to distribute dollar coins as change in its 3,000 outlets. Other such agreements were made with various organizations, including the baseball team the L.A. Dodgers.

The Mint also marketed the dollar coin to other local, state and federal authorities. The transit systems of large cities were targeted (New York, Chicago, Philadelphia and San Diego) with free distribution of a dollar with the purchase of a transit card. A new dollar event was also organized at the Pentagon.

Barriers

To the Mint, of the biggest barrier to the use of the dollar coin is the continuing existence of the one dollar bill. In many countries (France, Canada, UK) the introduction of coins for lower currency denominations was successful only with the withdrawal of the equivalent bank note. But, at least in part due to the rise of a 'save the bank note' lobbying campaign, the US government decided to have both paper and coin dollars in circulation at the same time. That situation implied that the Mint did not have a fixed goal in terms of circulation for the new dollar. It also explains its reluctance to show the benefits of coins at the detriment of the notes.

In its analysis of the campaign, the GAO underlines a number of elements limiting the wider use: 1) negative image from the public following previous failed attempts at introducing it; 2) the lack of knowledge on the population's part of the benefits and savings flowing from the use of dollar coins; 3) the comparative advantages of using coins; and 4) the fact that some consider it easier to use dollar bills rather than coins.

Distribution issues were also raised by a number of actors: 1) unavailability of coins at all banking institutions; 2) co-ordering of coins with the Suzanne B. Anthony; 3) packaging concerns (coins not available in rolls); and 4) higher fees for the delivery than with dollar bills. Departing from its usual procedures (recirculating 'used' coins before shipping out new ones), the Mint decided to ship the Sacagawea in priority. Unfortunately, the coin being so similar to the Suzanne B. Anthony, no bank or carrier had the necessary equipment to separate them. They were thus delivered commingled to the banks.

One of the goals of the introduction was saving money as well as generating revenues. Costs of money are more than simply the costs of production and of replacement. One has to account for the storage and handling as well as the seignorage, or profit, the government makes from putting currency into circulation. When a note or currency is produced, the American Mint 'makes' the difference between the cost of producing it and its face-value. The Mint evaluates that the new dollar coin has generated about 1.1 billion USD in revenues and 968 million in seignorage. The cost of producing the coin is estimated at $0.12 with the government receiving $1.00 for each, so a margin of $0.88 per coin. The cost of replacement of bank notes is higher, but the rate of replacement is gradually being lowered. In the early 2000s, a $1 note lasted about 18 months. It now lasts as long as 40 months.

Results

In a 2000 survey 57 per cent of those questioned said they would be using the coin more readily as it becomes more widely used. The problem for those marketing the dollar is circular. People will use it only when others are seen using it. In a 2001 survey, 66 per cent of the public mentioned that they were saving the coins rather than using them actively. In a 2002 report the Mint estimates that the dollar coin is used in 4 per cent of dollar transactions.

Other events were to punctuate the life of the Sacagawea, but the elements presented above suffice for our understanding of the marketing of money. Like its predecessor, and its successor, the Sacagawea failed to achieve widespread use.

In recent years Congress tried to increase the circulation and use of dollar coins. Notably it mandated

> the use of $1 coins by federal agencies, the United States Postal Service, all transit agencies receiving federal funds, and all entities operating businesses, including vending machines, on U.S. government premises; (2) required the Mint to promote $1 coins to the public; and (3) required the Secretary of the Treasury, in consultation with the Federal Reserve, to review the co-circulation of the different $1 coin designs and make recommendations to Congress on improving the circulation of $1 coins.
>
> (GAO, 2011, p.6)

But, despite these efforts, circulation is not on the increase. That might change following the GAO's 2011 proposal for the full replacement of the dollar bill for a dollar coin. The debate has been launched one again. 'According to GAO's analysis, replacing the $1 note with a $1 coin could save the government approximately

$5.5 billion over 30 years' (GAO, 2011, p.2). In the fiscal and financial situation of early 2011, these arguments might gain some resonance with politicians and citizens alike. But, in a 2006 survey, some 79 per cent of Americans said they were opposed to the disappearance of the $1 note.

MODERNIZING BANK NOTES

The replacement of bills by coins in lower denomination is not the only change occurring in the financial sector. New bank notes are also introduced, and with it marketing needs arise. In the United States the Bureau of Engraving and Printing is in charge of the creation of bank notes.

Despite some minor modifications in 1990, American paper currencies had not experienced important modifications since 1929. The desire to modify them in a series of modernizations starting in 1996, resulted from two central facts:

- US currency is one of the most widely used in the world.
- It is, almost logically, the most counterfeited currency in the world.

With counterfeiting technics always evolving, it became necessary to introduce the latest technological countermeasures: at the time, micro-impressions and more elaborate watermarks. The technical requirements seemed reasonable and a technical solution had been found for the modernization of the currency. This could have been the end of the story were it not for the communication and marketing efforts.

One key element is the international importance of the US currency. Due to the international circulation of American currency, the Federal Reserve had to plan ahead to counter any possible reaction of panic that might follow the introduction of a new $100 bill. One can refer to the reaction of the many Russians who keep in reserve a large number of US $100 bills. Would their old bill still be valid? Are their lifetime economies in peril? How to recognize the new bills? Won't they get swindled with fakes?

These questions were addressed in the introduction of the '1996 series'. The newer model was not a radical departure from the original note. This was deplored by, among other groups, by visually impaired. American bills are all the same colour and the same size. The goal of the project was guided by two main principles: 1) imposing as little a disturbance as possible on individuals and businesses and 2) achieving an expeditious substitution of pre-1996 notes. Several steps were taken with these two aspects in mind. It was estimated that some 60 per cent of all notes in circulation at the end of 1995 were held outside the United States (Federal Reserve note). This was seen as a consequence of the large dollarization of various economies in the 1990s. American dollars are also used as a store of value in high inflation countries.

As for validity the Federal Reserve has only one credo: value is guaranteed *ad eternam*. One first action was the holding of a joint press conference involving the Federal Reserve, the US Treasury and the Russian Central Bank in August 1995.

There will not be any requirement to exchange present design notes or any deadline for exchanging present design notes. There will be no recall or demonetization of the pre-1996 US banknotes. All genuine US currency notes whenever issued will always be valid.

(Kremlin International News Broadcast, 1995)

It is important to note that this is not the case in every country. For example, the introduction of a new £50 note by the British Central Bank gave people only two years to exchange them for the newer model. Despite this perpetual value of notes, the US government nevertheless instigated a conversion programmes to ensure the widest possible dissemination of the newer, safer notes (Allison and Pianalto, 1997).

The introduction of the 2003 new $20 bill as a case study in public sector communication and marketing in many ways travels the same route as the Sacagawea dollar. The campaign had a budget of some $32 million. The channels selected were numerous (print, TV, radio, internet), but to that was added product placement, just as with regular products being marketed. The campaign was termed 'the new colour of money' in reference to the new colour to be shown on $20 bills (peach and blue). This was the first time since 1905 that colours beside green and black were used on bills.

As with the other bills a marketing firm was hired, but this time it used the resources of a talent agency to secure the prominence of the 'product' in television shows and movies. 'We knew we couldn't rely on public service announcements and the news media alone to get the depth of information out about the bill's new design and security features,' said Thomas A. Ferguson, the bureau's director. 'We needed to look at different avenues. And we knew from our research that people get a lot of their information from entertainment and television' (Streisand, 2003). The campaign was to be focused on the United States with a part of the budget being allocated for overseas activities. A special emphasis was put on the people that handled cash as part of their daily job (cashiers) so that they would be aware of the new security measures.

According to representatives of the marketing company, the overall goal of the operation was quite straightforward: 'We want to build awareness – then we can begin to change behavior,' he said. The behaviour that he wanted to change included stuffing the $20 bill, the most frequently counterfeited in the United States, into a pocket or cash register before checking its authenticity by, say, holding it up to a light or feeling for the security thread (Streisand, 2003).

The strategy reflected in large part the failure of the campaign associated with the 1996 $100 series.

Tens of thousands of vending machines in post offices and train and subway stations hadn't been set up to accept the revised version, Mr. Lake said, and cashiers and other money handlers didn't always know what to make of the new money. Overseas, some consumers panicked, thinking that their old dollars would be worthless. Such confusion not only hurts sales for retailers, but can also give counterfeiters a wider berth to exploit the chaos.

(Streisand, 2003)

255 ■

Numerous communication activities were planned, including the rolling out of a new website: http://www.moneyfactory.gov/newmoney. The bill was featured on the David Letterman show as a prop for jokes, it made 'appearances' on *Wheel of Fortune*, *Who Wants to Be a Millionaire?*, *Jeopardy* and others. Joint marketing deals were made with Wal-Mart and with Pepperidge Farm that adorned the packaging of one of its products with the bill. Movies and TV placement was also ensured via *CSI:Miami*, *The West Wing* and others.

The results: 82 per cent awareness level. But problems were also identified, notably in terms of distribution. The new $20 bill received numerous prizes including one from the Public Relation Society of America, and the Best Product of 2003 award from *Business Week*.

The new $100 note is to be distributed in 2011. The bill has a number of new security features: 3D security ribbon, portrait watermark, raised printing, micro-printing, colour shifting, etc. Along with it will come another communication and marketing campaign.

EXERCISE A.1

Based on the preceding examples, and using some of the key resources identified, try to answer the following questions:

1 From a wider social point of view, what are the pros and cons of spending public monies on the marketing of currency?
2 Referring to Table 2.2, what are some of the main characteristics of currency 'product' that limit the use of marketing and communication tools?
3 What are the main 'alternatives' to using a coin?
4 Based on the distinction presented in Figure 4.4 between product and client orientation, can you identify the approach used by the US government in the marketing of its currencies (both coin and paper)?
5 For the Sacagawea and the new $20 bill, can you identify the various elements of the marketing mix (see Figure 4.6)?
6 Can you identify the various stakeholders in the marketing of both new coins and new bills? Do they differ? If so how, and what is the likely impact on the development of a marketing and communication campaign?
7 Following Figure 5.2, how would you classify the US government's attempt at gathering information on the potential users of the new denominations?
8 In your own country, what would be the main questions to be taken into account in the marketing analysis for a new bank note? (See Figure 6.5.)
9 Can you define the central and peripheral elements of the product that is a new bank note or dollar coin following the example of Figure 7.3?
10 Can you identify some of the elements of communication as presented in Figure 8.1 and define an integrated communication model based on Figure 9.3?

11 Based on the various communication instruments presented in Table 10.1, can you imagine other initiatives that might have been developed for the communication of these new 'products'?

12 One of the main worries in introducing these new currencies was the possible panic, notably abroad, of seeing one's savings vanish. In such a situation, where holders of American currency believe it to be losing its value, which elements of crisis communication would you use (see Chapter 12)?

13 The eventual success of the transition to a dollar coin could have an impact on other denominations. The GAO is, for example, envisaging a rise in the use of $2 notes. Can you imagine other consequences?

REFERENCES

Allison, T.E. and Pianalto, R.S. (1997) The Issuance of Series-1996 $100 Federal Reserve Notes: Goals, Strategy, and Likely Results, *Federal Reserve Bulletin*, July, 557–64.

General Accounting Office (2002) New Dollar Coin: Marketing Campaign Raised Public Awareness But Not Widespread Use, report of the Subcommittee on Treasury and General Government, Committee on Appropriation, US Senate, GAO-02-896.

—— (2011) Replacing the $1 Note with a $1 Coin Would Provide a Financial Benefit to the Government, report to Congressional Requesters, GAO-11-281.

Kremlin International News (1995) Press conference with representatives of the US Treasury, the Federal Reserve system and the Central Bank of the Russian Federation regarding a change in US currency notes, 4 August.

Streisand, B. (2003) Business; Need Change for a $20 Bill? Call Hollywood, *New York Times*, 28 September.

Index

sales orientation 65–6
sample data 75, 88–2
sampling errors 92
satisfaction surveys 84
'satisfiers' 51
segmentation strategies 100, 105
service provision, costs of 76
similarities in products and services 111
simple random sampling 89
Singapore 197
social consumerism 44
strained transparency 169
strategic decisions 114–20
strategic planning 100–14; and marketing
    strategy 105–6; and public organizations
    100–6
stratified random sampling 89
structuration of offers 111
substitutability 111
surveys 74, 77, 80; omnibus type 87;
    qualitative techniques for 80–3, 85–7;
    quantitative techniques for 80–2, 84–5;
    types of 80–3
Switzerland 64–5
SWOT analysis 69, 113
systemic analysis 59, 61–4

tangible services 126
target groups 181–2, 193
telephone surveys 84–5
test analysis 75, 80
de Tocqueville, Alexis 199
translation 100
transparency of communication 9, 163;
    definition of 164; development of 164–6;
    forms of 166–7; legal framework for 167–8;
    resistance to 168–70; and the Weber-ian
    model 8

unilateral communications 194
unique selling proposition (USP) 117
United States 64–5
users: citizens as 36, 41, 43–4; definition of
    35

vertical accountability 6, 9

Weber, Max 4, 6, 36
Weberian model 4, 6, 10–11; criticisms of
    7–8; definition of 4; movement away
    from 36–8
website design 208–11
welfare state 4